Tricks of the Trade

**Chicago Guides
to *Writing*, *Editing*,
and Publishing**

Tricks of the Trade

How to Think about Your
Research While You're Doing It

Howard S. Becker

The University of Chicago Press

Chicago and London

HOWARD S. BECKER is professor of sociology at the University of Washington and the 1987 winner of the George Herbert Mead Award for a Career of Distinguished Scholarship. He is the author or editor of sixteen books, including *Writing for Social Scientists* (1986) and *Symbolic Interaction and Cultural Studies* (1990), both published by the University of Chicago Press.

The University of Chicago Press, Chicago 60637
The University of Chicago Press, Ltd., London
© 1998 by The University of Chicago
All rights reserved. Published 1998
Printed in the United States of America
07 06 05 04 03 02 01 00 99 98   2 3 4 5

ISBN: 0-226-04123-9 (cloth)
ISBN: 0-226-04124-7 (paper)

Library of Congress Cataloging-in-Publication Data

Becker, Howard Saul, 1928–
    Tricks of the trade : how to think about your research while you're doing it / Howard S. Becker.
        p.   cm.—(Chicago guides to writing, editing, and publishing)
    Includes bibliographical references and index.
    ISBN 0-226-04123-9 (alk. paper).—ISBN 0-226-04124-7 (pbk. : alk. paper)
    1. Social sciences—Authorship.   2. Sociology—Authorship.
    3. Academic writing.   I. Title.   II. Series.
    H91.B38   1997
    300'.72—dc21   97-19618
                                                                                        CIP

For Dianne

CONTENTS

PREFACE

Much of this book results from my experience teaching. Having to explain what you do to students pushes you to find simple ways of saying things, examples that give concrete form to abstract ideas, and exercises that give students practice in new ways of thinking and manipulating what they learn in their research. As you listen to the individual, seemingly idiosyncratic problems students find in their work, you begin (like the local computer guru, who accumulates knowledge by solving individual problems) to see family resemblances among them. You learn to identify the idiosyncratic as a variant of some general problem. But every new problem is just different enough from all the others to give you something to add to your understanding of the general class of difficulties.

After a while, I began to keep track of my ad hoc inventions, concocted for the needs of a particular day's class or a particular student's research problem. And then, having written a book on the problems of academic writing (Becker 1986b), I decided I could follow that up with a book on "thinking" if I started with the materials in the file of "tricks" I had started. Some of these ideas first saw daylight in earlier publications, articles written for this or that occasion, and I have borrowed freely from those earlier formulations (at the end of this preface is a list of the publishers to whom I am indebted for permission to do that).

Most of my work has been autobiographical, explicitly or otherwise, and this is especially so. I have drawn on my own experiences extensively and repeatedly. Perhaps most importantly, I have recalled the way I was taught, the sociologists from whom I learned what sociological work could be and what a sociological life could be. In a certain way, this book is an homage to the people who taught me, many of them while I was in school, others after I had left school (but not stopped my education). I've paid my respects by often tying what I have to say to the words of people I

PREFACE

learned from, using their thoughts as a springboard for my own. I have learned, over the years, what most people learn, which is that my teachers usually weren't as dumb as I sometimes thought.

I've also learned from a number of people who have read what I write over the years with appreciation, but without sparing the criticism. Several of them read an earlier version of this manuscript, and I'm grateful for their extended commentaries, even though it meant more work. (Better I should hear it from them!) So I thank Kathryn Addelson, Eliot Freidson, Harvey Molotch, and Charles Ragin for their thoughtful critiques.

Doug Mitchell is the editor authors dream about working with. He has waited for this book patiently, offered interesting and useful ideas, encouraged my flagging interest and confidence, and generally kept the project alive.

Dianne Hagaman and I share an intellectual as well as a domestic life, and our mutual explorations of all sorts of research and conceptual problems have informed the whole book in ways that can't be separated out and pointed to. She has, in addition, listened to practically everything here—in the form of disjointed monologues, casual remarks, and even readings aloud—and her reactions and ideas helped to shape the final version.

I am grateful to a number of individuals and publishers for permission to reprint materials that originally appeared in other publications. Scattered portions of this book first appeared in Howard S. Becker, "Tricks of the Trade," in *Studies in Symbolic Interaction,* ed. Norman K. Denzin (New York: JAI Press, 1989), 10B:481–90. The photograph of René Boulet in chapter 2 originally appeared in Bruno Latour, "The Pedofil of Boa Vista," *Common Knowledge* 4 (1995): 165. Portions of the text in chapter 2 originally appeared in Howard S. Becker, "Foi por acaso: Conceptualizing Co-incidence," *Sociological Quarterly* 25 (1994): 183–94; Howard S. Becker, "The Epistemology of Qualitative Research," in *Ethnography and Human Development,* ed. Richard Jessor, Anne Colby, and Richard A. Shweder (Chicago: University of Chicago Press, 1996), 53–71; Howard S. Becker, "Cases, Causes, Conjunctures, Stories, and Imagery," in Charles C. Ragin and Howard S. Becker, *What Is Case?* (Cambridge: Cambridge University Press, 1992), 205–16, © 1992 by Cambridge University Press, reprinted with the permission of Cambridge University Press. Portions of chapter 3 appeared in Howard S. Becker, "Letter to Charles Seeger," *Ethnomusicology* 33 (spring—summer 1989): 275–85, reprinted by permission of *Ethnomusicology.* Portions of chapter 4 originally appeared in Howard S. Becker,

"Generalizing from Case Studies," in *Qualitative Inquiry in Education: The Continuing Debate,* ed. E. W. Eisner and A. Peshkin (New York: Teachers College Press, Columbia University), 233–42, © 1990 by Teachers College, Columbia University, all rights reserved, reprinted by permission of Teachers College Press. Portions of chapter 5 originally appeared in Howard S. Becker, "How I Learned What a Crock Was," *Journal of Contemporary Ethnography* 22 (April 1993): 28–35. In addition, chapters 1, 3, and 5 contain excerpts of Everett C. Hughes, *The Sociological Eye* (New Brunswick, N.J.: Transaction Books, 1984), © 1984 by Transaction, Inc., all rights reserved, reprinted by permission of Transaction Publishers; chapter 3 contains excerpts of James Agee and Walker Evans, *Let Us Now Praise Famous Men* (Boston: Houghton Mifflin, 1941), 125–26, 162–65, © 1939, 1940 by James Agee, © 1941 James Agee and Walker Evans, © renewed 1969 by Mia Fritsch Agee and Walker Evans, reprinted by permission of Houghton Mifflin Co., all rights reserved; chapter 5 contains an excerpt of Arthur Danto, "The Artworld," *Journal of Philosophy* 61 (1964): 571–84, reprinted by permission of the *Journal of Philosophy.*

1

TRICKS

Undergraduates at the University of Chicago, when I was a student there, learned to deal with all difficult conceptual questions by saying, authoritatively, "Well, it all depends on how you define your terms." True enough, but it didn't help us much, since we didn't know anything special about how to do the defining.

I stayed at the University of Chicago for my graduate training and so met Everett C. Hughes, who became my adviser and, eventually, research partner. Hughes was a student of Robert E. Park, who could be considered the "founder" of the "Chicago School" of sociology. Hughes taught me to trace my sociological descent, through him and Park, back to Georg Simmel, the great German sociologist who had been Park's teacher. I am still proud of that lineage.

Hughes had no love for abstract Theory. A group of us students once approached him after class, nervously, to ask what he thought about "theory." He looked at us grumpily and asked, "Theory of what?" He thought that there were theories about specific things, like race and ethnicity or the organization of work, but that there wasn't any such animal as Theory in general. But he knew what to do when a class or a student got into a tangle over what we thought of as "theoretical" questions, like how to define ideas or concepts. We would wonder, for instance, how to define the concept of "ethnic group." How did we know if a group was one of those or not? Hughes had identified our chronic mistake, in an essay he wrote on ethnic relations in Canada:

> Almost anyone who uses the term [ethnic group] would say that it is a group distinguishable from others by one, or some combination of the following: physical characteristics, language, religion, customs, institutions, or "cultural traits." (Hughes [1971] 1984, 153)

That is, we thought you could define an "ethnic" group by the traits that differentiated it from some other, presumably "nonethnic," group; it was an ethnic group because it was different.

But, Hughes explained, we had it backwards. A simple trick could settle such a definitional conundrum: reverse the explanatory sequence and see the differences as the result of the definitions the people in a network of group relations made:

> An ethnic group is not one because of the degree of measurable or observable difference from other groups; it is an ethnic group, on the contrary, because the people in and the people out of it know that it is one; because both the *ins* and the *outs* talk, feel, and act as if it were a separate group. (Hughes [1971] 1984, 153–54)

So French Canadians were not an ethnic group *because* they spoke French while other Canadians spoke English, or *because* they were usually Catholic while the English were usually Protestant. They were an ethnic group because both French and English regarded the two groups as different. The differences in language, religion, culture and the rest we thought defined ethnicity were important, but only because two groups can treat each other as different only if "there are ways of telling who belongs to the group and who does not, and if a person learns early, deeply, and usually irrevocably to what group he belongs." The heart of the trick, which can be applied to all sorts of other definitional problems (for example, the problem of deviance, to which I'll return later in the book), is recognizing that you can't study an ethnic group all by itself and must instead trace its "ethnicity" to the network of relations with other groups in which it arises. Hughes says:

> It takes more than one ethnic group to make ethnic relations. The relations can no more be understood by studying one or the other of the groups than can a chemical combination by the study of one element only, or a boxing bout by the observation of only one of the fighters. (Hughes [1971] 1984, 155)

That's what a trick is—a simple device that helps you solve a problem (in this case, the device of looking for the network in which definitions arise and are used). Every trade has its tricks, its solutions to its own distinctive problems, easy ways of doing something lay people have a lot of trouble with. The social science trades, no less than plumbing or carpentry, have their tricks, designed to solve their peculiar problems. Some of these tricks are simple rules of thumb derived from experience, like the advice that putting colorful commemorative stamps on the return envelopes will get more people to send their questionnaires back. Others come out of a social scientific analysis of the situation in which the problem arises, like Julius Roth's (1965) suggestion that researchers consider the problem of cheating survey interviewers not as a kind of police matter, a problem of chasing down irresponsible employees, but rather as the way people who have no interest or stake in their work are likely to behave when their only motivation is economic.

The tricks that make up the content of this book help solve problems of thinking, the kind of problems social scientists usually see as "theoretical." Defining a term by looking for how its meaning arises in a network of relations is just the kind of trick I'm talking about, but it's not the usual way of settling theoretical questions. Social scientists typically discuss "theory" in a rarefied way, as a subject in its own right, coordinate with, but not really related to, the way we do research. To be sure, Merton's two classic papers (Merton 1957, 85–117) outline the close relations he thought theory and research ought to have to one another, but students studying for examinations used those ideas more than working researchers ever did. Hughes, who oriented his own methodological work to the practical problems of finding out about the world, always threatened to write "a little theory book," containing the essence of his theoretical position and somehow different from the nuggets of sociological generalization scattered through his essays and books.

Hughes's students, me among them, all hoped he would write that theory book, because we knew, when we listened to him and read his work, that we were learning a theory, though we couldn't say what it was. (Jean-Michel Chapoulie [1996] analyzes the basic ideas of Hughes's sociological style perceptively.) But he never wrote it. He didn't, I think, because he didn't have a systematic theory in the style of Talcott Parsons. He had, rather, a theoretically informed way of working, if that distinction conveys anything. His theory was not designed to provide all the conceptual boxes into which the world had to fit. It consisted, instead, of a collection of generalizing tricks he used to think about society, tricks that helped him interpret and make general sense of data. (The flavor is best conveyed in his essays, collected in Hughes [1971] 1984.) Because his theory consisted of such analytic tricks rather than a Theory, students learned it by hanging around him and learning to use his tricks, the way apprentices learn craft

ONE

skills by watching journeymen, who already know them, use them to solve real-life problems.

Like Hughes, I have a deep suspicion of abstract sociological theorizing; I regard it as at best a necessary evil, something we need in order to get our work done but, at the same time, a tool that is likely to get out of hand, leading to a generalized discourse largely divorced from the day-to-day digging into social life that constitutes sociological science. I've tried to tame theory for myself by viewing it as a collection of tricks, ways of thinking that help researchers faced with concrete research problems make some progress.

To repeat and amplify, a trick is a specific operation that shows a way around some common difficulty, suggests a procedure that solves relatively easily what would otherwise seem an intractable and persistent problem. The tricks that follow deal with problems in several areas of social science work, which I've roughly divided under the headings of imagery, sampling, concepts, and logic.

My descriptions of the tricks frequently consist of extended examples that might serve as exemplars in one of the Kuhnian senses, as models you can imitate when you run into a similar problem. I've been guided in this preference for examples, as opposed to general definitions, by my experience in teaching. When I taught the sociology of art, at a time when I was writing what became the book *Art Worlds* (Becker 1982), I was eager to share with students my theoretical framework for understanding art as a social product. But, of course, to fill out the class hours I told a lot of stories. One of my best lectures was on the Watts Towers, the incredible construction an Italian immigrant mason made in Los Angeles in the 1930s, and then left to take care of itself. I told his story and showed slides of the work. I meant it as a limiting case of the social character of an art work. Simon Rodia, who made the Towers, really did it all himself, with no help from anyone, no reliance on art theories or ideas or art history or art supply stores or museums or galleries or any organized art anything—and I explained how the work exhibited that independence and showed how you could see the marks of most works' dependence on all that stuff in the way they were made. To me, the point was the way the marginal case explained all the other cases. It was chastening, therefore, when students later told me that the thing they really remembered from that course was the Watts Towers. Some of them, with the story in mind, remembered the point I had been at such pains to make with the Towers too, but most of them just re-

4

membered the fact of the Towers' existence, the story of this crazy guy and his crazy art work. That taught me that stories and examples are what people attend to and remember. So there are plenty of both here.

(Some readers will note that many of my examples are not exactly up-to-date, not the latest findings or ideas. I've made that choice on purpose. It surprises me how much good work of the past is forgotten, not because it isn't good, but because students have never heard about it, never had their attention drawn to it. So I have often picked my examples from work that is thirty, forty, even fifty years old, in hope of giving it a deserved new life.)

These tricks, then, are ways of thinking about what we know or want to know that help us make sense of data and formulate new questions based on what we've found. They help us get all the good we can out of our data by exposing facets of the phenomenon we're studying other than those we've already thought of.

Sociologists of science (e.g., Latour and Woolgar 1979 and Lynch 1985) have shown us how natural scientists work in ways never mentioned in their formal statements of method, hiding "shop floor practice"—what scientists really do—in the formal way they talk about what they do. Social scientists do that too, using a workaday collection of theoretical tricks when they're actually doing social science, as opposed to talking about Theory. This book deals with what are often thought of as theoretical problems by cataloguing and analyzing some tricks social scientists use, social science's shop floor practice. I'll describe some of my favorites, as well as some I learned from Hughes, noting their theoretical relevance as I proceed. I've occasionally given them names to serve as mnemonics, so you'll encounter such creatures as the Machine Trick, the Wittgenstein Trick, and many others.

Calling this book *Tricks of the Trade* creates some ambiguities that should be cleared up right away. The phrase has several potential meanings, most of which I don't intend. Some may hope that I'm going to pass on tricks of getting along in academia: how to get a job, how to get tenure, how to get a better job, how to get your articles published. I'm always willing to discuss such things. My unconventional academic career, in which I spent many years as what used to be called a "research bum" before finally entering academia as a full professor, might have given me some special insights that come with marginality. But times change and the economic and political situation of universities has changed sufficiently that I doubt I any longer have any inside information on those chancy processes. In any event, academia isn't the trade I have in mind. (Aaron Wildavsky [1993] covers a lot of that ground.)

Others may think I mean technical tricks of writing or computing or "methods" or statistics (though not many expect statistical tricks from me). I've told what I know about technical writing tricks elsewhere (Becker 1986b), and probably have a similar collection of folkloric tips on other areas of social science practice to pass on. But those, while they are tricks of our social science trade, are too specific, not generalizable enough to warrant lengthy discussion. They are appropriately handed on in the oral tradition.

So I am talking about the trade of sociologist or (since so many people do work that I think of, imperialistically, as sociology even though they themselves think they are some other breed of social scientist or humanist) about the trade of studying society, under the aegis of whatever professional title suits. The tricks I have in mind are tricks that help those doing that kind of work to get on with it, whatever professional title they use. As a result, I have been somewhat carefree in using "sociology" and "social science" interchangeably, even though that occasionally creates ambiguities with respect to disciplines on the margin, like psychology.

Another thing I hope will be clear, but probably need to say explicitly, is that my thoughts are not restricted to what is usually called "qualitative" research. It's the kind of research I've done, but that represents a practical, rather than an ideological, choice. It's what I knew how to do, and found personal enjoyment in, so I kept on doing it. But I've always been alive to the possibilities of other methods (so long as they weren't pressed on me as matters of religious conviction), and have found it particularly useful to think about what I did in terms that came from such other ways of working as survey research or mathematical modeling. So the ideas contained here are not meant for the initiates of anthropological-style fieldwork alone, though they will, I hope, find its contents familiar though not soothing. It's also meant for people who work in the variety of styles and traditions that make up contemporary social science.

The word "trick" usually suggests that the device or operation described will make things easier to do. In this case, that's misleading. To tell the truth, these tricks probably make things harder for the researcher, in a special sense. Instead of making it easier to get a conventional piece of work done, they suggest ways of interfering with the comfortable thought routines academic life promotes and supports by making them the "right" way to do things. This is a case where the "right" is the enemy of the good. What the tricks do is suggest ways to turn things around, to see things differently, in order to create new problems for research, new possibilities for comparing cases and inventing new categories, and the like. All that is work. It's enjoyable, but it's more work than if you did things in a routine way that didn't make you think at all.

Clifford Geertz has given a good description of the work these tricks are supposed to do:

> What recommends them ["figurations" describing an ethnographic result], or disrecommends them, is the further figures that issue from them; their capacity to lead on to extended accounts which, intersecting other accounts of other matters, widen their implications and deepen their hold. We can always count on something else happening, another glancing experience, another half-witnessed event. What we can't count on is that we will have something useful to say about it when it does. We are in no danger of running out of reality; we are in constant danger of running out of signs, or at least of having the old ones die on us. The after the fact, *ex post,* life-trailing nature of consciousness generally—occurrence first, formulation later on—appears in anthropology as a continual effort to devise systems of discourse that can keep up, more or less, with what, perhaps, is going on. (Geertz 1995, 19)

Every section of the book thus takes up the theme of convention—social convention and scientific convention—as a major enemy of sociological thought. Every subject we study has already been studied by lots of people with lots of ideas of their own, and is further the domain of the people who actually inhabit that world, who have ideas of their own about what it's about and what the objects and events in it mean. These experts by profession or group membership usually have an uninspected and unchallenged monopoly of ideas on "their" subject. Newcomers to the study of the subject, whatever it is, can easily be seduced into adopting those conventional ideas as the uninspected premises of their research. The estimable activity of "reviewing the literature," so dear to the hearts of dissertation committees, exposes us to the danger of that seduction.

So we need ways of expanding the reach of our thinking, of seeing what else we could be thinking and asking, of increasing the ability of our ideas to deal with the diversity of what goes on in the world. Many of the tricks I describe are devoted to that enterprise.

The book's sections concern major aspects of the work of social science research. "Imagery" deals with how we think about what we are going to study before we actually start our research, and how our pictures of what that part of the social world is like, and what the work of the social scientist is like, get made. It discusses the various forms imagery about society takes, and suggests ways of getting control over how we see things, so that we are not simply the unknowing carriers of the conventional world's thoughts.

"Sampling," the next section, recognizes that our general ideas always reflect the selection of cases from the universe of cases that might have been considered. It takes up the question of how we choose what we actually look at, the cases we will have in mind when we formulate our general ideas explicitly. It suggests the necessity of choosing cases in ways that maximize the chance of finding at least a few that will jar our ideas, make us question what we think we know.

"Concepts," the third section of this book, takes up the making of our ideas. How shall we put together what we learn from our samples in the form of more general ideas? How can we use the world's diversity, which our efforts to improve our imagery and sampling have delivered to us, to create better, more useful ways to think about things?

Finally, "Logic" suggests ways of manipulating ideas through methods of more or less (mostly less) formal logic. This section borrows heavily from materials already constructed and diffused by others (notably Paul Lazarsfeld, Charles Ragin, and Alfred Lindesmith—an unlikely trio). A major theme here, borrowed from Ragin, is the usefulness of focusing on a diversity of cases rather than on variation in variables. (That shorthand will be explained in "Logic.") I don't apologize for my borrowings, except to say that I've taken only from the best and given credit, as best I can remember, for what I've taken.

Readers will soon discover, so I might as well confess, that there is a certain arbitrariness in where topics are discussed. Most topics could have been (and sometimes are) taken up in more than one place. The section headings are only rough guides to the section contents. The ideas are not a seamless web of logically connected propositions (don't I wish!), but they are an organic whole. That is, they all pretty much imply one another. The book is a network or web rather than a straight line.

The sections seem to have a kind of rough chronological order, too. You might think that researchers naturally begin their work by having images of various kinds about what they are going to study and then, on the basis of those images, develop ideas about what to study and how to choose cases (in other words, how to devise sampling schemes). You might think further that, having picked the cases to be studied and having studied them, researchers then develop concepts to use in their analyses, and apply logic in the application of those concepts to their cases. You might reasonably think all that because most of the books on theory building and methods of research specify such an order as the "right way." But if you did, you'd be wrong. The various operations have that kind of logical connection among themselves—imagery, in some sense, certainly underlies and seems to dictate a kind of sampling—but that doesn't mean you do them in that order, not if you want to get any serious work done.

Serious researchers repeatedly move back and forth among these four areas of thought, and each area affects the others. I may choose my sample in a way that takes into account my image of what I'm studying, but I will surely modify my image on the basis of what my sample shows me. And the logical operations I perform on the results of some part of my work will probably dictate a change in my concepts. And so on. There is no sense imagining that this will be a neat, logical, unmessy process. Geertz again:

> One works *ad hoc* and *ad interim*, piecing together thousand-year histories with three-week massacres, international conflicts with municipal ecologies. The economics of rice or olives, the politics of ethnicity or religion, the workings of language or war, must, to some extent, be soldered into the final construction. So must geography, trade, art, and technology. The result, inevitably, is unsatisfactory, lumbering, shaky, and badly formed: a grand contraption. The anthropologist, or at least one who wishes to complicate his contraptions, not close them in upon themselves, is a manic tinkerer adrift with his wits. (Geertz 1995, 20)

None of the tricks of thinking in this book have a "proper place" in the timetable for building such a contraption. Use them when it looks like they might move your work along—at the beginning, in the middle, or toward the end of your research.

2

IMAGERY

Herbert Blumer (1969) was another of my teachers at the University of Chicago. A former football player, he was tall, heavy, and imposing, with a voice that rose to an incongruously high squeak when he got excited over some abstract theoretical point. He taught us social psychology and an idiosyncratic version of methodology, one aspect of which was the habitual, even obsessive, way he called attention to the underlying imagery with which sociologists approach the phenomena they study. What do they think they are looking at? What is its character? Most importantly, given what they think it is, do they study it and report their findings about it in a way that is congruent with that character? He made this point often and forcefully:

> One can see the empirical world only through some scheme or image of it. The *entire act* of scientific study is oriented and shaped by the underlying picture of the empirical world that is used. This picture sets the selection and formulation of problems, the determination of what are data, the means to be used in getting the data, the kinds of relations sought between data, and the forms in which propositions are cast. In view of this fundamental and pervasive effect wielded on the entire act of scientific inquiry by the initiating picture of the empirical world, it is ridiculous to ignore this picture. The underlying picture of the world is always capable of identification in the form of a set of premises. These premises are constituted by the nature given either explicitly or implicitly to the key objects that comprise the picture. The unavoidable task of genuine methodological treatment is to identify and assess these premises. (Blumer 1969, 24–25)

Blumer was primarily interested in scolding sociologists for basing their work on imagery that was blatantly incompatible with what people knew, in particular for working with images of society that contradicted the way their own daily experience told them things were. I was a student of Blumer's and learned the importance of this through an exercise he urged on us: take any ten minutes of your own experience and try to explain and understand it using any of the currently fashionable theories of social psychology. As you tried to apply, say, stimulus-response psychology (then quite popular) to such mundane activities as getting up and having breakfast, you realized that you couldn't identify the stimuli or connect them in any sure way to the way you were "responding." We got the point soon enough. No available theory gave you the words and ideas, the imagery, with which to do justice to the multitude of things you saw and heard and felt and did as you went about doing the things your life was made up of.

But once you've accepted the idea that our usual social science imagery is lacking something, what do you do? Why is our imagery so bad? How do we improve it? I suffered, with other students, the difficulties that came from seeing the problem but no solution. Blumer let us down there. He was merciless in exposing the failure of sociologists to respect, or even to know much about, what he always called "the obdurate character of social life as a process of interacting selves."

> [A]lmost by definition the research scholar does not have a first-hand acquaintance with the sphere of social life he proposes to study. He is rarely a participant in that sphere and usually is not in close touch with the actions and the experiences of the people who are involved in that sphere. His position is almost always that of an outsider; as such he is markedly limited in simple knowledge of what takes place in the given sphere of life. The sociologist who proposes to study crime, or student unrest in Latin America, or political elites in Africa, and the psychologist who undertakes to study adolescent drug use, or aspirations among Negro school children, or social judgments among delinquents exemplify this almost inevitable absence of intimate acquaintance with the area of life under consideration. (Blumer 1969, 35–36)

Blumer never pursued this line of thought to the point of providing specific remedies. He did not tell us what would be good images for us to work with, except at the most abstract level, or how to create them, other than to achieve a firsthand knowledge of the area of social life we were interested in. That was clearly necessary, but it wasn't sufficient guidance for us. In this chapter I'm going to try to remedy that lack of specificity, and discuss the images social scientists use, look at where they come from, and provide specific tricks for improving them.

Substantive Imagery

To begin again, Blumer thought, and so do I, that the basic operation in studying society—we start with images and end with them—is the production and refinement of an image of the thing we are studying. We learn a little (maybe a lot) about something we're interested in. On the basis of that little, we construct (or imagine) a pretty complete story of the phenomenon. Suppose I decide to study a city neighborhood. I might begin by consulting a book of local statistics (the *Chicago Community Fact Book* or the relevant Census publications) to see what kind of people live there. How many men? How many women? How old are they? What is their median education? Their median income? With this basic information, I can work up a complete, if provisional, mental picture—an image—of the neighborhood, deciding on the basis of the figures on income and education that it is a working-class neighborhood, using the age distribution to guess at the nature of family life, seeing it as an area of people retiring or getting ready to retire or, conversely, as an area filled with young people just beginning their families. When I add the variables of race and ethnicity my picture becomes still more detailed.

My picture is more than a compilation of statistics. It includes details that are not in the books and tables I consulted, details I invented on the basis of what those books told me. This takes us to the second part of Blumer's critique of the imagery of social scientists:

> [D]espite this lack of firsthand acquaintance the research scholar will unwittingly form some kind of picture of the area of life he proposes to study. He will bring into play the beliefs and images that he already has to fashion a more or less intelligible view of the area of life. In this respect he is like all human beings. Whether we be laymen or scholars, we necessarily view any unfamiliar area of group life through images we already possess. We may have no firsthand acquaintance with life among delinquent groups, or in labor unions, or in legislative committees, or among bank executives, or in a religious cult, yet given a few cues we readily form serviceable pictures of such life. This, as we all know, is the point at which stereotyped images enter and take control. All of us, as scholars, have our share of common stereotypes that we use to see a sphere of empirical social life that we do not know. (Blumer 1969, 36)

So, after gathering these few preliminary facts about the neighborhood I intend to study, I "know," for instance, what kinds of houses these people live in—I can almost see, as if in a photograph, the neat lawn with the plastic flamingos, the furniture "suites" from the credit furniture store and whatever else my stereotype of that kind of population produces. None of this is based on any real knowledge of the area. It is imagery I have constructed imaginatively, just as Blumer says I would, from a few facts and the stock of stereotypes my own experience of society has provided me with. It includes, if I'm imaginative enough, the look of the streets and the smell of the kitchens ("Italians? Garlic!"). If I'm well read enough in social science, I can even add to my picture of the neighborhood some idea of, say, the kind of talk that goes on over the dinner table ("Working class? Restricted code—a lot of grunts and monosyllables, as described by Basil Bernstein").

Imaginative, well-read social scientists can go a long way with a little fact. Since, however, we all claim to be social *scientists,* we don't stop with imagination and extrapolation, as a novelist or filmmaker might. Because we also know that our stereotypes are just that, and are as likely to be inaccurate as not. We find Blumer waiting for us here, with another damning complaint:

> [T]he research scholar in the social sciences has another set of pre-established images that he uses. These images are constituted by his theories, by the beliefs current in his own professional circles, and by his ideas of how the empirical world must be set up to allow him to follow his research procedure. No careful observer can honestly deny that this is true. We see it clearly in the shaping of pictures of the empirical world to fit one's theories, in the organizing of such pictures in terms of the concepts and beliefs that enjoy current acceptance among one's set of colleagues, and in the molding of such pictures to fit the demands of scientific protocol. We must say in all honesty that the research scholar in the social sciences who undertakes to study a given sphere of social life that he does not know at first hand will fashion a picture of that sphere in terms of pre-established images. (Blumer 1969, 36)

As he says, our imagery at this level determines the direction of our research—the ideas we start with, the questions we ask to check them out, the answers we find plausible. And it does that without us thinking much about it, because these are things we scarcely know we "know." They are just part of the baggage of our ordinary lives, the knowledge we rely on when we aren't being scientists and don't feel we need to know things in that special scientific way that would let us publish in reputable scientific journals.

Some social scientists will stop me here and say that they never talk about things for which they have no data. I don't believe them. Let's consider the obvious case to which Herbert Blumer, and many others since, have devoted a lot of attention, the imputation of meanings and motives to social actors. (The same problems arise with respect to matters that seem less amorphous, events and other "harder" facts; I'll get to those in later sections.) We social scientists always, implicitly or explicitly, attribute a point of view, a perspective, and motives to the people whose actions we analyze. We *always,* for instance, describe the meanings the people we have studied give to the events they participate in, so the only question is not whether we should do that, but how accurately we do it. We can, and many social scientists do, gather data about the meanings people give to things. We find out—not with perfect accuracy, but better than zero—what people think they are doing, how they interpret the objects and events and people in their lives and experience. We do that by talking to them, in formal or informal interviews, in quick exchanges while we participate in and observe their ordinary activities, and by watching and listening as they go about their business; we can even do it by giving them questionnaires that let them say what their meanings are or choose between meanings we give them as possibilities. The nearer we get to the conditions in which they actually attribute meanings to objects and events, the more accurate our descriptions of those meanings will be.

What if we don't find out directly what meanings people are actually giving to things. and to their own and others' activities? Will we, in a spasm of scientific asceticism, rigorously abstain from any discussion of motives and purposes and intents? Not likely. No, we will still talk about those meanings, but we will, by necessity born of ignorance, make them up, using the knowledge that comes out of our everyday experience (or lack of it) to argue that the people we are writing about must have meant this or that, or they would not have done the things they did. But it is, of course, dangerous to guess at what could be known more directly. The danger is that we will guess wrong, that what looks reasonable to us will not be what looked reasonable to them. We run this risk all the time, largely because, as Blumer indicated, we are not those people and do not live in their circumstances. We are thus likely to take the easy way, attributing to people what we think we would feel in what we understand to be their situations, as when scholars studying teen-age behavior (more than likely middle aged, more than likely men) look at comparative rates of pregnancy, and the correlates thereof, and decide what the young women who had these babies "must have been" thinking in order to get themselves into such a fix. In the absence of real knowledge, our imagery takes over.

The study of drug use is filled with such errors. Experts and lay people alike commonly interpret drug use as an "escape" from some sort of reality the drug user is thought to find oppressive or unbearable. They conceive drug intoxication as an experience in which all painful and unwanted aspects of reality recede into the background and need not be dealt with. The drug user replaces reality with gaudy dreams of splendor and ease, unproblematic pleasures, perverse erotic thrills and fantasies. Reality, of course, is understood to be lurking in the background, ready to kick the user in the ass the second he or she comes down.

This kind of imagery has a long literary history, probably stemming from De Quincey's *Confessions of an English Opium Eater* (De Quincey 1971). (A wonderful nineteenth-century American version is Fitz Hugh Ludlow's *The Hashish Eater* [Ludlow 1975].) These works play on the imagery analyzed in Edward Said's dissection of Orientalia, the Orient as Mysterious Other (Said 1978). A more up-to-date version, more science-fiction, less Oriental, and less benign, can be found in William Burroughs's *Naked Lunch* (1966).

Such descriptions of drug use are, as could be and has been found out by generations of researchers who bothered to ask, pure fantasies invented (with help from the literature I cited) by the researchers who publish them. The fantasies do not correspond to the experiences of users or of those researchers who have made the experiment of using drugs themselves. They are concocted out of a kind of willful ignorance. Misinterpretations of people's experience and meanings are commonplace in studies of delinquency and crime, of sexual behavior, and in general of behavior outside the experience and lifestyle of conventional academic researchers.

Since our lay imagery influences our work so much, we should take care that it is accurate. But how can you do that? Imagery enters our heads as the residue of our everyday experience; so, to get better imagery in there, we have to do something about the character of our ordinary lives. That is what Blumer, ponderously and abstractly, hinted at.

Harvey Molotch (1994), feelingly and tellingly, has expanded and given texture to Blumer's diagnosis and prescription. He begins by quoting Patricia Limerick's assertion that academics are the people nobody would dance with in high school and adds, on his own account, that they are also the last people chosen for gym class ball teams. He describes his own youthful image of sociology as the work of some kind of amalgam of C. Wright Mills, Jack Kerouac, Lenny Bruce, and Henry Miller, "all heroes who knew the world through its edges—deviant, strident, and/or dirty mouthed." That is, if you want to write about society, you have to know about it firsthand, and particularly have to know about the places respectable people have little experience of: "the taxi-dance hall, the housing projects, the protest marches, the youth gang, and the dark places most of us know only as haunting hints of the possible."

But, Molotch says, sociologists are not only not Kerouac, they are not even Louis Wirth or Herbert Gans (who studied Jewish and Italian ghettoes, respectively), and cannot "sustain a pattern of taking on even the ordinary outside settings. Sociologists often know no world outside their own academic and family daily round; they do not hang around commodity trading floors, or holy roller churches, or exclusive golf clubs. Committee meetings, teaching loads, peer reviews, and writing essays like this are the occupation, leaving little space for walking through the world." Without fuller participation in society (the title of Molotch's essay is "Going Out"), we don't know the first things that would keep us from making dumb mistakes.

(Molotch makes another interesting point, tangential to what I'm arguing here, but worth noting. Without knowledge based on firsthand experience to correct our imagery, we not only don't know where to look for the interesting stuff, we also don't know what doesn't need extensive investigation and proof. Lacking personal knowledge, we assume that many ordinary things are among those great social science mysteries that need to be cleared up with a big study and a lot of data. An early version of Molotch's diagnosis defined a sociologist as someone who spends a hundred thousand dollars studying prostitution to discover what any cab driver could have told him. I had a wonderful example of this myself some years ago when I described the study of regional American theater Michal McCall and I (Becker, McCall, and Morris 1989) wanted to do to a distinguished and very smart sociologist who just happened to have been born and raised in New York City. When I explained that we wanted to study the network of regional theaters that had replaced New York as the center of the theater world, he insisted that we could not do our study without a preliminary study that would prove that New York had been replaced, which his provincial pride told him just could not be true. I got off by citing a hard-to-counter statistic: that while, in the old days, circa 1950, almost all theatrical employment in the United States was in New York, by the late 1980s half the paid days of theater work occurred outside the New York area. New Yorkers don't take the downgrading of their town lightly.)

Science Imagery

Because we are, after all, social *scientists,* we aren't satisfied to stop with the imagery of daily life we bring to a new object of study, no matter how detailed and imaginative it is. We do a little checking to see if we're right. Research. We gather data. We construct hypotheses and theories.

Now, however, we enter the more abstract realm of imagery whose origins Blumer traced to our professional lives and the groups they embed us in. This imagery is "scientific." Perhaps it is less presumptuous just to say that it is professional. That is, it is not the imagery embodied in the lay stereotypes I spoke of earlier ("Italians? Garlic!"). It is the imagery shared by a professional group whose members make their living studying and writing about such matters for the edification and judgment of professional peers.

Professional imagery is not tied to such specifics as garlic. Some social science imagery, of course, is specific ("Working class? Restricted speech codes!"). But the imagery I am most concerned with now is abstract. It envisions not such specifics as the working class of London, but, instead, abstract entities recognized only by people who have been trained to see the world in a professional way. We use these images to embody, and to help us produce, knowledge and understanding about large, abstractly defined classes of stuff, not just about single members of those classes. Social scientists usually think of these images as theories or explanations of something, stories about how events and people of a certain kind come to be the way they are. (If that sounds abstract and a little unreal, it is in direct imitation of the kind of knowledge I'm talking about.) I will for the moment use the word "story" as the generic term for these explanations and descriptions, since they can almost always be understood as some kind of narrative about how something happened in the past, happens now, and will happen in the future. Since they are told to a professional audience, these stories have certain generic features and problems. (I'll use "story" or "narrative" later on to describe a particular kind of science story.)

Telling Scientific Stories

Creating an acceptable scientific theory or explanation of some phenomenon constrains the telling of the story in two ways. The story must first of
all "work," be coherent in any of the many ways stories can be of one piece.
It has to get us from here to there in such a way that when we reach the end
we say yes, that's the way it has to end. So we try to construct a story about
our topic, a story that includes everything we think it ought to have (or else
the story will be incomplete in some crucial way) and puts it together in a
way that "makes sense." It's not obvious what "makes sense" means here.
What I, at least, mean is that the story must embody or be organized on
some principle that the reader (and author) accept as a reasonable way to
connect things. Robert E. Park told a story about the *race relations cycle,* a
story about how different kinds of relations between blacks and whites followed one another. It was acceptable to people, in part, because the idea of
a cycle, in which one set of affairs creates the conditions under which the
next stage arises, made sense to them.

The other constraint is that the story must be congruent with the facts
we have found out. I suppose there's also an argument about what it would
mean for stories and facts to be congruent. Thomas Kuhn taught us that
our observations are not "pure," that they are shaped by our concepts—we
see what we have ideas about, and can't see what we don't have words and
ideas for. So, in a strong sense, there aren't any "facts" independent of the
ideas we use to describe them. That's true, but irrelevant here. Recognizing the conceptual shaping of our perceptions, it is still true that not everything our concepts would, in principle, let us see actually turns up in what
we look at. So we can only "see" men and women in the Census, because,
providing only those two gender categories, it prevents us from seeing the
variety of other gender types a different conceptualization would show us.
The Census doesn't recognize such complicating categories as "transgen-
der." But if we said that the population of the United States, counted the
way the Census counts, consisted of fifty percent men and fifty percent
women, the Census report could certainly tell us that that story is wrong.
We don't accept stories that are not borne out by the facts we have available.

"Not accepting a story" means believing that the story's imagery of how
this thing really works is wrong in some important way—we can't understand it or we know that it's not true because some facts inconveniently

refuse to be congruent with it. When that happens, and we can't elude or finesse it, we try to change the story.

There's a tension here, between changing stories to make the logic better and changing stories to take better account of the facts. Which should we do? Which do we do? This is, of course, a phony question: we should and do do both. A more reasonable question is when we should or do do one or the other. Sometimes we want to produce a very complicated story, and don't worry about loose ends and not too much coherence. At such times, we immerse ourselves in facts—read a lot about neurophysiology or interview a lot of theater people or observe a group of Hungarian steel workers—so that we know a lot of discrete facts about our topic. That means we can find, any time we want to look hard enough, something inconvenient for the picture we already have of what neurophysiology or steel working or whatever is like. When we do that, we push ourselves to extend our ideas and images to accommodate more of the "real world," as we usually call it.

Sometimes, though, we look for the kind of nice, neat story we like to think, when we are feeling scientific, can be told about the world. We try to identify some of the things we have discovered as things people in our kind of science have already discovered and named, and about whose interconnections our kind of scientist has already worked out such a story. Then we need only show that we have another case of one of those already-known stories and everyone will be happy and relieved, especially us. Working in that style, we push ourselves to be ingenious and connect the things we're telling about in ingenious ways that remove anomalies and make our basic picture simple, clean, intuitively apprehensible, "obvious." If we tell such a story, we need only cite some facts and everyone will believe it; we will believe it ourselves and be relieved that we have after all found some order in the world. We have a neat story or image. Unfortunately, it is one easily punctured by inconvenient facts.

Within the limits created by our solutions to these problems, we have a wide choice of kinds of imagery. Generally speaking, professionalized imagery has to do with the kind of causality we think might be operating. Do we think the phenomenon we're studying is totally governed by chance, so that a model of random activity is appropriate? Do we think it is partly chance and partly something more deterministic? Do we think it is best described as a narrative, told as a story? In other words, in thinking about the phenomenon, we include in the picture we build up some notions about the kind of conclusion we will draw about it, the kind of paradigmatic thinking we will assimilate it to. These paradigms come to us out of our participation in a world of professional social scientists. (My debt to Kuhn [1970] here is obvious.)

That specialized occupational world gives us many images of the way the social world in general works. Blumer's notion of society as made up of interacting selves is one such. Others include a world governed by random activity; the social world as coincidence; the social world as machine; the social world as organism; the social world as story. Each of these images helps you get at some things and keeps you from getting at others. I'll take them up in turn, detailing, with examples, their characteristic features, and describing the kinds of analytic tricks they make possible.

The Null Hypothesis Trick

Our imagery need not always be accurate. Blumer was wrong about that. Inaccurate images of things, as long as they are eventually checked against reality, can be very useful, showing us how things would be if they were a certain way we're pretty sure they aren't.

RANDOM ASSIGNMENTS

The classic version of this trick is the null hypothesis, which asserts a hypothesis the researcher believes is not true. Proving the null hypothesis wrong proves that something else must be right, though it doesn't tell you what that something else is. Its simplest form, well known to statisticians and experimentalists, asserts that two variables are related only by chance. The image is one of numbered balls being drawn by a blindfolded person from an urn, each ball having an equal chance of being chosen. Or of particles bumping around in an enclosed space, each equally likely to bump into any other one. Nothing operates to "bias" the outcome. No influences make any outcome any more likely than any other.

Scientists who do experiments do not announce the null hypothesis—that the differing results of treating the same stuff in two different ways are random, that the "treatment variable" they introduced into their experimental situation has no effect—because they think it's true. On the contrary, they hope and trust that they are wrong and their null hypothesis will be disproved. When they find some kind of relationship (and thus can reject the null hypothesis of no relationship at a given level of significance), that becomes presumptive evidence for whatever theory they were propounding. It gives them a basis on which to say that there is very little chance that these results would have occurred if their theory weren't true. They never believed there was no relationship at all, they just said that in order to focus the investigation and provide a way to state a result. The hypothesis that the world runs on random numbers serves them analytically by showing what the world would be like if it really did. The experiment gets its import and its punch from showing that the world is, exactly, not like that.

(There's a problem with this, which Anatole Beck showed me years ago. This device tells you the chance of getting a particular result, given that your theory is true. But that isn't what you want to know. You already know that you *have* gotten these results, and talking about the probability of getting them is somehow silly. What you want to know is the probability of your theory being true, given that you got these results. And, according to Beck, there's no mathematical way of turning the result you *can* get into the result you'd *like* to get.)

My null hypothesis trick is a qualitative or theoretical version of the statistical device. You start by observing that any social event consists of the joint activity of a lot of people. Typically, we want to understand the activities of the people who have been chosen, or have volunteered themselves, or have in some other way been led to participate in this event, who come from a much larger aggregate of people who in some sense were "eligible" or "available" or "likely candidates" for participation. That is, out of the large pool of people who might have chosen or been chosen, only some were.

The null hypothesis trick is to hypothesize that the selection of participants *was* random, that everyone in the larger pool of potential participants was equally likely to be chosen, that no "selection" was being made by anyone or even by the workings of social structure. Participants were assembled in some analog of assigning everyone a number and then using a table of random numbers to assemble the required cast. The thousand children in a neighborhood with a high juvenile delinquency rate were all equally likely to become delinquent. Some got their numbers picked up, others didn't. That's it.

Of course, in social reality everyone is not "eligible," or not equally "eligible," to participate in any specific event. The workings of social life almost always ensure that only a very small and highly selected collection of people will be chosen or be eligible to be chosen. That's the point of this trick. Just as in the statistical version, you pretend there was a random selection exactly in order to see how the population selected to participate varies from the population random selection would have produced. You assume that it *will* so vary, and want to know *how* so that you can then see what social practices or structures produced that deviation from random assignment.

Here's an example. Lori Morris, Michal McCall, and I wanted to know, among other things, how the social organization of a theater community leads to the productions playgoers eventually see (Morris 1989; Becker, McCall, and Morris 1989; Becker and McCall 1990). One aspect of this process is the casting of actors in roles in plays. We could, using the null hypothesis trick, assume (for the sake of argument, remember!) that directors cast shows by picking actors from a list of those available by using random numbers. In such purely "blind" casting, the people doing the choosing wouldn't worry about age, gender, race, physical type or anything else. A seventy-year-old black woman might play Romeo. Under slightly less stringent rules, the director could take account of those variables, but nothing else.

These "less stringent rules" I just invoked so blithely are actually the beginning of the analysis, because (since very few plays are cast with such disregard for these basic social variables) they show that directors actually are constrained in their choice of actors by their acceptance, more or less unconsciously (and I do mean *more* or *less*), of the rules governing what kind of socially defined person can play what kind of dramatically defined person. So they will not assign a male to a female part unless they specifically want, for some special purpose, the effect that would create (which is what Caryl Churchill did in *Cloud 9*). Or, to make the analysis a little more realistic, they cast an "inappropriate" person because they have no choice, because no one of the "right" physical type is available. The reason so many smaller theaters cast Lears who are obviously too young for the role is that there are many more young actors than old ones, especially in theaters that don't pay very well or at all.

Very often, especially in a "well-defined" problem like the one I have posed, we ignore this sort of prior selection as obvious, don't notice it until the people in the world we are studying turn it into an issue they are conscious about (as socially stereotyped casting eventually became an issue, largely though not only with respect to race, under the heading of "non-traditional casting"). Which is to say that a "well-defined problem" is one for which we have already ruled out of consideration a lot of potentially very interesting processes.

So our "well-defined problem" about theater casting focused us (until Lori Morris's fieldwork [Morris 1989] made us see some of these other considerations) on the processes that grew more naturally out of community organization and the way that organization interfered with random selection. In an organized theater community, selective interaction gets people acquainted with one another in such a way that the people who make casting decisions "know" enough about actors to know what they can do and how they are to work with. This mainly happens when directors have already worked with actors in previous shows. So the processes of casting either keep directors from learning this much about very many people (as would be the case in a tightly organized theater world in which the same few people always worked for the same director who never worked with people from outside that group) or allow them to learn a lot about a lot of people (as would be the case if every show was cast strictly from well-attended auditions) or, naturally, everything in between.

In short, Morris looked at who got cast and asked (knowing in advance that the answer would be "No") whether they had been chosen by some version of random numbers. Sure enough, the answer was "No," which then pushed her to find out just how the selection varied from random and how that result came about. And that pointed her to the processes of professional community organization we were looking for.

Were we really that dumb? Didn't we know before going through such a naive exercise that the selection wasn't random? Yes, of course we knew that, and the above is a little bit of a fairy tale about how we actually did things. In real life, you use a trick like this at any stage of your work, even after you have some idea of what's going on. You use it not because it produces a result you could not have imagined otherwise, but to help you formalize your thinking and perhaps see some connections you might not have noticed or taken seriously.

So far, I've talked about how people are selected for participation in social events—that is, in any kind of collective action. But there's no reason to limit the use of this trick to the selection of people. People, singly and together, make choices of things to do, and they choose the things they do in a particular situation from a larger number of things they might have chosen to do. Some of these other choices will be things they know about as possibilities and have decided not to choose for reasons they are well aware of and can, if they want, describe to an inquiring sociologist. Some of the possibilities may occur to them so fleetingly, be rejected so quickly, as not to be remembered even as potential choices. And still others will be things that just don't seem to them possible, not even for a minute.

Whatever combination of these three is the case, we can use the same trick as before. We can begin with the null hypothesis that the choice of what to do was made by using random numbers to choose from a complete list of possible actions. Again, we know that this is not how it happens, but think we will learn something by making that unrealistic assumption.

And we will. What we will learn, as in the first case, is what constraints make people decide that this particular choice is, after all, the best one or, perhaps, the only (practical) one. Constraints are one of the major things social science studies. Joseph Lohman used to say that sociology studied what people *had* to do, the things they did whether they liked it or not. (That's not completely true, because people often do what has to be done because they've learned to like doing it, but that's another story.) In any event, this trick shows us, by highlighting the deviations from randomness, what constraints are operating and thus what the nature is of the social organization we are studying.

This means that a scientifically adequate analysis of a situation will lay out the full range of constraints operating. To get that full range we need to know, as well as we can, the complete range of possibilities from which the choices we observe have been picked. To know that, we have to make ourselves as aware as we can of all the kinds of possibilities there are in the world from which the things that did happen were chosen. We need to do whatever we can to make ourselves think of unlikely possibilities, and we also need to take stern precautions against dropping any possibilities from our analysis just because they seem unlikely or are too much trouble to look into. I will take this question up later, in the section on "Sampling."

What Is a Nice Girl Like You Doing in a Place Like This?

There are other possible and useful null hypotheses—hypotheses you take up because you think they're not true and think that searching for what negates them will get you to what is true—besides the random assignment model. For instance, people often explain conduct they don't like or don't understand by saying that it is crazy (or some tonier word or phrase that means the same thing, like "psychologically disturbed" or even "socially disorganized"). The sign that the conduct is crazy is that it serves no useful purpose the analyst can imagine. In the folklore about prostitutes, their customers are always asking why a seemingly "nice" woman like the one they are with is doing this kind of work. The classic question about why a nice girl like you is doing this reflects a cultural contradiction: the woman seems nice (that is, not weird and unusual, not a member of a different species), but "nice girls" don't sell their cooperation in a sexual act. The motives that explain the behavior of "normal" women don't seem to explain this behavior, but the woman looks and acts normal. The sociological analyst who looks for unusual motives that differ from those that lie behind normal behavior is betraying the same naiveté as the customers who ask for those explanations.

Smoking marijuana, to take another example, serves no useful purpose. To understand why some folks nevertheless smoke it, we can use the version of the null hypothesis that says an action doesn't make any sense, actions like marijuana smoking being a good example. We try to disprove this null hypothesis, by showing that things that look crazy or erratic or capricious might make sense, if you knew more about them. In this case, we look for the reasons why smoking marijuana makes perfect sense to the smoker. An answer might be that it gives the smoker pleasure inexpensively and without significant social sanctions.

It's not just marijuana smoking that can be made sense of that way. It's generally a good sociological alternative to the null hypothesis of craziness to assume that the action to be studied makes perfect sense, only we don't know the sense it makes. You might say, in a variant of an expression that was very popular in my high school as a way of explaining something stupid you had done, "it seemed like a good idea at the time." In fact, it's probably a very good hypothesis about seemingly unintelligible acts that they seemed like a good idea at the time to the people who did them. This makes the analytic task the discovery of the circumstances which made the actor think it was a good idea.

An obvious way to begin that analysis is to see that things often seem like a good idea because their consequences aren't visible when the action is undertaken. It's only in hindsight, after the house whose value you and everyone else were sure was going to go up goes down, that you see that buying it wasn't a good idea after all. It's worth remembering that no one can ever predict the result of any human action with perfect confidence, and therefore that even the seemingly safest choice can turn out badly. Reasonable people, and experts, often disagree about the likely outcome of an action, so a lot of things that looked like good ideas will turn out, in the end, to have been dumb.

(One reason the null hypothesis of craziness is interesting is that other disciplines—some versions of psychology especially—make a living by insisting that some actions *really* don't make any sense and are in fact the result of mental disorder of some kind, so we're not just fighting a hypothetical null hypothesis, so to speak, we're fighting another discipline's positive hypothesis.)

Things also often look incomprehensible to us simply because we are too far away from the situation to know the actual contingencies under which the action was chosen. Take the rather gaudy, but nevertheless interesting, example of sex change operations. It's possible to ask the question this way: What would lead a seemingly normal American man to have his penis and testicles amputated? To put it that way makes the act completely unintelligible. "Hi! Like to have your genitals amputated?" "No, thanks!"

But, as James Driscoll's (1971) research (done early in the history of sex change surgery) showed, that isn't how it happens. Men don't suddenly decide, whether in the grip of hidden motives or drives or not, to have such surgery. That final decision is the end of a long line of prior decisions, each of which—and this is the key point—did not seem so bizarre in itself. Here is one, not necessarily the only, typical trajectory. First, perhaps, a young man finds himself drawn to some version of homosexual activity. His initial impulse, perhaps (and each of these perhapses represents a contingency point at which some portion of the group that has taken this step turns in another direction we are not going to investigate because we are only interested in the ones that take this path toward a sex change operation), leads him into a social world in which homosexual activity is neither frowned on nor unusual.

The potential candidate for an operation now finds himself among people who suggest actions he may not previously have known about, actions he might find interesting or pleasurable. These new companions, anticipating the fears and doubts that stop him from immediately accepting some of their suggestions, may have ideologies and rationales ready that explain why the ideas holding him back are wrong. He may decide to try some of the recommended possibilities, and perhaps finds that he likes doing these new things (perhaps, of course, not). He has now acquired some new motives. He has some new things he likes to do, and he has names for them and routine ways of doing them, and these are names and routines he shares with many others. So engaging in these acts is relatively easy, no longer frightening and unknown.

If you asked this young man at this moment whether he would like to have a sex change operation he would probably think you completely crazy. If you ask him whether he thinks he is a woman, he will probably think the same thing. But he might, as a result of his new abilities and motives, meet some new people who suggest to him that, if he likes what he has been doing, he might begin to consider that he really is in some part a woman, and that he might find it incredibly interesting to play that role, and even perhaps (another "perhaps") to dress like a woman. He may not have thought of doing that himself (even though he was well aware that others do), but now he does, and finds himself learning a new set of skills and motives. He learns, for instance, how to buy women's clothing in sizes big enough for a man. He may learn the skills of applying makeup and doing his hair in a way more common among women. He may start observing and trying to imitate the physical mannerisms he takes to be prototypically feminine.

He may thus become what is known as a transvestite. (Note that not all transvestites are gay, nor are all gay men transvestites. In Driscoll's interviews, however, this was a pattern.) But now he may find the role intriguing enough to wonder what it would be like to live as a woman all the time. And perhaps he will do that, and thus find himself in the situation of Agnes, the transsexual made sociologically famous by Harold Garfinkel (1967, 116–85), and now have to remake not just his physical behavior but his entire past.

At each of these points, our mythical young man finds himself doing some things he had at some earlier time never heard of and, having heard of them, had not imagined he might do. The steps he does take are never so very radical. Each one is simply another small step on a road from which he might at any minute turn to some other of the many roads available. Each small step is intellectually and emotionally understandable to people who themselves are nothing like this young man, *once the circumstances are made intelligible to them*. If we continue, which I won't, we will eventually see that, when it comes to the sex change operation, the young man is only taking another relatively small step not very different from all the other small steps along the way.

In short, he didn't decide one day, for almost no reason or because of some inner prompting, to have this surgery. That would be hard to understand, if that were how it happened. But it isn't. He took dozens of relatively small steps, each of them small enough not to require any elaborate or unusual form of explanation. It will turn out, if we really investigate all the circumstances and processes, that every one of these steps seemed, in a way that will be intelligible, like a good idea at the time.

Analytically, that means discovering something that seems so bizarre and unintelligible that our only explanation is some form of "They must be crazy" should alert us that we don't know enough about the behavior under study. It's better to assume that it makes some kind of sense and to look for the sense it makes.

Coincidence

Another kind of useful imagery, one that is perhaps quite realistic in a way null hypotheses usually aren't, is the notion of "coincidence." That is, things aren't exactly random, but they aren't completely determined either. There is what you could call a coincidental quality to them. Though none of the particular actions involved in a particular event we want to explain are random, though each of them can be accounted for in a quite sensible sociological way, what can't so easily be explained is their intersection. It may be explicable that I decided to go to work at my government job that day; after all, it's my job and I will experience negative sanctions, as we sociologists say, if I don't go, so I go to work every day. For good sociological reasons, I went to work that day as well. And it may be explicable that two other people, through a conversion sequence not unlike what I described for the candidate for a sex change operation, should decide that the United States government is an enemy they should and can deal with by bombing some building it owns. And some combination of socially determined propinquity and special local knowledge may lead them to pick the building I work in as their target. But what does not seem explicable as a result of any causal social process is how their choice of a building to bomb coincided with my working in that building. What explains how I, as opposed to thousands or millions of other people, became one of their victims?

Coincidence seems like a good word for what's involved. I actually became interested in this problem in a way that embodies the process. Here's what happened.

In April 1990, I went to Rio de Janeiro as a Fulbright Scholar, to teach in the Programa de Pós-Graduação em Antropologia Social at the Museu Nacional. It was my third visit to Rio, my second experience teaching in that program. I got there the first time through an odd conjuncture of circumstances. A friend, whom I had met through our mutual connection to the Haight-Ashbury Free Medical Clinic in San Francisco (a story in itself), was now in charge of higher education for the Ford Foundation's Brazilian operation. He had met Gilberto Velho, who taught in this graduate program and whose specialty was urban anthropology. Gilberto had read my book *Outsiders,* and many of his students were studying the phenomenon of deviance. So Richie Krasno called me and suggested that I come to Rio as part of the Ford-supported program at the Museu.

This came out of the blue. The only thing I knew about Brazil was bossa nova, and that because of my past in the music business. But, for some reason I never understood or tried to explain to myself, I decided that this was something I should do. I spent a year studying Portuguese, read (with enormous difficulty) the two books of his own Gilberto sent me (Velho 1973, 1974), and went there in the fall of 1976. I had a wonderful time and maintained the connection, reading work the people I had met there sent me, sending my own work there for them to read, visiting one other time, seeing Brazilians who came to the United States, and working with several Brazilian students who came for advanced degrees or just for a year's study abroad.

I went to Rio again in 1990 for what felt to me like a long overdue return. I taught a course with Gilberto on, roughly, the "Chicago School of sociology," a topic he had long been interested in and which, having become fashionable in Paris, was becoming more interesting to others in Rio. Since I was using Gilberto's office as my headquarters, I had plenty of time to explore the debris on his work table, an enormous pile of magazines, journals, newspapers, books, and papers. I had been reading a lot of Portuguese since I arrived, and one of the things I read was an article he gave me by Antonio Candido, whom I had never heard of but who was in fact one of the most important literary figures in Brazil. The sophistication and literary grace of the article impressed me greatly, and I wanted to know more about its author.

Candido, it turned out, had been trained in sociology and had in fact taught sociology for many years before becoming a professor of comparative literature; his dissertation (Candido [1964] 1987) was a study of the way of life of rural villagers in the state of São Paulo. And, in consequence, Mariza Peirano, an anthropologist interested in the development of Brazilian anthropology, had interviewed him for her dissertation. Nurturing my developing interest in Candido, Gilberto gave me an article Peirano had written about him based on that interview (Peirano 1991, 25–49), and another article that discussed an interesting phenomenon she had discovered during her research (Peirano 1995, 119–33).

I found that article intriguing, from the very first paragraph, which went like this:

> Eleven years ago, while doing a series of interviews with social scientists, I noticed a curious phenomenon. My objective then was to clarify matters which had until then remained cloudy to me, even after having read the works and studied the intellectual careers of these authors, who I considered fundamental for understanding the development of social science in Brazil. Most of them had been born during the Twenties and were, therefore, in their fifties and sixties. They included Florestan Fernandes, Antonio Candido, Darcy Ribeiro and, the youngest, Roberto Cardoso de Oliveira. In these interviews, each of which lasted about two hours, I was surprised to hear, again and again, the expression "It was by chance" or "It's a matter of a chance phenomenon" [in Portuguese, "foi por acaso"] offered as an explanation of a change of course at a specific moment in their careers. They all used the explanation of "chance" or "coincidence" in our conversations. (Peirano 1995, 119–20)

Peirano was surprised because, she says, the work of all of these authors was utterly committed to highly deterministic models of social causation. It was only in discussing their own lives that the deterministic theories were not adequate explanations; when they talked about other people, more conventional social science talk worked just fine.

She gave several examples of how the lives of these scholars reflected chance events. One dealt with the way Roberto Cardoso de Oliveira, a leader in the development of professional anthropology in Brazil, became an anthropologist:

> At the end of 1953, Darcy Ribeiro [a pioneer in Brazilian anthropology] gave a talk at the Municipal Library in São Paulo. He was looking for an assistant for a course he was going to teach at the Museum of the Indian, and thought that Roberto, who was introduced to him by a mutual acquaintance, looked like the

most capable and intelligent person for the job. Roberto was re-
luctant, since his training was in philosophy and sociology, but
this did not convince Darcy, who argued that since Lévi-Strauss
had learned ethnology after his formal education was finished,
why not Roberto? Thus, owing to this "purely accidental" beginning, a meeting in the Municipal Library, Roberto Cardoso
de Oliveira made the transition from sociology to anthropology,
learning from Darcy the lesson of "indigenism," keeping from his
sociological training with Florestan [Fernandes] the ambition to
be theoretical as well. Thus was born a sociological anthropology
in which the concept of "interethnic friction" gave evidence that
Roberto Cardoso had created an "Eve" from a rib taken from the
distinctive sociology taught at the University of São Paulo.
(Peirano 1995)

I myself was, by another set of circumstances that had led to my recent
marriage, peculiarly open to the recognition of what I thought of as the
"chance" elements in social life. Like so many people who reflect on how
they met their mate, I was tremendously aware of the many things that, had
they happened differently, would have sent me somewhere other than Columbia, Missouri, on the day I met Dianne Hagaman. I could deliver an
endless lecture on how easily it might have happened that we would not
have met. So I read Peirano's paper with great interest and attention.

I delivered the lecture on how Dianne and I met, as much as Gilberto
would listen to, to him one day, and we ended up discussing the topic for
the remaining weeks of my stay in Rio. In other words, to bring this self-
exemplifying digression to an end, I became interested in the problem of
the role of chance and coincidence in social life quite by accident.

As I thought about it, the chief problem seemed to be that while everyone recognizes that stories like these are "really the way things happen,"
there is no conceptual language for discussing this thing that everyone
knows. When we talk as professional social scientists, we talk about
"causes" in a way we don't recognize in daily life. That disparity would not
bother a lot of sociologists, but it bothers me.

The above discussion surely leads, practically speaking (and in spite of
my perennial complaints about such woolly notions as the ones I'm about
to utter), to the idea that things don't just happen, but rather occur in a series of steps, which we social scientists are inclined to call "processes," but
which could just as well be called "stories." A well-constructed story can
satisfy us as an explanation of an event. The story tells how something hap-

pened—how this happened first and led, in a way that is reasonable to see, to that happening, and then those things led to the next thing . . . and right on to the end. And how, if all that hadn't happened, the event we're interested in wouldn't have happened either. We could describe the conditions necessary for an event (call it *It*) to occur as the story of how one thing after another happened until it was almost certain that *It* would happen. Assembling all the necessary components for a symphony concert certainly won't cause the concert to happen, and in no way guarantees that it will, but if we get all the musicians assembled to play a symphony concert . . . and if the audience shows up . . . and if there is no fire or tornado or other unexpected natural obstacle . . . then it is hard to see what would prevent the concert from taking place.

If two people meet, however, it is not as certain as that that they will fall in love. Far from it. Mostly people do not fall in love with people they meet casually. Friends are always scheming, bringing likely pairs together, only to have their plans fall through. So having all the preconditions in place doesn't mean that *It* will happen. The anthropologist Lloyd Warner used to tell of investigating the Australian aboriginal society whose members, earlier anthropological accounts had alleged, did not understand the physiological basis of pregnancy. When he asked them where babies came from, they told him just what they had told earlier investigators: babies wait in the clan's spirit well until a woman has a special dream; then one baby's spirit leaves the spirit well and enters her stomach. He pursued it. "What about when men and women, you know, have intercourse? Doesn't that have something to do with it?" They looked at him pityingly, as if at a stupid child, and said that, of course, that's what made the baby. But, they reminded him, men and women do that all the time, but women only get pregnant once in a while—only, they pointed out triumphantly, when the mother dreamed of the spirit well.

I learned, largely through the influence of Everett C. Hughes, to think of these dependencies of one event on another as "contingencies." When event A happens, the people involved are now in a situation where any of several things could happen next. If I graduate high school I can go to college, to the Army, to trade school, to jail . . . those are among the possible next steps. There are a large number of possible next steps, but not an infinite number, and usually only a relatively small number are more or less likely (though the unlikely ones can happen too). Which path is taken at such a juncture depends on many things. We can call the things that next step depends on "contingencies," and say that event A being followed by B, rather than C or D, is contingent on something else, X. My going to college is contingent on my getting sufficiently high test scores to be accepted by the college I want, on my having enough money, on having sufficient desire to go to college that I will put up with some of the associated inconveniences, and so on.

(Stephen Jay Gould, the biologist, describes this as the fundamental character of history and of all historical explanation: "A historical explanation does not rest on direct deductions from laws of nature, but on an unpredictable sequence of antecedent states, where any major change in any step of the sequence would have altered the final result. This final result is therefore dependent, or contingent, on everything that came before—the unerasable and determining signature of history" [1989, 283].)

So the pathway that leads to any event can be seen as a succession of events that are contingent on each other in this way. You might envision it as a tree diagram in which, instead of the probability of getting to a particular end point getting smaller the farther you get from the starting point, the probability of reaching point X increases the nearer you get to it. (Von Wright 1971 uses tree diagrams effectively in his analysis.)

The chain of events that leads up to the event that is important to me, the one for which I want a detailed explanation, involves many other people. So the chain of events that led to me being interested in this problem required, among many other things (not the least of which is my having gone to Brazil in the first place), that Mariza Peirano interview a number of Brazilian social scientists, that they all use this form of explanation, that she write a paper about it, that the paper be on Gilberto Velho's desk where I could find it (which in turn requires that he know Peirano, that she send him this then unpublished work), and so on. Any one of these other people might have done something different such that my interest would not, or could not, have been aroused in the way it was.

The Swiss playwright Max Frisch, in his play "Biography: A Game," embodied this thought in an interesting dramatic situation. A mysterious stranger ("The Recorder") appears to the main character, Hannes Kürmann, one day, offering him the opportunity to go back over his life, the details of which are available to him through a computer terminal and operator located stage right throughout the action (in the staging I saw in Minneapolis, though not in the published script [Frisch 1969]), and change anything he likes. The hero relives a number of crucial moments in his life. The play begins with him trying to change the episode of the party at which he first meets, and eventually sleeps with Antoinette Stein, who, as he knows, he will marry and finally kill. When the taxi driver who was called to take her home from the party rings the bell, they both ignore it. Now, looking back, he wants, instead of getting involved with her, to send her away politely, but finds that he cannot change his actions—his character apparently does not have the will to do it—in such a way as to change the eventual outcome. Finally, when the Recorder asks if he wants to change the murder itself, they have this exchange:

> KÜRMANN. I know how it happened.
> RECORDER. By chance?
> KÜRMANN. It wasn't inevitable.

Which expresses nicely my first point, about the nature of this sort of explanation, which conceives events as neither random nor determined.

But, having chosen not to commit the murder, Kürmann learns that, instead of spending at least twelve years in prison, he now gets cancer, and is on his way to a mean death, with his wife, whom he meant to give a new life by making this new choice, now condemned to visit him religiously.

So far, contingency. But now the Recorder turns to Kürmann's wife, Antoinette:

> RECORDER. Frau Kürmann.
> ANTOINETTE. Yes?
> RECORDER. Do you regret the seven years with him? [*Antoinette stares at the Recorder.*] If I told you that you too have the choice, you too can start all over again, would you know what you would do differently in your life?
> ANTOINETTE. Yes.
> RECORDER. Yes?
> ANTOINETTE. Yes.
> RECORDER. Then go ahead. . . . You too can choose all over again.

They then replay the opening scene, in which she meets Kürmann for the first time. But this time, when the taxi driver rings, she says goodbye, and walks out of Kürmann's apartment, and his life, for good.

> KÜRMANN. What now?
> RECORDER. Now she has gone.
> KÜRMANN. What now?

RECORDER. And now you're free.
KÜRMANN. Free . . .

And so we are reminded that everything that happened in Kürmann's life, of course, depended not only on his actions and choices, but also on what all the other people he was involved with did. If Antoinette changes her life, his will necessarily change as well. He cannot marry and murder someone who walked out of his life so definitively. We might call the dependence of his actions on hers *intercontingency.*

Peirano quotes Norbert Elias speaking of much the same thing:

> In contrast [to "determinism"], when the indeterminacy, the "freedom" of the individual is stressed, it is usually forgotten that there are simultaneously many mutually dependent individuals. . . . More subtle tools of thought than the usual antithesis of "determinism" and "freedom" are needed if such problems are to be solved. (Elias 1970, 167)

This is a sort of imagery for which social scientists do not now have very good conceptual tools. But it is always worth considering as a candidate for the explanatory image that fits a case.

Society as a Machine

There is essentially nothing wrong with the basic forms of social science thinking. It's just that social scientists don't actually use those forms when they should. They get into their worst troubles and make their biggest mistakes when they forget how they are supposed to do things, forget because some political or temperamental commitment leads them to see a problem in a narrow way and to forget the full range of things their basic theories would force on them if they paid attention. The Society is a Big Machine trick is designed to take care of this. First I'll explain what difficulty the trick is meant to overcome.

We suffer these memory lapses (I don't exempt myself from the charge) especially when we want to change the world so that it will be a better place for democracy or the middle class or honest law-abiding citizens or mental patients or . . . . Whenever we want to improve things, we are likely to forget (conveniently, it might be said, except that the inconvenience that results is usually astronomical) many of the people, groups, or things that contribute to the result we want to change. If mental patients are ill treated and the so-called treatment they receive in mental hospitals does not help them in any way, if we can see how hospitals deprive them of the most elementary rights and dignities, then it seems obvious what ought to be done: get them out of the hospitals. The striking analyses of mental illness and hospitalization by Goffman (1961), Foucault (1965), and Szasz (1961) made us see all this clearly.

What was left out of those analyses was: where would these patients go when they left the hospital? When you closed the state hospital in Napa, where did all those people who had been incarcerated unjustly (Goffman and Foucault and Szasz were right about that, I think) go? The theory of "deinstitutionalization" was that they would be absorbed into "the community," and would no longer be subject to the major and minor humiliations that went with the label of "mentally ill." Having regained all their rights as citizens, they would go about their business like anyone else: get a job, rent an apartment, go shopping for food and make their own meals, marry, raise children—in short, become ordinary normal productive citizens. They might, of course, actually have been too crazy to do any of that or too involved in their own internal concerns to make accurate calculations about what the results of their activities would be or too unable to control their impulses to make the adjustments that would let them fit what they did to what others were doing and so become part of the social world. Even if they did not have any of these difficulties to contend with, they had often been out of civil society for a long time and their skills and smarts were no longer adequate to the daily hustle. The idea of deinstitutionalization didn't take account of these possibilities.

The newly released mental patients did not, as it turned out, go to live in the communities they had left for the hospital. Those communities—to be more accurate, the families the patients had left—were not anxious to have them back. Patients mostly become patients when their families and friends will no longer tolerate the disruption they cause. So the newly released patients went to live in halfway houses, run by entrepreneurs who were ready to accept what the state paid for patient upkeep (still cheaper than the expense of a large hospital), in neighborhoods that were unable to protect themselves against the invasion of such businesses. In a short time, many large cities had mental patient ghettoes—Chicago's Uptown or the corresponding area in San Jose. These ghettoes were not the welcoming "normal" communities envisioned in the liberating idea of deinstitutionalization (although they were certainly the money savers foreseen by some of the advisers of politicians like Governor Ronald Reagan of California). The released patients, now "normal citizens," could not or would not live the normal lives the theory expected and become self-sufficient. Instead, they learned to manipulate the systems of service set up to facilitate their reentry into society, and to exploit the spaces and opportunities afforded by the looseness of urban social organization. They became a noticeable part of the group that came to be known as "the homeless."

No one, no politician, no social scientist, had foreseen this. Why not? The introductory course in sociology would alert you to just such a possibility, by insisting that you find out about all the people involved in the situation: not just the patients, but also the families, and not just "the community" in the abstract, but the community as a specific social and political organization. Following that injunction, you would inquire, as part of your standard procedure, about how those people were organized, what they understood to be their interests, and what resources they had to defend those interests. And you would then not be surprised when middle-class communities used their political power to keep halfway houses out of their neighborhoods. In fact, had you read Suttles's (1972) analysis of the "defended community," you would have seen the whole thing coming.

So the failure to think about all the people involved, which the most elementary conception of society requires, led to a gross misunderstanding of the situation, and a bad set of policies, which never achieved what they were intended to.

Take another example: theories of deviance. The so-called "labeling theory" revolution should never have been required. It was not an intellectual or scientific revolution (though it might be said to have been a political one, because of the shifting allegiances and changes in opportunities and organization in the professional fields it touched). No basic paradigms of sociological thought were overturned. The "definition of the situation," for instance—W. I. Thomas's great contribution to sociology's vocabulary and way of thinking—directs us to understand how the situation looks to the actors in it, to find out what they think is going on so that we will understand what goes into the making of their activity. If criminologists and others who studied what later came to be called deviance had paid attention to that, they would routinely have asked about criminals' viewpoints, instead of assuming that criminals had personality disorders or came from pathogenic environments. They would have understood that they should have made what law enforcement people did problematic, instead of taking it for granted.

Far from being a revolution, you could say that labeling theory was a counterrevolution, a conservative return to a strand of basic sociological thinking that had somehow gotten lost in the discipline's practice.

But that "somehow" should not go by unquestioned. These basic sociological ideas were lost not by accident, but because sociologists had acquired commitments that pushed them to define problems in ways that left out some of the most important actors in the drama of deviance. These sociologists did not allow the definition of some activities as "wrong" (whatever term was used to register that judgment) to become an object of investigation. Who successfully defined some activities as deviant and how they did that were not discussable questions. Conventional social scientists treated those definitions as obvious or God-given; who but a fool would question whether murder or child prostitution or drug use were evil activities?

In the same way, studies of education often focused on why students did not learn what they ought to have learned in school. Researchers typically looked for the answer in something about the students: personality, ability, intelligence, and social class culture were, and still are, frequent candidates for the guilty factor. They never looked for the answer in the teachers or in the organization of school life. This reflected, as do the earlier examples, where the money was coming from. No one, after all, pays you to tell them that what they're complaining about is their own fault. Educators do not like to have researchers around who will tell them that their schools' shortcomings result from their own activities, rather than from the failings of their students, or the students' parents or communities. They like to see research so organized that such a finding could not possibly come up. They make sure that no such answer will be found by not allowing themselves to become the object of study. (A faculty member in a school I studied said to me, in irritated surprise when he realized I was interviewing him, "You mean you're studying me too?" and couldn't understand why I thought that was necessary, since he wasn't "the problem.")

In short, sociologists forget their own theories when anything important in the world is at stake. They fail to follow the clear instructions those theories imply, and to look at all the people and organizations that contribute to a result.

The Machine Trick is meant to deal with this problem, to push us into not leaving out crucial elements of the situation. It requires us to think like engineers who want the machine they design to do what it is supposed to do. Here is the trick:

> Design the machine that will produce the result your analysis indicates occurs routinely in the situation you have studied. Make sure you have included all the parts—all the social gears, cranks, belts, buttons, and other widgets—and all the specifications of materials and their qualities necessary to get the desired result. Since social scientists often study "problem situations," the machine's product will often be something we wouldn't in fact want to produce, and the exercise of figuring out how to produce it is inevitably ironic, but that shouldn't prevent us from taking it seriously.

Let's apply the trick. Consider some phenomenon we don't like: our students don't learn what we teach, our representatives in legislatures behave corruptly, our physicians are more interested in making money and playing golf than in stamping out disease. Now assume that, far from being an unwanted result, this is exactly what some omniscient and omnipotent Creator intended. With care and craft, the Creator organized an elaborate machine that would produce exactly the result we have before us. We would love to reproduce this machine, so that we too could produce corrupt politicians or students who don't learn or golf-playing doctors; unfortunately, the Creator being out to lunch or not answering the phone, the plans are not available to us. So we have to do what people in the computer business call "reverse engineering." We will take this machine apart, find out how it works, what the parts are, how the parts connect, and what goes on inside the black box so that we too can cause exactly this wonderful result to occur.

Suppose we want to make sure that schools teach students exactly the amount they now teach them, no more or less, so that the students will continue to leave school with at least the same degree of incapacity they now exhibit. What kinds of students will we have to recruit? What kinds of teachers will we need? What should the teachers do so that students will be no more motivated than they are? How will they keep students who might want to learn more from doing so? How will we keep the parents under control so that they don't do anything to interfere with our desired result? How shall the school system's budget be constrained so that money cannot be spent on things that would affect our result in ways we don't want?

We can find the answers to these questions in many researches done in schools. We can, for instance, tell teachers to kill students' interest in school by keeping them waiting for long periods of time during which they learn nothing (see Jackson 1990), we can reward students for memorizing and regurgitating and punish them for thinking for themselves (see Holt 1967 and Herndon 1968), and so on. This is a very biased summary of what can be learned from published research on schools, but it makes the point clear.

Similar exercises might consist of designing a machine, using Alfred Lindesmith's (1947) analysis of the addiction process, for producing heroin addicts; or a machine for producing an ethnically biased labor force distribution, based on the analyses of such processes found in the writings of Everett Hughes (1943) and Stanley Lieberson (1980).

Imagining such a machine gives us a good reason for including what we might otherwise leave out, what our sentiments, commitments, and interests would lead us to forget or ignore. Our machine will not work if it doesn't have everything it needs to get the job done.

We won't always find it easy to design such machines. We seldom know with such assurance just what we want the machine to do, what result we would like to see. And when we are sure, at least some of our colleagues will usually disagree with us. Even if we did achieve such a consensus, few social phenomena have been studied well enough that we could provide the specifications of parts and materials that would let us design a machine that would really do the job. Most social phenomena are connected in so many ways to so many environing conditions that we may never be able to get an adequate design. The classic way out of this dilemma is to do the job over and over, to keep looking, adding as we go to the contraption's design: build a small piece that does some part of the job, add it to other pieces already designed, see what is still needed, go out and find its specifications, design and test it, and repeat the process until our machine produces a reasonable approximation of the product we want (Geertz 1995 describes this process nicely). Remember that we don't really want these results but engage in this machine-designing exercise as a way of systematically looking for everything that contributes to their occurrence.

Society as Organism

The image of the machine will not always be useful or appropriate. It works best when the social world acts in a very repetitive way, delivering essentially similar products by following a systematic procedure, no matter how complicated that might be (the way, we might say, schools routinely and stubbornly continue to graduate pupils who aren't what we hope for). Or, I might better say, it works when we decide to think about the repetitive aspect of what we are studying. Most social organizations have such repetitive aspects. That, in fact, is one way to understand what we mean by social organization: a situation in which most people do pretty much the same things in pretty much the same way most of the time.

Suppose, as Everett Hughes liked to suggest, a major revolution were to take place tomorrow, one akin in scope and magnitude to the ones social scientists most like to study, like the French or Chinese revolutions. What would change and what would stay the same? The newspapers might be different, the television programs would almost surely be different. Would the system of collecting garbage change? Perhaps. Would the water distribution system change? Almost surely not. But this is not a matter to be decided by theoretical analysis. These things will be decided when the revolution happens and we see what changed.

Nonetheless, the exercise makes us realize that, very likely, not everything would change. Many things would probably continue to happen just as they did before. And it is those things for which the model of the machine is the most appropriate, and to which we will want to apply it in our day-to-day work.

But sometimes we want to think about social life in another way, as a series of interconnected processes. When we think this way, we emphasize the connectedness rather than, as with the machine image, the repetition. Things won't always be the same, but from day to day they will be connected to one another in much the same way, the way the parts of an animal's circulatory system are connected, so that what happens in the heart affects and is affected by what's going on in the blood vessels and the lungs and the central nervous system.

"Connection" is a vague word and I use it because there are many modes of connection, for which we use words like "influence" or "causality" or "dependence." All these words point to variation. Something will vary and something else, dependent on what happens to the first thing, will undergo some change as well. The things that so vary will often influence each other in complicated ways, so that "causality" is not really an appropriate way to talk about what we want to emphasize. You could say that the pieces of the system in question are connected in such a way that the output of each of the sub-processes that make it up provides one of the inputs for some other processes, which in turn take results from many other places and produce results that are inputs for still other processes, and so on.

Nineteenth-century social thinkers often used the metaphor of society as an organism to express this insight. Their overly enthusiastic and overly literal uses—the upper classes of the society being its brain, the working classes its muscles, for instance—discredited the metaphor. But the revitalized discipline of ecology, whose basic imagery stresses exactly such multiple connections, revived it. So it is a good trick to think of some set of social activities as having just that organic character, looking for all the connections that contribute to the outcome we are interested in, seeing how they affect one another, each creating the conditions for the others to operate. Arthur McEvoy's (1986) detailed analysis of the California fisheries exemplifies this kind of analytic approach. I'll give a small piece of the whole historical analysis, which starts with the Indian communities before the invasions of Europeans and ends with the passage of the Fishery Conservation and Management Act in 1976 and its immediate aftermath.

McEvoy begins his analysis by noting that the Pacific Ocean and the rivers that ran into it from the California coast gave a home to a great variety of marine life: kelp, sea otters, whales, sea lions, abalone, shellfish (shrimp, oysters, mussels), and all sorts of fish, but most especially salmon. These species were complexly connected:

> Abalone and sea urchin graze voraciously on kelp, which provides food and shelter for a great many fishes important to market and recreational fisheries alike. Where there are even a few otters to keep the grazers thinned out, the kelp grows luxuriantly. Coastal waters with abundant kelp support a greater total mass of living matter than they would otherwise, and more of that mass is concentrated in the bodies of animals high enough on the food chain to be useful to people. Where there are no otters, there are more grazers but less kelp and, on the whole, less productive waters. (McEvoy 1986, 81)

Different human societies and populations have different eating habits, different ways of organizing fishing and the harvesting of seafood, different cultures, all of which affect the connections between the species in different ways, causing great variations in the numbers of plants and animals of each kind that exist at any particular time. In the 1820s, Russian, Yankee, and Spanish traders greedily exploited the seemingly insatiable

Chinese market for sea otter pelts and depleted the otter population dramatically. Which meant that forty years later, some of the Chinese who had come to California, like everyone else, to find gold, but who had been excluded from the hunt on racial grounds, could make a living by fishing for abalone to sell to other Chinese, for whom it was a prized foodstuff. Because the otters were gone, the abalone population had grown to the point where huge bales of abalone, dried in a way familiar and palatable to Chinese consumers, were piled up on the San Diego wharves (McEvoy 1986, 76).

When the Chinese fishers, following their cultural ways, thus lowered the abalone population dramatically (at the same time that the killing of seals for the fur trade expanded), the catch of such edible fish as barracuda, bonito, grouper, and sea bass (which were prized as food by other population groups—another cultural phenomenon) increased greatly. The complexity of that sentence only hints at the complexity of the social and ecological reality. A far more complicated sentence would be needed to explain the connections between the cultures of the variety of Native American tribes who inhabited California, their religious rituals and economic life, their diets and food gathering habits—all that on the one hand—and the economic and political motives that brought large numbers of people of European descent from the Eastern parts of the United States to fish for and can the salmon that was so important a part of Indian diets, and to kill the salmon by mining gold and harvesting timber in ways that polluted the streams the salmon spawned in.

The genetically rooted habits of the fish, the cultural habits of the humans, and the geographical features of the landscape interacted in ways of which the above is only the tiniest sample. McEvoy's book tells a lot more and gives enough detail to make summaries like mine intelligible and believable. I've described it here to indicate the kind of useful analysis the "society is an organism" metaphor can produce. Seeing society as an organism isn't itself an analytic trick, just a general caution to pay attention to all the things connected to what you're interested in. The society-as-organism view works especially well when we want to acknowledge and make room in our analysis for the independent variation of whole subsystems of phenomena that are neither totally unrelated nor related in any profoundly deterministic way. The relations of fish, people, weather, culture, and geography along the California coast are just such a mishmash of systems, and we often have reason to recognize that many of the things we want to explain are just like that, rather than like some machine we could reverse engineer.

Some specific tricks, however, flow from such a point of view. Here are several. The first consists of forgetting about types of people as analytic categories and looking instead for types of activities people now and then engage in. The second consists of viewing objects as the embodied residue of people's activities. Both tricks flow from the organism metaphor in this way: looking at people and objects as fixed entities with an inherent character makes them analytically immune to context—if not in theory, certainly in practice. Making activities the starting point focuses analysis on the situation the activity occurs in, and on all the connections what you are studying has with all the other things around it, with its context. Activities only make sense when you know what they are a response to, what phenomena provide inputs and necessary conditions for the thing you want to understand. If the character of the person or object is so immutable as to resist all situational variation, so unchanging that no input is a necessary condition for it to do whatever it does, that will be an empirical finding rather than a theoretical commitment made before the research began and thus immune to disproof by evidence.

Turning People into Activities

This trick offers a replacement for the habit social scientists have of making typologies of people. A classic example is the division sociologists habitually make between deviants and nondeviants, between people who conform to existing social rules and those who break them. What's wrong with that? And what's the alternative?

What's wrong is that such an analysis makes the basic unit of the analysis a kind of person, treated analytically as though that's what he or she is, that's all he or she is, and as though what such people do or are likely to do makes sense, has been "explained" causally, by the kind of person they are. Analysts do this with psychological types, but also with types based on social characteristics: class types, ethnic types, gender types, or occupational types as well as introverts and extroverts, deviants as well as psychopaths.

This is a mistake, to start with, because it's easily observed that no one ever acts completely in character, just like their type. Everyone's activity is always more various and unexpected than that. I'm not making an argument here about how human freedom will burst through the shackles of sociological theorizing—just a simple empirical observation. Types that don't actually predict what they are supposed to aren't much use.

The conventional answer to that objection is that if you insist that using these constructed types must enable the analyst to predict people's behavior with a very small margin of error you are being anti-science. Why? Because insisting on such perfection rules out the realistic and attainable scientific goal of modest predictive success. I won't plead guilty to that charge of being anti-science, since there is a simple and easily available solution, which consists of substituting types of activity for types of people. The theoretical rationale for the substitution is that to talk about types of people makes the strong and empirically unfounded assumption that people act consistently in ways determined by their makeup as people, whether that's psychological or sociological. The alternate assumption, more seemly for a sociologist to make and more likely to be empirically correct, is that, taking everything into consideration, people do whatever they have to or whatever seems good to them at the time, and that, since situations change, there's no reason to expect that they'll act in consistent ways.

Dietrich Reitzes (Lohman and Reitzes 1954) demonstrated this by giving a questionnaire that measured racial attitudes to white members of an interracial labor union who lived in a racially segregated neighborhood. When they answered the questions at work they were as racially tolerant as their union membership suggested; when they answered it at home, they were as racially bigoted as their neighbors. If you try to think of them as tolerant or bigoted people, you have a big problem. If you think of them as people who act like bigots sometimes and other times like racial liberals, you still have to explain the difference in their behavior, but you don't have a major problem of understanding how a person's basic nature, expressed in the type, could change so quickly. Turning a kind of person into a kind of activity makes the problem much more tractable.

The kind of solution to such a problem you can more reasonably expect to find is that activities will be responses to particular situations, and that the relations between situations and activities will have a consistency that permits generalization, so that you can say something like this: people who are in a situation of kind X, with these kinds of pressures, and these possibilities of action to choose from, will do this. Or you might be able to say that a certain sequence of situations constitutes a pathway likely to be followed by people who have done the thing you're interested in (Driscoll's analysis of men who have had sex change operations is an example of that).

Lindesmith's study of opiate addiction (to which I've already referred, and will again) embodies this strategy. He didn't suppose there were types of people who became addicts; rather, he guessed there was an addictive kind of behavior that, under the right circumstances, people would engage in. He studied addictive behavior, not addicts. In the same way, in my own research I spoke of marijuana use as a kind of activity, not marijuana users as a kind of people.

Having said that, I have some explaining to do. Both Lindesmith and I talked (as everyone else does) of kinds of people. In fact, he did write about addicts and I did write about marijuana users. But we used those expressions as a kind of shorthand, a way of noting that some people engaged in these activities in a more or less routine or regular way. We meant readers to understand (though they often didn't) that these usages *were* shorthand, and that the subjects of our research were just ordinary people who happened to do these particular things a lot.

Our analyses recognized that engaging in a particular act created conditions that affected whether and how you did it again. Doing X might lead to a reaction by other people that would make it more likely that you would continue doing X. Doing X might lead to some physical result (as drinking a lot might injure your liver) that would then affect what you did or could do in the future. Most important, doing X might set in motion a variety of processes that would make it more likely that you would continue to do X, again and again.

Typing people is a way of accounting for regularity in people's actions; typing situations and lines of activity is a different way. Focusing on activities rather than people nudges you into an interest in change rather than stability, in ideas of process rather than structure. You see change as the normal condition of social life, so that the scientific problem becomes not accounting for change or the lack of it, but accounting for the direction it takes, regarding as a special case the situation in which things actually stay the same for a while.

Things Are Just People Acting Together

Physical objects, while real enough physically, don't have "objective" properties. Neither do more intangible social objects. We give them those properties, for social purposes, by recognizing that they have them. Sociologists often assume that the physical properties of an object constrain what the people involved with it can do, but that almost invariably means those properties are constraining if, and only if, people use the object the way everyone recognizes it is usually used. A drug may have measurable effects on the central nervous system, but it won't get you "high" if you don't recognize that those effects have occurred or that they are what being "high" consists of. There are indisputable limits to this; no one can breathe underwater forever (although, having said that, I can easily imagine someone writing to say that I'm wrong, there is a way that can be done).

We get some idea of the interaction between social definitions and physical properties in operation by looking for those situations (and we can always find them) in which the object seems not to have its normal properties, as when a narcotic drug doesn't get someone high or cause addiction. Then we can see that the constraints we thought ineluctably built into the physical object have a social and definitional component. Even better, we can watch objects change character as their social definition changes. We can see that the object is, as I said above, the embodiment in physical form of all the actions everyone took to bring it into being. A musical instrument, for all its indubitable physical reality, is the physical embodiment of all the experiments in acoustics that made it possible, but also of the choices made by many, many generations of performers and composers to compose for and play the instrument in a certain way, and of the listeners who accepted the resulting sounds as music, and of the commercial enterprises that made all that possible (I've written about this and related examples at great length in Becker 1982).

An elegant example of the way physical objects get their character from the collective activities of people is Bruno Latour's (1995) analysis of the way a clod of Brazilian soil changes as scientists handle it. Latour had studied science in the up-to-date, high-tech laboratory of a biological scientist who was searching for the molecular structure of a growth hormone. And he had studied it in the state of the art, for its day, laboratory of Louis Pasteur in Paris, and in the quasi-laboratory Pasteur had constructed on a farm in order to test his theories about the causes of bovine anthrax. Latour had concluded that laboratories were crucial to the making of science, since they allowed scientists to isolate the thing they were interested in (the hormone, the microbe, the whatever) from everything that interfered with its activity and survival in ordinary life. Once you isolated a microbe, and protected it from all its natural predators, you could grow enough of them to experiment with, and thus apply the methods of laboratory science to. No laboratory, no science.

But how can you do science when laboratory experimentation isn't possible, as it so often isn't? Latour decided, in a wonderful sampling strategy (a topic we'll take up in the next chapter), to accompany some French soil scientists to the forest of Boa Vista, in the very center of tropical Brazil, to watch them solve that problem. The soil scientists wanted to know if, in the particular place they were studying, the forest was encroaching on the savanna or the savanna was taking land away from the forest (a topic that was of interest to them, and the world of their scientific peers, far more than this particular patch of land). You can't study this encroachment in the lab; you have to go to the frontier between the two and see what's going on. Furthermore, the process goes slowly. You can't just sit and watch it happen. You have to make inferences from samples of soil dug up here and there in the area.

The forest and savanna, however, are wild and not set up for scientific activity, so the scientists have first to impose an order of their own on them. They nail numbers on trees to establish reference points; how else could they tell one tree from another?. Because the land has never been cleared they cannot use conventional surveying instruments and methods, which assume clear sightlines; they have to use a special instrument (the Topofil Chaix) to lay threads on the ground at measured intervals and thus mark out a grid. They can then take cores of earth from each box in the grid, and so compare the nature of the soil from one part of the research site (one cell in their grid) to another. They make that comparison systematically by putting each clod of earth into one of the hundred little boxes arranged in the 10×10 "pedocomparator" in strict correspondence to the hundred squares marked out on the ground by the signs and threads.

Latour follows the process through many more steps than I will pay attention to here; it is worth reading the article to grasp the subtlety of the argument I have diverted to my own purposes. The crucial step, for me, is contained in Figure 12 of the article, a photograph of one of the soil scientists, René Boulet, taking a clod of earth, extracted from the ground at a depth specified by the research plan, and putting it in one of the cubes of the pedocomparator:

> Consider this lump of earth. Held partially in René's right hand,
> it still retains all the materiality of soil—"ashes to ashes, dust to
> dust." Yet partially inside the cardboard cube held in René's left

hand, the earth becomes a sign, takes on a geometrical form, becomes the carrier of a numbered code, and will soon be defined
by a color. In the philosophy of science, the left hand does not
know what the right hand is doing. In anthropology, we are am-
bidextrous: we focus the reader's attention on this hybrid, this
moment of substitution, the very instant when the future sign is
abstracted from the soil. We should never take our eyes off the
material weight of this action. The earthly dimension of Platon-
ism is revealed in this image. We are not jumping from soil to the
Idea of soil, but from the continuous and multiple clumps of
earth to a discrete color in a geometrical cube coded in x and y

coordinates. And yet René does not impose predetermined categories on a shapeless horizon; he loads his pedocomparator with the meaning of the piece of earth; he *educes* it. Only the movement of substitution by which the real soil becomes the soil known to pedology [soil science] counts. The immense abyss separating things and words can be found everywhere distributed to many smaller gaps between the clods of earth and the cubes-cases-codes of the pedocomparator. (Latour 1995, 163–65)

Latour goes on to make this moment the prototype of all the moments in which something that seems "real" enough (a clod of Brazilian earth) is "abstracted" scientifically to make yet another "real" object (a sample of earth in a device for making systematic comparisons), which in turn is abstracted to become still another real object—part of a table or a chart in a scientific article. For our purposes, the point is that a piece of dirt, physically real as it is, is what we make of it. To us it might just be a piece of dirt, but to Boulet and his colleagues it is a piece of scientific evidence.

Most objects, of course, do not change their character this radically. In fact, people usually quite successfully treat objects as though they have stable properties and are unchanging. It then becomes an interesting problem for the social scientist to account for how they do that. The general answer is that objects continue to have the same properties when people continue to think of them, and define them jointly, in the same way. Agreeing on what objects are, what they do, and how they can be used makes joint activity much easier. Anyone who wants to change the definition may have to pay a substantial price for the privilege, so most of us accept current definitions of objects most of the time.

Objects, then, are congealed social agreements, or rather, congealed moments in the history of people acting together. The analytic trick consists of seeing in the physical object before you all the traces of how it got that way, of who did what so that this thing should now exist as it does. I often act out the exercise in class: picking up any object that comes to hand—a student's notebook, my shoe, a pencil—and tracking down all the earlier decisions and activities that produced this thing sitting before us.

An easy way to make yourself aware of the social agreements embodied in physical objects is to find places where that agreement has produced a different object than the one we're used to. A classical example is the QWERTY keyboard, an inefficient and dysfunctional arrangement of typewriter keys that highlights the enormous influence of early steps in the creation of standard objects. Once the keyboard had been arranged that way—so that typists could be slowed down, since fast typing jammed the early machines—it proved totally resistant to the introduction of better arrangements (like the Dvorak keyboard, whose users are faster and more accurate). Too many people already knew the old way to make changing "practical." (This example is described in David 1985.)

Everything Has to Be Someplace

Although sociologists (people in other social science disciplines less so and in history, of necessity, not at all) have made a fetish (reasonably or not) of keeping the identities of the people they study "confidential," they also almost invariably give a short description of the setting of their research, the place their data came from. Such a researcher might say: "I gathered my data [whether the data are qualitative or quantitative is irrelevant] from children in a working-class neighborhood made up of equal numbers of blacks, whites, and Latinos. It sits on a hill overlooking a large river in which barges hauling freight can be seen, on the western edge of a large midwestern city. The city had experienced a net loss of jobs during the previous twenty years, and its tax base had shrunk." And so on, trying to give in a roundabout way information that could more handily be expressed by saying "I studied such-and-such a neighborhood in Cleveland [or Detroit]."

When my colleagues and I reported on our study of college undergraduates (Becker, Geer, and Hughes [1968] 1994), we did name the place—the University of Kansas—but we still gave such a thumbnail description:

> The university (except for the medical school, which is located in Kansas City, Kansas) has its home in Lawrence, Kansas, a town of more than 32,000 (hence one of the larger cities in the state, exceeded in population only by the Kansas City suburban ring, Wichita, Topeka, and Salina). Downtown Kansas City is about forty-five minutes away by car, and Topeka less than that. Though the city has other industries, the University is its biggest business. Lawrence is a college town.
>
> Situated in the rolling hills of the more heavily populated eastern third of the state, most of the University sits atop Mount Oread, a high hill that looks out across the plains to the hundreds of smaller cities and town that make up its constituency. Bigger than most of them, Lawrence is something of a cultural and intellectual center for the state, despite the competition from

Kansas City and Topeka (which has more of such amenities than its size warrants, because of its position as a world-famous center of psychiatric treatment and research).

Lawrence looks a lot like a Midwestern college town. The University, with its old and new school buildings, its dormitories, fraternity and sorority houses, its football stadium, and its tree-lined streets filled with students, stands at the center. Beyond it lie the comfortable homes of the faculty and townspeople, and beyond that the suburban developments found around every American city. Just to the north, within walking distance, are downtown Lawrence, the shopping and business center, the Kaw River, and the Kansas Turnpike. ([1968] 1994: 16–17)

Why do social scientists provide these descriptions? Why did we go into these details about the University of Kansas and the town of Lawrence? (See the related discussion in Hunter 1990, 112–17.) After all, social scientists like to make generalizations, and so they like to minimize the ways "their case" differs from other cases. We like to say that our case is "representative," that it resembles many or most other cases of things like it. This lets us argue that we have discovered important general results about some social phenomenon or process, not just some interesting stories or facts. (I'll take this topic up again in the section on sampling.)

But, remember, I said "case." Every research site is a case of some general category, and so knowledge about it gives knowledge about a generalized phenomenon. We can pretend that it is just like all the other cases, or at least is like them in all relevant ways, but only if we ignore all its local, peculiar characteristics. If our case is located in California, it will differ in some ways from a case located in Michigan or Florida or Alaska, because anything related to or contained in or dependent on (there are a lot of possibilities to choose from) the geographical location necessarily affects what we are studying.

What sorts of things? The weather, for one. The student uprisings that took place in California in the 1960s could hardly have happened in the same way in Minnesota; it makes a difference in the incidence of outdoor demonstrations if you have mild weather all year long or if you only have a few months of school before it gets really cold. If a necessary prelude to a spontaneous demonstration is that a large number of people routinely hang around in public places where they are available to be mobilized by organizers, orators, and the simple flow of events, that condition is more likely met when the weather is conducive to eating on the grass, Frisbee throwing, and just hanging around. It is much less likely to be met when the temperature is measured in wind chill factors and standing outside for any length of time invites frostbite (though it is not impossible; Irving Horowitz reminds me that some of the most important episodes of the Russian Revolution took place in the coldest parts of that country—a useful reminder that "influences" or "affects" is not the same as "determines").

Population characteristics also make a difference: whether the population is educated or not, the percentages of various ethnic and racial groups, the prevalence of particular work skills. These and similar facts are relevant to any investigation of stratification processes and patterns of behavior and organization indirectly tied to those processes. And the connections can be very complex, progressing through a long series of linked phenomena. Here's an extended example.

Suppose we are studying the organization of medical practice.

1. Populations that differ in race and class also often differ in their eating habits; some groups customarily eat lots of meat and other high-cholesterol foods.

2. Eating habits have a strong connection to disease patterns; differences in rates of heart disease, for instance, are thought to be connected to differences in the amount of saturated fat (meat contains a lot of such fats) a population ingests. So populations whose culinary culture differs may also differ in disease patterns.

3. The work situations of doctors who practice in an area will vary depending on the distribution of medical problems and events characteristic of that area. That distribution depends in turn on the area's population and its culture. A doctor who opens an office in an area where people eat high-cholesterol diets as a matter of cultural routine will probably see many patients with heart disease.

4. Add now the physical characteristics of the area. It is hilly. Some residents work off some of the physical effects of their diet by routine strenuous exercise, walking up and down the hills. Others don't, and increase the risk of cardiac problems by occasional massive overexertion. And it snows heavily in the winter, so that overweight people with cholesterol-clogged arteries periodically engage in very strenuous shoveling almost guaranteed to increase that risk further.

5. Although doctors specialize to some extent, so that they do not all see the same distribution of diseases, many doctors in this area will

see patients with the same cultural/medical syndromes related to high-cholesterol diets: high blood pressure, heart attacks, and related difficulties.

6.   Professionals who have similar work problems develop, when they have the opportunity to discuss them, shared understandings that specify, in the case of physicians, such matters as how patients got their disease, whose "fault" it is that they have them, what these patients will or won't do to take care of themselves. They will develop patterns of cooperation (covering for each other so that vacations and weekends can go undisturbed) attuned to the problems the area's "typical" diseases produce (one kind of cooperation for an older population with heart trouble and Alzheimer's, another for a younger group with many pregnancies).

I won't go on to list all the other aspects of the place that might come into such an analysis. What I've said is enough to suggest that patterns of professional culture—this would be a good working guess—will have something to do with *where* the professionals are working.

We give that sort of "background information," as it is usually called, because we know that it is relevant, even if we can't specify exactly how it's relevant, even if we don't make what we mention an explicit part of our analysis. Sometimes we explain the inclusion of such detail by saying that it gives people a "feel" for the locale or a "sense" of what it was like there. There's a little (sometimes more than a little) literary pretense in this.

But the "background details" we include are, in fact, much more important than mere background, not just local color thrown in to give off a little verisimilitude. They are the environing *conditions* under which the things we studied—the relationships we uncovered, the general social processes whose discovery we want to brag about—exist. When we say that Lawrence, Kansas is thirty or so miles from Kansas City, that's not just an "interesting" fact. It points to characteristic features of that campus that would not have existed on a campus differently situated. We did not make explicit use of these features in our analysis, but we nevertheless knew that they were there and true and that they influenced what went on. For instance: Kansas City, being so near, was a place you could go and return in an evening, a place you could buy a beer or a drink over the counter, as you could not then in Lawrence. So it was a place where you could go to hear a band and drink while you did it, therefore a place where you could take a date, therefore a place from which you could, if you were no more thoughtful than an average undergraduate, drive home with your date half-tanked. Whatever kinds of trouble students at Kansas State, 100 miles farther west in the town of Manhattan, could get into, they couldn't do that.

Maybe more importantly, being so near to Kansas City and being thought by many (though certainly not everyone) to be far superior academically and socially to the University of Missouri in Columbia, which was considerably farther from Kansas City than Lawrence, it attracted more than its share of well-to-do students from Missouri. That no doubt had something to do with the relatively sophisticated and intellectual air of the campus. Well-to-do middle-class youth are not as worldly as they like to think, but they have a certain style, and a large clump of them from the nearest metropolis was something to take into account.

As I said, we knew these things, but didn't take them into account in our book. Our book was about collective student resistance to the academic and intellectual demands and requirements faculty made of them and for them—what we and others have called "student culture." We ignored in our analysis the geographic features (and I haven't mentioned all of them) of the place where KU student culture was being constructed, and left their consequences for readers to deduce for themselves explicitly, if they were so inclined, or just read into what we said as "obvious" things anyone (any American of a certain age and background, anyway) would understand. But they were facts, aspects of what the University of Kansas *was,* that conditioned the forms of collective action that made up campus life.

Another way to say this is that there were other relationships than the ones we analyzed involved in what we were trying to understand. No doubt student cooperation to minimize the coercion of faculty-and administration-imposed academic organization was crucial. That's a story with a long history, as Helen Horowitz (1987) has shown. But this particular case of it took place where it did, and where it took place made a difference.

More formally still, the environing conditions of an event or organization or phenomenon are crucial to its occurrence or existence in the form it eventually takes. Making those dependencies explicit helps you make better explanations.

Recognizing the dependency of social organization on its environment brings into focus the problem many researchers have when they write those little accounts of where they did their research. Since it's clear we can't include everything, which things related to where our case is located should we take into account? That's a tactical question. The provisional answer is that you include anything that tells you it can't be left out by sticking its nose up so that it can't be ignored. If the psychoanalysts you interview tell you that self-help groups and lay therapies like est successfully compete with them for patients, and those therapies and groups are very common in California, then you know that when you study the careers of analysts geography and local culture cannot be ignored (see Nunes 1984). We accumulate knowledge by finding more and more things that, in this sense, can't be left out, things that are, in the first instance, tied to the local circumstances of the cases we study.

So, rather than trying to ignore or "control" local variation, we should find these local peculiarities and build them into our results. An excellent example is Thomas Hennessy's (1973) study of the development of big dance bands among black musicians between 1917 (the end of World War I, when many black musicians returned from service, where they had played in segregated bands) and 1935 (when the new form of the traveling big band became a national phenomenon). The bands, and the music they played, developed differently depending on where in the country the development occurred and, specifically, on the nature of the black and white populations in those metropolitan centers and the relations between them. New York had sophisticated black and white populations; black musicians learned to read music of all kinds; white audiences were accustomed to having black musicians perform for them, so black musicians performed in a great variety of circumstances, and tailored their music to the occasion. Black musicians in Atlanta were much less schooled in conventional European music and mainly played for tent shows for the black population.

All this leads to, and can be summarized in, two tricks.

> *Everything Has to Be Somewhere.* The import of everything being somewhere is that what you are studying is taking place somewhere specific. Not in the world in general, or in "a social setting," but in this place, right here, and whatever is true of this place is going to affect it. So take a close look, and keep looking, at the features of that place: the physical features (where it is and what kind of place that is to live, work, and be) and the social features (who is there, how long they've been there, and all the other things demographers, sociologists, anthropologists, and

historians tell you to attend to). It helps to repeat "Everything has to be somewhere" to yourself frequently.

Put In What Can't Be Left Out. Following the previous rule is clearly impossible, since it requires you to know everything about everything and write about all of it when the time comes. Therefore, as you think about what you are studying, notice what features of the place you are invoking as ad hoc explanations of the specific social features you want to talk about. If you find yourself referring to the weather as a partial explanation of some event, the weather belongs in your introductory description. And if it belongs in that description, it belongs in your analysis.

Just as everything has to happen somewhere, so it has to happen sometime, and when that sometime is makes a difference. The problems and solutions for the problem of time resemble those of place closely; I will leave, as mathematicians say, as an exercise for the reader to work out the implications of the trick called "Everything has to be sometime."

Narrative

Narrative styles of analysis focus on finding stories that explain what It is ("It" being whatever we want to understand and explain) and how it got that way. When an analyst of causes has done the job well, the result is a large proportion of variance explained. When an analyst of narrative has done the job well, the result is a story that explains why this process had to lead to this result.

Narrative analysis produces something causal analysts are suspicious of, and properly so, given their presuppositions and working practices: perfect correlations. Probabilistic causal analyses that produce a perfect correlation are dismissed as necessarily containing sizable errors. Researchers know that there is too much noise in their data, too many measurement and other errors, for perfect correlations to occur. They expect imperfect correlations, even when their theory predicts a perfect one. But while they know that there is error in their data (the errors that stand in the way of better correlations), they do not throw their imperfect data out, for they don't know which cases or measurements contain the errors. To be honest, they include all the cases and thus guarantee a probabilistic result. This upsets narrative analysts who see the unexplained variance as a problem, not a natural feature of the landscape. (These matters get a more thorough airing in the discussions of property space analysis and qualitative comparative analysis in chapter 5.)

Narrative analysts, on the other hand, aren't happy unless they have a completely deterministic result. Every negative case becomes an opportunity to refine the result, to rework the explanation so that it includes the case that seems anomalous. A second way of dealing with anomalous cases, however, one that upsets probabilistic causal analysts, is to throw them out. Not exactly throw them out but, rather, decide by inspecting them carefully that they are not after all a case of the sort of thing we are explaining. Part of the process of constructing a narrative is a continuous redefinition of what the theory is explaining, of what the dependent variable actually is. (This is taken up more thoroughly in the discussion of analytic induction in chapter 5; see also Abbott 1992.)

ASK "HOW?" NOT "WHY?"

Everyone knows this trick. But, like many other things everyone knows, the people who know it don't always use it when they should, don't follow the prescription to ask how things happened, not why they happened. Why people do that is an interesting problem, though I suppose this sentence contains the answer: it seems more natural to ask why, as I just did. Somehow "Why?" seems more profound, more intellectual, as though you were asking about the deeper meaning of things, as opposed to the simple narrative "How?" would likely evoke. This prejudice is embodied in the old and meretricious distinction, invariably used pejoratively, between explanation and "mere" description.

I first understood that "How?" was better than "Why?" as a result of doing field research. When I interviewed people, asking them why they did something inevitably provoked a defensive response. If I asked someone why he or she had done some particular thing I was interested in—"Why did you become a doctor?" "Why did you choose that school to teach at?"—the poor defenseless interviewee understood my question as a request for a justification, for a good and sufficient reason for the action I was inquiring about. They answered my "Why?" questions briefly, guardedly, pugnaciously, as if to say, "OK, buddy, that good enough for you?"

When, on the other hand, I asked how something had happened—"How did you happen to go into that line of work?" "How did you end up teaching at that school?"—my questions "worked" well. People answered at length, told me stories filled with informative detail, gave accounts that included not only their reasons for whatever they had done, but also the actions of others that had contributed to the outcome I was inquiring about. And, when I interviewed marijuana users in order to develop a theory of the genesis of that activity, "How did you happen to start smoking grass?" evoked none of the defensive, guilty reaction evoked (as though I had accused them of something) by "Why do you smoke dope?"

Why does "How?" work so much better than "Why?" as an interview question? Even cooperative, nondefensive interviewees gave short answers to "Why?" They understood the question to be asking for a cause, maybe even causes, but in any event for something that could be summarized briefly in a few words. And not just any old cause, but the cause contained in the victim's intentions. If you did it, you did it for a reason. OK, what's your reason? Furthermore, "Why?" required a "good" answer, one that made sense and could be defended. The answer should not reveal logical flaws and inconsistencies. It should be socially as well as logically defensible; that is, the answer should express one of the motives conventionally accepted as adequate in that world. In other words, asking "why?" asks the interviewee for a reason that absolves the speaker of any responsibility for whatever bad thing's occurrence lay behind the question. "Why are you late for work?" clearly asks for a "good" reason; "I felt like sleeping late today" isn't an answer, even though true, because it conveys an illegitimate intention. "The trains broke down" might be a good answer, since it suggests that the intentions were good and the fault lay elsewhere (unless "You should leave early enough to take account of that possibility" lies in wait as a response). "It was foretold in my horoscope" will not do the trick in many places.

"How?" questions, when I asked them, gave people more leeway, were less constraining, invited them to answer in any way that suited them, to tell a story that included whatever they thought the story ought to include in order to make sense. They didn't demand a "right" answer, didn't seem to be trying to place responsibility for bad actions or outcomes anywhere. They signaled idle or disinterested curiosity: "Gee, what happened on the way to work that made you so late?" They didn't telegraph the form the answer had to take (in the case of "why," a reason contained in an intention). As a result, they invited people to include what they thought was important to the story, whether I had thought of it or not.

You might not welcome an interviewee having that sort of freedom if you were doing a certain sort of research. If you wanted to get everyone to choose answers to your questions from the same small number of choices (as is sometimes, but not necessarily, the aim in survey research), so that you could count how many had chosen each, you wouldn't want to hear about possibilities not contained in your list; those would have to go under "other" and couldn't be used to do anything you had in mind to do.

But the kind of research I was doing, and still do, was after something else. I wanted to know all the circumstances of an event, everything that was going on around it, everyone who was involved. ("All" and "everything" here are hyperbolic; I wouldn't really want all that, but certainly a lot more than social scientists often do.) I wanted to know the sequences of things, how one thing led to another, how this didn't happen until that happened. And, further, I was sure that I didn't know all the people and events and circumstances involved in the story. I expected to keep adding to that collection, and making my understanding, my analysis, more complicated, as I learned from the people I talked to. I wanted to maximize their freedom to tell me things, especially things I hadn't thought of.

There's an important exception to my condemnation of "why" questions. Sometimes researchers want to know, exactly, what kinds of reasons people give for what they have done or think they might do. When Blanche Geer and I interviewed medical students (Becker et al. [1961] 1977, 401–18) about the choices they intended to make of medical specialties—since they were still students, these choices were all hypothetical—what we wanted to know was, precisely, the kinds of reasons they would give for their choices. We wanted to chart the framework of acceptable reasons for choosing and the way those choices mapped onto the range of available specialties. We didn't expect these choices to predict the choices students would actually make when, in the future, they entered one or another specialty. We wanted to know their reasons as part of our description of the perspective that guided their thinking while they were in school.

So, in the field, you learn more from interview questions phrased as "how" than from those phrased as "why." Effectiveness as an interview strategy does not warrant an idea's theoretical usefulness. Still, it's a clue.

PROCESS

The clue leads to a general way of thinking that is a good theoretical trick. Assume that whatever you want to study has, not causes, but a history, a story, a narrative, a "first this happened, then that happened, and then the other happened, and it ended up like this." On this view, we understand the occurrence of events by learning the steps in the process by which they came to happen, rather than by learning the conditions that made their existence necessary.

But you aren't looking for particular stories, of the kind novelists or historians tell. You aren't looking for the specifics that distinguish this story from any other story. Instead, you are looking for typical stories, stories that work out pretty much the same way every time they happen. You don't look for invariant effects of causes, but for stories whose steps have a logic, perhaps even a logic as inevitable as the logic of causes. From this point of view, events are not caused by anything other than the story that led them to be the way they are.

Social scientists call stories with these characteristics *processes*. Abbott (1992, 68–69) quotes Robert E. Park's explanation of this idea in his introduction to a study of revolutions (Edwards 1927, x, xiii):

> [That there are tactics of revolutions] presupposes the existence of something typical and generic in these movements—something that can be described in general terms. It presupposes in short the existence of materials for a scientific account of revolution since science—natural science—in the long run is little more than a description in conceptual terms of the processes by which events take place, together with explanations which permit events to be predicted and controlled.

This is not just a matter of saying the right words, "process" instead of "cause." It implies a different way of working. You want to understand how a couple breaks up? Don't look, as a generation of family researchers did, for the factors in the backgrounds or present circumstances of those who break up that differentiate them from those who don't. Instead, look, as Diane Vaughan (1986) did, for the story of how the breakup occurred, for all the steps in that process, for how the steps connected to each other, for how one step created the conditions for the next step to occur—for the "description in conceptual terms of the processes by which events take place." The explanation of the breakup is that the couple went through all those steps, not that they were these or those kinds of people.

You might want to ask, "Well, OK, but why do they go through all those steps? What's the cause of that?" Empirically, when you look into that, you find that people of all kinds go through those steps, that there doesn't seem to be any one kind of person who goes through these steps or any specific situation that leads to the participants going through them. One of Vaughan's surprising findings about the way couples break up is that the process is the same whether the couple are married or unmarried, straight or gay, working class or middle class. Even more surprisingly, it happens the same way whether the person who initiates the breakup is male or female. Either way, the "initiator" starts the process and then the rest of the sequence unfolds, according to a logic that depends very much (in the case of couples breaking up) on who knows what about the state of the relationship at each step in the process. The initiator, for instance, knows that a breakup is coming, because he or she intends it, and the "partner" doesn't, and so can't be prepared for it as the first party is.

Process narratives don't have a predestined goal. They can have more than one ending (although we may only be interested in one of the possible endings, which is another story, taken up in chapter 5), and in some of those endings the thing we set out to explain doesn't happen. The couple, for instance, doesn't break up after all. As the story unfolds, you can see how one or another background factor or set of circumstances makes it more or less likely that the story will unfold in the way that leads to breakup. But that outcome isn't a sure thing. The sure thing is just that stories that turn out this way get there by this path.

This kind of narrative imagery will make a lot of social scientists nervous, because they want to find invariant laws, of the form "A → B, under conditions C, D, and E." They want to be able to say that something had to happen, could not have happened otherwise, because there is a law of social science that shows its logical and empirical necessity. If they get a story instead, especially a story that could have turned out some other way, they feel cheated. They don't accept a mere story as science, because there's nothing compelling the result to be what it is. They don't think they've learned anything. If you are seriously attached to that version of the "science" in "social science," that's a big problem.

Stephen Jay Gould (1989, 48–50) describes this problem as the question of, if we rewound the tape of history—he's talking, of course, about the story of biological evolution on earth—and played it again, would it come out the same way? He says "No."

Georg von Wright (1971) has given a helpful, though complicated, formal analysis of the complexities involved in constructing such a language. His most useful contribution is to distinguish two kinds of explanations.

One shows *"why* something was or became *necessary;"* the other shows *"how* something was or became *possible."* When we know how something became possible we still do not know enough for prediction, only for what he and others have called "retrodiction" (1971, 58): "From the fact that a phenomenon is known to have occurred, we can infer back in time that its antecedent necessary conditions must also have occurred, in the past. And by 'looking into the past' we may find traces of them (in the present)" (1971, 58–59).

Causes

A final form of imagery needs to be considered: causality. Social scientists like to think, and to say, that something "causes" something else. The imagery of causality, and the logic it implies, is very tangled philosophically, at least (to my meager knowledge) since Hume, and it is especially hard to separate from the simple fact of sequence, of one thing following another. Billiard ball A hits billiard ball B. Billiard ball B moves. Did A's hitting B "cause" it to move?

Leave these philosophical tangles aside. Sociologists typically solve the problem of cause by embodying it in procedures we agree will serve as the way we know that A caused B, philosophically sound or not. These procedures have the status of paradigmatic methods. They are parts of packages of ideas and procedures that some community of scientists has agreed to accept as plenty good enough for the purpose of establishing cause. For all the reasons that Thomas Kuhn (1962) pointed out, these paradigmatic ideas are double-edged. Without them we can't get anything done. But they never really do what they say they do. They leave terrible anomalies in the wake of their use. They have terrible flaws in their supporting logic. They are thus always vulnerable to attack, to being shown to be and do less than they pretend.

Sociologists have agreed on paradigms for establishing causality many times, generally describing their procedures in the language of variables. The analyst identifies a "dependent variable," some phenomenon that varies along some dimension, and then attempts to identify the "independent variables" whose own variation "causes" the variation of the dependent variable. The definition of cause is covariation. If the measure of dependent variable A changes in some regular way when the measure of the independent variables changes, cause has been demonstrated or, at least, researchers who accept this paradigm agree that evidence of causation has been produced. (I have relied extensively in what follows on Ragin's 1987 discussion, although I've adapted his arguments to my uses. And I'll return to his ideas later, in chapter 5.)

Naturally, such procedures have many difficulties. Students learning correlation techniques traditionally also learn that correlation is not causation. A long list of troubles can derail the easy identification of covariation and causality. Nevertheless, sociologists routinely use this form of explanation, in a variety of forms, particularly in such paradigmatic applications as figuring out, say, what factors affect social mobility: to what degree do parental social position, education, occupation, and similar variables covary with (and thus cause) someone's class mobility?

One standard procedure (or, better, family of procedures) has been a kind of quasi-experimental factoring out of the relative influence of the several causes we can imagine might explain or account for (a variety of terms have been used to describe this connection) the outcome we are interested in. Lieberson (1985) has criticized this family of statistical procedures profoundly, arguing that the notion of estimating the influence of a variable by holding other factors constant is untenable, because of the nonrandom distribution of the variables so introduced, the "selection" problem. He has (1992) nevertheless tried to keep that logic going by cleaning up the occasions of its use.

The procedures used in studies based on this logic depend on comparing cells in a table (the cells containing cases that embody different combinations of the variables being studied), and the comparisons will not withstand standard criticisms unless they rest on large numbers of cases. The results of such studies consist of probabilistic statements about the relations between the variables, statements whose subjects are not people or organizations doing things but rather variables having an effect or producing some measurable degree of variation in the dependent variable. The conclusions of such a study—that the cases studied have a particular probability of showing this or that result—are intended to apply to an entire universe of similar cases.

The logic of this approach, even in the cleaned up version advocated by Lieberson, requires us to imagine that all the causes involved in the production of an effect operate more or less simultaneously and continuously, as in the well-known laws governing the relations between pressure, temperature, and volume of gases. Even when we know better and know that

A must precede B, the analytic procedures require us to treat them as though that were not true.

These procedures also require us to imagine that the variables proposed as causes operate independently. Each makes its own contribution to the variation in the dependent variable. To be sure, the analyst may have to contend with interaction effects—the effects on the dependent variable of the effects the independent variables have on each other. But these too are treated as though they are all happening simultaneously and continuously.

Finally, such procedures treat causes as additive. A number of things may be found to contribute to a result we're interested in. The imagery of this kind of causality suggests that each of them could, if there were enough of it, produce the result by itself. Put more generally, any combination of "contributions" to the result will produce it, as long as they add up to enough.

To say that this family of techniques treats causes as operating in these ways does not imply that analysts using them are so stupid as not to recognize that variables have a temporal order, that they occur in recognizable and variable sequences, but rather that the techniques offer no simple way of dealing with this knowledge. The analysis proceeds "as if" all the above were the case. The logic of the techniques does not provide any special way of dealing with these problems. Such visual devices as path diagrams, which lay variables out in a diagram connected by arrows, purport to deal with temporal sequence, but time is only a visual metaphor in them.

Another approach, which Ragin (1987) describes as multiple and conjunctural, has a quite different image of causality. It recognizes that causes are typically not really independent, each making its independent contribution to some vector that produces the overall outcome in a dependent variable. It suggests instead that causes are only effective when they operate in concert. Variable X_1 has an effect, but only if variables X_2 and X_3 and X_4 are also present. In their absence, X_1 might as well have stayed home. That's the "conjunctural" part. Another way to put it, to make the difference from the earlier model clear, is to say that it is multiplicative. As we all learned in school, if you multiply a number, no matter how large, by zero, the result is zero. In multiplicative images of causality, all the elements have to be there to play their part in the conjunction or combination of relevant causal circumstances. If any one of them is missing, no matter how big or important the others are, the answer will still be zero—the effect we are interested in will not be produced.

The "multiple" part of the argument says that more than one such combination can produce the result we're interested in. In these causal images, there's more than one way to get there. Which combination works in a case depends on context: historically and socially specific conditions that vary from case to case.

This approach is often seen as necessary in studies that accumulate a great deal of information about a small number of cases, as is typical of detailed cross-national historical studies (such as studies of revolution or the development of state welfare policies in a few countries). Here, the analyst tries to deal with all the complexity of real historical cases, rather than the relations between variables in a universe of hypothetical cases. The conclusion is intended to make historical cases intelligible as instances of the way the posited variables operate in concert. (Ragin's "Boolean algorithm" is a method for producing results that do just this. I take it up in detail in chapter 5.)

I'll conclude this chapter by referring to another kind of image, our image of the social scientist at work. A standard image in contemporary social science is of the brave scientist submitting his (I use the masculine pronoun because the imagery is so macho) theories to a crucial empirical test and casting them aside when they don't measure up, when it isn't possible to reject the null hypothesis. Ragin draws a contrasting picture that I find quite compelling, of a social scientist engaged in "a rich dialogue" of data and evidence, a picture that looks a lot more like the scientific activity Blumer envisioned: pondering the possibilities gained from deep familiarity with some aspect of the world, systematizing those ideas in relation to kinds of information one might gather, checking the ideas in the light of that information, dealing with the inevitable discrepancies between what was expected and what was found by rethinking the possibilities and getting more data, and so on, in a version of Kuhn's image of the development of science as a whole.

3

SAMPLING

What to Include

Sampling and Synecdoche

Sampling is a major problem for any kind of research. We can't study every case of whatever we're interested in, nor should we want to. Every scientific enterprise tries to find out something that will apply to *everything* of a certain kind by studying *a few examples,* the results of the study being, as we say, "generalizable" to all members of that class of stuff. We need the sample to persuade people that we know something about the whole class.

This is a version of the classical trope of *synecdoche,* a rhetorical figure in which we use a part of something to refer the listener or reader to the whole it belongs to. So we say "The White House," and mean not the physical building but the American presidency—and not just the president, but the whole administration the president heads. Synecdoche is thus a kind of sampling, but meant to serve the purpose of persuasion, rather than that of research or study. Or perhaps it would be better to say that sampling is a kind of synecdoche, in which we want the part of a population or organization or system we have studied to be taken to represent, meaningfully, the whole from which it was drawn. Logics of sampling are arguments meant to persuade readers that the synecdoche works, because it has been arrived at in a defensible way. (I only discovered the discussion of sampling and synecdoche in Hunter 1990, which parallels mine in several ways, as this book was being readied for publication.)

The problem with synecdoche, or sampling, seems at first to be that the part may not represent the whole as we would like to think it does, may not reproduce in miniature the characteristics we are interested in, may not allow us to draw conclusions from what we do know that will also be true of what we haven't inspected ourselves. If we pick a few men and women off the streets of Paris and measure their height, will the average we calculate from those measurements apply to the whole population of Paris? Can we compare a similar average, computed from the heights of a few people picked off the streets of Seattle, to the Parisian average? Will the average height of all the inhabitants of each of these cities be the same, more or less, as the average height of the few we did measure? Could we, with these samples, arrive at a defensible conclusion about the comparative height of people in France and people in the United States? Can we use the sample as a synecdoche for the population? Or will our research be open to the kind of carping criticism students soon learn to address to any finding, the one that announces triumphantly "your sample's deficient!"?

Random Sampling: A Perfect Solution (For Some Problems)

The procedure of random sampling, so beloved of those who want to make social science into "real science," is designed to deal with this difficulty. Suppose we want to know what fraction of a city's population think of themselves as Democrats, or voted Democratic in the last election, or think they are going to vote for the Democratic candidate in an upcoming election. For the sake of efficiency, we don't want to ask every inhabitant about their identifications or actions or intentions. We want to ask some of them and reason from the some we talk with to the whole population of the city. If 53 percent of those we talk to say "Democrat," we'd like to be able to say that if we had asked everyone, the proportion would have been pretty much the same.

Statistical sampling procedures tell us how to do that. We can choose the people we will interview by using a table of random numbers, numbers arranged in an order guaranteed not to contain any bias. That is, there aren't any patterns in the numbers that will give some people a greater chance of being chosen. We have to use such an arcane procedure because almost any other way of picking cases you can think of will turn out to have such a bias built in.

Here's a frightening example of the kind of mistake you can make. Hatch and Hatch (1947) decided to study "criteria of social status" by gathering biographical data about the participants in weddings announced in the Sunday *New York Times,* on the assumption that people whose weddings got into the *Times* probably occupied "a superior position in the New York social system." Well, maybe so; it's the kind of thing sociologists are always assuming in order to get on with their research. The researchers further decided (it seems a reasonable way to get a large number, though the researchers did not make an argument for it) to study all the weddings announced in June over a period of years. They reported (this was only one of many findings) that "no announcement acknowledged marriage in a Jewish synagogue or gave any indication of association with the Jewish faith." They don't comment on this result, although they do make some interpretations of other findings, mostly pointing to the social characteristics of their families people thought worth emphasizing in their announcements. Still, it's quite striking that, in a city with as large a Jewish population as New York then had, no Jewish weddings were announced in the place where such announcements were customarily made.

The explanation was not long coming. A "Letter to the Editor" (Cahnman 1948) reported replicating the study, at least with respect to the proportions of Jewish weddings, in Sunday editions in October and November (because that was when Professor Cahnman read the offending article). In this sample, he reported, "[Of the] 36 marriage announcements [in these editions] no less than 13, that is 36.1% of the total, were performed by a rabbi. (The rabbi, to be sure, is labeled 'The Reverend So-and-so,' but there is a way to find out who is a rabbi, for one who knows.)"

Why the discrepancy? Cahnman explains:

> [T]he fact which the authors could easily have ascertained from any rabbi or otherwise Jewishly informed scholar is that Jewish weddings are not performed in the seven weeks between Passover and the Feast of Weeks and in the three weeks preceding the day of mourning for the destruction of the Holy Temple in Jerusalem. Almost invariably, June falls into the one or the other period. All orthodox and conservative rabbis, and the great majority of reform rabbis, adhere to the observance.

Cahnman concludes that the authors should have, on getting such a seemingly unusual result, looked into the matter further, become more knowledgeable, or at least gotten some expert advice—in short, done something to undo the effects of their ignorance of this feature of Jewish practice.

But Josephine Williams, from whom I was taking a course in statistics at the University of Chicago when the article and letter appeared, drew a different and in some ways more practical conclusion. Recognizing that (a) there might be many such problems buried in the data, and (b) not all of them would produce "amazing" conclusions of the kind that alerted

Cahnman, she showed us that any and all problems of this general type would have been avoided had the authors used a table of random numbers to pick their months, instead of the cute device of studying June weddings.

Using such a method, we pick our cases (usually people, but they could easily be issues of the *New York Times*) in such a way that every member of the population has a known (usually, but not necessarily, equal) chance of being chosen for the sample. Then existing formulae, whose mathematical logic is thoroughly defensible, can tell you how probable it is that the proportion of Jewish weddings reported in the issues you looked at (or the proportion of Democrats you found in your sample of interviewees) could have come from a population where the "true" proportion of Jewish weddings (or Democrats) was different.

Such a result is well worth getting, but only when it is what you want to know. That's why I said above that the problem *seems* to be that the part might not accurately represent the whole, faithfully reproducing its important characteristics: average height, proportion of Democratic voters, proportion of Jewish weddings. The relation of a variable's value in the sample to its value in the population is a problem, but it isn't the only sampling problem, because the average or proportion of some variable in a population might not be what you want to know. There are other questions.

Some Other Sampling Problems

We might, to take another kind of problem social scientists often try to solve, want to know what kind of an organization could be the whole of which the thing we have studied is a part. Using "the presidency" to refer to the whole administrative apparatus of the executive branch of the United States government raises the question of what kind of phenomenon that apparatus is. If we talk about the executive in charge, does our synecdoche communicate anything meaningful or reliable about the rest of it? We're not interested in proportions here, but in the way the parts of some complicated whole reveal its overall design (see the discussion in Hunter 1990, 122–27).

Archeologists and paleontologists have this problem to solve when they uncover the remnants of a now-vanished society. They find some bones, but not a whole skeleton; they find some cooking equipment, but not the whole kitchen; they find some garbage, but not the stuff of which the

garbage is the remains. They know that they are lucky to have found the little they have, because the world is not organized to make life easy for
archeologists. So they don't complain about having lousy data. Instead,
they work on getting from this thigh bone to the whole organism, from
this pot to the way of life in which it played its small role as a tool of living.
It's the problem of the Machine Trick, of inferring the organization of a
machine from a few parts we have found somewhere.

We might want to know a third thing social scientists often concern
themselves with: the full range of variation in some phenomenon. What
are all the different ways people have organized kinship relations? What is
the full range of variation in the ways people have organized keeping
records or designing clothing? We ask those questions because we want to
know all the members of the class our generalizations are supposed to apply to. We don't want our synecdoche to have features that are specific to
some subgroup of the whole, which the unwary (among whom we must
include ourselves) will take as essential characteristics of the class. We don't
want, simple-mindedly, to assume that some feature contained in our example is just "naturally" there in every class member and thus does not require explanation. Is it just "instinctive" and "natural" that people don't
have sexual relations with close relatives? If it turns out that that "natural"
restriction didn't hold for the royalty of ancient Egypt, then we have to revise our conclusion about how "natural" the restriction is. We have to recognize that its existence requires a more detailed and explicit explanation.

Where Do You Stop? The Case of Ethnomusicology

Before considering some tricks that will help us arrive at synecdoches that
will be helpful and withstand the "bad sample" criticism, let's return to an
alternative approach I dismissed out of hand above, an approach that,
though not practical, is something most social scientists have now and then
dreamed about: to forget about sampling and, instead of relying on synecdoche, just get "the whole thing" and present it to our colleagues as the result of our work. This produces such chimeras as "complete description"
and "reproducing the lived experience of people," among others.

We can investigate the result of trying to have it all by looking at ethnomusicology, that interesting, and usually happy, hybrid of anthropology
and musicology. As a discipline, it aims to improve conventional musicology by getting rid of its ethnocentrism, and to improve anthropology by

giving it access to a subject matter nonmusicians find hard to describe and discuss. In pursuit of these worthy goals, it sets out to solve the sampling problem by describing, as I will explain, all the music there ever was or is.

But such an inclusive goal immediately creates a terrible problem. If you don't limit the scope of your discipline—the range of material whose explanation and understanding its ideas and theories are responsible for—to conventional Western music (that's the usual solution), what do you count as the music you ought to be studying and theorizing and generalizing about? (Remember that this is only a special case of a problem all the social sciences share, whether they recognize it or not. Try it for yourself with religion or economy or any of the standard social science objects.)

An outsider approaching ethnomusicology can't help noticing the ambitious nature of the enterprise. The simple but unsatisfactory answer the discipline long gave to itself, and to anyone else who asked, was a list of all the things that were patently music but had usually been left out of musicological thinking and theorizing. It thus proposed to study and take intellectual responsibility for all the world's musics, all the music made anywhere by anyone in any society. Not just Western symphonies and operas, and Western popular music, but Javanese *gamelan* and Japanese court music and Native American musics and African drumming and Andean pipe playing, and anything else an exhaustive survey could uncover. Later ethnomusicologists added to the list: folk musics of all kinds, jazz, the transformations of Western pop music found in other parts of the world (as in Waterman 1990). But a list is not a definition.

In addition to taking all that on, ethnomusicology, as the plural form—"musics"—implies, proposed to treat all those musics on their own terms. Every music has an aesthetic ethnomusicological researchers have enjoined themselves to take as seriously as the people who perform it and listen to it do. Researchers therefore do not treat other musics as degenerate or incompletely realized versions of "our" music; rather, they give each one the same serious consideration musicologists give to music in the Western ("our") tradition. If you accept this view of the job, there isn't anything that might be considered music that one shouldn't, in principle, be studying. Such catholicism has been traditional in comparative studies of the arts, and comparative musicology has always been omnivorous, collecting instruments and sounds and compositions and performances from anywhere a practitioner could get to with notebook, still camera, movie camera, and state-of-the-art sound recording equipment.

This definition of the job, of course, has never been completely honored in ethnomusicological practice. The discipline has always had to struggle against a chronic highbrow prejudice, a tendency to give greatest attention to what counts as art music in other "high" cultures, musical traditions we think as aesthetically worthy as our own: Indian *ragas* or Japanese *gogaku*. The discipline has often overcome that prejudice, but practicing ethnomusicologists always feel a strong obligation to go beyond such parochialism. Their worries about that obligation show up in the general statements about the field made in textbooks and on such ceremonial occasions as the presentation of presidential addresses.

Such a definition of ethnomusicology's domain creates terrible problems because, in practice, the comprehensiveness can't really be honored. You can aim at collecting all the music, but then collecting takes precedence over everything else. You never get beyond the collecting, because there is so much music to collect. Surely there has to be a principle of selection. What music can we safely leave out? How about children's nursery rhymes? Can we ignore them? Well, no, we wouldn't want to leave those rhymes out. They're so important in understanding how children are taught the ways of thinking and feeling and acting characteristic of their society—how they are, in a word, socialized. And the way children learn music, their "mistakes," the salience of one or another aspect of music to them, that's all interesting and important. Look what John Blacking (1967) did with such material, or at Antoine Hennion's study (1988) of the way French children are taught (whether they learn, as he shows, is another matter) music in school.

Can we leave out what isn't "authentic"? Authenticity has off and on been a problem for ethnomusicologists, at least some of whom used to have that sort of bias, a predilection for what people used to do rather than what they're doing now—a greater interest, let's say, in the remnants of authentic Polynesian musics than in the "Hawaiian" songs like "Sweet Leilani" that Don Ho was singing in a hotel on Waikiki Beach. Ethnomusicologists have often wished people wouldn't change their musical habits and tastes the way they do, that they would keep their music "pure," unadulterated by the inexorable spread of Western (mostly North American) rock and roll, jazz, and the rest of it. Ethnomusicologists have in this way resembled those naturalists who want to save endangered creatures so that the earth's gene pool will contain maximal variety.

These complaints often merge with those of musical nationalists, who want to preserve the "traditional" music of their people or country, even when that tradition is newly invented. Hermano Vianna (1995) has described how the samba, itself a mixture of a variety of musics from Europe and Africa, became the "traditional" national music of Brazil, a claim to which it had no more right than many other musics played and heard in Brazil at the same time.

Preserving all these changing musics sounds like a noble idea, but the world seldom accepts such noble ideas as guides to action. People pick up on the music they like, the music that seems attractive to them, that represents, however inchoately, what they want represented, the music that will make a profit for those who do the producing and distributing, and so on. So it seems wiser, even more practical, if you're interested in the world's musics, to study what people are playing and singing now, no matter what bastard combination of raw materials it comes from, as well as whatever you can recover of those musics they are deserting.

But, far from solving the problem of what to study, that really opens the door. I worked my way through graduate school playing piano in taverns and strip joints in Chicago. Should ethnomusicologists study what every tavern piano player (the kind I was) plays in all the joints on all the streets in all the world's cities? No one would have thought it worthwhile to do that around 1900, when a definitive study could have been done, say, of the origins of ragtime. But wouldn't it be wonderful if they had? And had carried that study through with the same care and attention that have been devoted to Native American music? Of course it would.

But why limit ourselves to the professionals who make music as a job? Should we study, as we might study the similar musical rituals in a Melanesian society, every singing of "Happy Birthday" in the United States or, to be a little reasonable, a sample of such singing? And if not, why not?

I won't continue with the examples because the point's clear. We'd like, in retrospect, to have everything, because all of it will fit the definition and all of it could be made the object of serious study. (By now it should also be clear that I'm not just talking about music.) But we can't have everything, for the most obvious practical reasons: we don't have the people to collect it and we wouldn't know what to do with the mass of detail we'd end up with if we did. It resembles oral history in that way. The "new" historians (see McCall and Wittner 1990) have convinced us that everyone's life is important; but we can't collect *everyone's* life, and if we did we'd drown in the detail of all those lives. And no computerized database could help us, because the drowning is conceptual, not mechanical.

Social science has no simple answer to this problem. A social scientist might put it in comparative perspective and note that every global definition of a field creates just such an undoable job, certainly in the social sciences. A sociologist of science and scholarship might note further that the practical answers to these unanswerable questions—and practitioners always have practical, everyday answers to unanswerable questions—do not come from logic or argument, but are based in solid social facts of organizational resources and competition. Ethnomusicology's scope has, I assume (though I haven't done the work to justify saying this), been determined by its position in the academic hierarchy and the resources for research and other scholarly activities that position makes available. That's a topic ethnomusicologists might want to confront directly, rather than continuing to debate the proper boundaries of the field, taking as a model the discussions of the effect of anthropology's position in the academy on anthropological work in George Marcus (1986) and Paul Rabinow (1986, esp. 253–56).

Other social scientists might at this point be feeling superior to these benighted ethnomusicologists, who haven't grasped the impossibility of "getting it all," and haven't understood that the point is to find ways to avoid having to do that. But they needn't feel superior. Every field of social science has its own yearnings for completeness. For some it is the archive that will contain all the data from all the polls ever made; for others it is the will-of-the-wisp of "complete description" made possible by such new machines as audio or videotape recorders. We all know better, but we all lust after "getting it all" just the same.

Harold Garfinkel, the founder of ethnomethodology, has made generations of researchers of every methodological tribe uneasy by insisting that social science is, after all, a "practical activity," which is to say, among other things, that the work has to get finished sometime. No one can spend forever doing their study, so short cuts have to be taken and these invariably lead to violations of "the way research is supposed to be done."

This long example is just one version of how and why we are stuck with the synecdoche of sampling. Let's return to the idea of sampling understood in this extended way, as a question of what we can say about what we didn't see on the basis of what we did see, keeping in mind that there are several reasons for doing that, and not just the conventional one of estimating, within a given range of confidence, a measure of something in a population from a sample of that population.

Having just given up on the idea of completely describing everything, I now want perversely to return to it, to use it as a benchmark, to consider every way of creating the synecdoches of sampling as methods whose results we should assess against the "ideal" of full and complete description of everything that might be or is relevant to whatever we want to say with assurance about some social phenomenon. I suggest this not because I think such description is possible, but because such a benchmark shows us what choices we make when we do, inevitably, leave things out.

What, then, would "full and complete description" mean?

How Much Detail? How Much Analysis?

When I teach field research, I always insist that students begin their observations and interviews by writing down "everything." That is, I claim that I don't want them to sample but rather to report the universe of "relevant" occurrences. This generally leads to a good deal of foot dragging by them and nagging by me. They say they can't do it, or can't do it "honestly" (by which they mean that what they write will be neither complete or fully accurate). I say they will never know whether they can do it unless they try and that their attempts to write everything down will be no less accurate than an account that leaves a lot out. I suggest that they buy a rubber stamp that says "This transcript is not complete or fully accurate" and stamp every page of their notes with it, to assuage the combination of guilt and sloth that attacks them. Though I make fun of them, beneath their reluctance lies a healthy wariness at being asked to do what we have already seen is, on the large scale, undoable.

The job is, of course, undoable on the small scale as well. You can't write down "everything." That doesn't mean that you can't write down a good deal more than students ordinarily do. But the students are right, they can't write it all down.

I also insist that what they think is straight description is usually nothing of the kind, but rather a sort of analytic summary of what they have seen, designed to evade the requirement not to sample, but to report it all. Thus: "Patients came into the office, and waited impatiently for the doctor to see them." That sentence contains no report of an observation of someone actually exhibiting impatience, no sample of such descriptions on which a conclusion might be based. Instead, it summarizes and interprets many things its author surely did see: people walking in and out of the office, fidgeting, looking at their watches or the clock on the wall, making ritualized sounds of impatience aimed at no one in particular, perhaps soliciting an expression of similar feeling from others, and so on.

What would straight, uninterpreted description—supposing one did it—actually look like? Granting that it is, in principle, impossible to avoid all interpretation, you can still go a lot farther in the direction of pure description than most of us ever go. Georges Perec, the French novelist, was a great experimenter with "plain description," and conducted one of his experiments for a French radio network, the experiment here described by his biographer, David Bellos:

> On 19 May, 1978, a mobile recording studio drew up outside L'Atrium (Perec usually called it L'Acquarium) at Place Mabillon, on Boulevard Saint-Germain. One of the strangest experiments in radio history was about to begin. A writer well known for his attention to detail and to the "infra-ordinary" was to spend an entire day describing what passed in front of his eye, into the microphone, in real time. Obviously, Perec took a few breaks for coffee and meals and so on, and the experiment was brought to a close with about five hours of tape in the can. This was later edited by Perec and René Farabet, the producer, into a hallucinatory aural experience some two hours in length, broadcast in February 1979 as *Tentative de description de choses vues au carrefour Mabillon le 19 mai 1978* (An attempt at a description of things seen at Mabillon Junction on 19 May 1978).
>
> What does the experiment prove? That trivia can become poetry when pushed beyond reasonable limits; that repetition can become rhythm. That there is a thin borderline between punishment and intoxication. And perhaps no one but Perec could have had the combination of self-restraint (he never comments on what he sees, he just says, *another 68 bus, three red cars, a lady with a dog* . . .), modesty, and sheer gall to carry on for hours on end, to the end.
>
> The art of enumeration is not easy. (Bellos 1993, 640)

Right. The art of enumeration is not easy. Understand what enumerating without ever commenting implies here. Perec did not say "He looks like he's in a hurry to get home with his shopping" or "Those two look like they're gossiping about someone they know slightly," the kind of thing you might expect a novelist to say, the kind of thing you might expect anyone to say. Here's what he did say (and this quotation comes from a published fragment drawn from a different occasion of such observation and recording, the material from the day Bellos talks about not being available in print):

Saturday, June 12, 1971, Around three o'clock.
Cafe l'Atrium.
A gray police car just stopped in front of Lip's clothing store. Three women cops got out, their traffic ticket books in their hands.
Next to Lip's, a black building is being repaired or torn down. On the wooden enclosure hiding its ground floor, three advertisements, one for the "House Under the Trees" (the title hidden by a row of yellow portraits under which I believe I can read "Passionaria"), the second for "Taking Off," the third for "You're Always Too Good to Women" (the title hidden by violet and white question marks which I know, because I saw them from much closer up a second ago, belong to a poster for a public discussion with Laurent Salini (Communist Party)).
At the intersection of Buci and Saint-Germain, a pole with a French flag and, a third of the way up, a banner announcing the Roualt exhibition.
In the foreground, chains which prevent crossing the boulevard. Someone has hung small placards for the magazine CREE "The First French Magazine for the Design of Art and the Contemporary Environment" on them; the cover of the magazine represents a fence.
Light traffic.
Not many people in the café.
Pale sun coming through the clouds. It's cool.
The people: generally alone, sullen. Sometimes in couples. Two young mothers with their young children; girls, in twos and threes; very few tourists. Long raincoats, a lot of army (American) jackets and shirts.
A newspaper stand across the street:
Automobile: Le Mans
Romy Schneider charged!
Week-end: A camera shows the winners
(I still have a good view!)
Another police car (the third since I got here)
A friend who I often see strolling along the streets shuffles by.
(Sketch of a typology of walking? Most of the passersby stroll, shuffle, seem to have no precise idea of just where they are).
A couple on the terrace block my view.
It begins to rain. (Perec 1980, 33–34)

This is description without the interpretations that, we might say, make sense of the simple facts of observation, the interpretations the students in my fieldwork classes so often want to substitute for sheer observation.

Social scientists, like those students, ordinarily expect to be given such interpretations in what they read and to rely on them in what they write. They think of the details of their work as the basis for generalizations, as samples whose interest lies in their generalizability, in the interpretations that explain what the details stand for. But perhaps these interpretations aren't as necessary as we think. We can get a lot from simpler, less analyzed observations. The appropriate ratio of description to interpretation is a real problem every describer of the social world has to solve or come to terms with.

(Everyone knows that there is no "pure" description, that all description, requiring acts of selection and therefore reflecting a point of view, is what Thomas Kuhn said it was, "theory laden." That it is not possible to do away entirely with the necessity of selection, and the point of view it implies, does not mean that there aren't degrees of interpretation, that some descriptions can't be less interpretive (or perhaps we should say less conventionally interpretive) than others. We might even say that some descriptions require less inference than others. To say that someone looks like he is hurrying home with his shopping requires an inference about motivation that saying that he is walking rapidly doesn't.)

So social scientists expect interpretations from themselves and each other. They typically want to reduce the amount of stuff they have to deal with, to see it as examples of and evidence for ideas they have, not as something to be dished up in quantity for its own interest. They don't want a lot of (what is often labeled "mere") description, or a lot of detail. John Tukey, the statistician, once remarked that most tables contain far more information than anyone wants or needs, that mostly what we want to do is compare two numbers and see if they are the same or if one is bigger than the other; the rest of the numbers in all those cells are just noise, drowning out the message we are looking for.

Still, massive detailed description has something substantial to recommend it, beyond the possibilities of poetry and rhythm to which Bellos alluded, which we can't expect social scientists to take seriously. An occasional researcher still finds the accumulation of enormous detail to be just the ticket. Roger Barker, in a wonderful but never imitated book (Barker and Wright 1966), described one Kansas boy's day in that kind of detail. Gregory Bateson and Margaret Mead (1942) described the psychological life of Balinese villagers in something like such detail, adding several hundred photographs to the verbal descriptions. A well-known example of such description is *Let Us Now Praise Famous Men,* by photographer Walker Evans and writer James Agee, from which I will take an extended example.

In 1936 James Agee and Walker Evans, writer and photographer, went to Alabama to do a story, text and pictures, for *Fortune* magazine. Their book, *Let Us Now Praise Famous Men: Three Tenant Families* (Agee and Evans 1941), was not successful when first published but has since been recognized as a classic of—well, it isn't exactly clear what genre it's a classic of. Literature, perhaps. I would be glad to claim it for sociology, although I think a lot of sociologists would be unhappy about that (bad sample, not very scientific, etc.). In any event, one thing it is certainly a masterpiece of is minute, detailed description, the kind of description that lets you see how much summary, how much generalization, is contained in the most exhaustive social scientific descriptions. So it raises the question of sampling in an even stronger form than Perec's description of the Paris street corner. This is what description would look like if it were a much more detailed and complete sampling of what is there to describe.

The book's extended table of contents gives an idea of this detail. A section called "Shelter: An Outline," in the subsection devoted to "The Gudger House," contains the following headings, each referring to a substantial (that is to say, several printed pages) description of the kind I will shortly quote:

> The house is left alone
> In front of the house: its general structure
> In front of the house: the façade
> •
> The room beneath the house
> •
> The hallway
> Structure of four rooms
> Odors
> Bareness and space
> • •
> I. The Front Bedroom
>   General
>   Placement of furniture

Fifty-four pages are devoted to this description of a sharecropper family's shack, which the reader already knows from the portfolio of photographs by Walker Evans that precedes the book's text. Here are the two pages devoted to "the altar" (already pictured in one of the Evans photographs, so the reader can check the words against the picture):

The three other walls [of the front bedroom] are straight and angled beams and the inward surfaces of unplaned pine weatherboards. This partition wall is made of horizontals of narrow and cleanly planed wood, laid tightly edge to edge; the wood is pine of another quality, slenderly grained in narrow yellow and rich iron-red golds, very smooth and as if polished, softly glowing and shining, almost mirroring bulks: and is the one wall of the room at all conducive to ornament, and is the one ornamented wall. At its center the mantel and square fireplace frame, painted, one coat, an old and thin blue-white: in front of the fireplace, not much more than covering the full width of its frame, the small table: and through, beneath it, the gray, swept yet ashy bricks of the fireplace and short hearth, and the silent shoes: and on the table, and on the mantel, and spread above and wide of it on the walls, the things of which I will now tell.

On the table: it is blue auto paint: a white cloth, hanging a little over the edges. On the cloth, at center, a small fluted green glass bowl in which sits a white china swan, profiled upon the north.

On the mantel against the glowing wall, each about six inches from the ends of the shelf, two small twin vases, very simply blown, of pebble-grained iridescent glass. Exactly at center between them, a fluted saucer, with a coarse lace edge, of pressed milky glass, which Louise's mother gave her to call her own and for which she cares more dearly than for anything else she possesses. Pinned all long the edge of this mantel, a broad fringe of white tissue pattern-paper which Mrs. Gudger folded many times on itself and scissored into pierced geometrics of lace, and of which she speaks as her last effort to make this house pretty.

On the wall, pasted or pinned or tacked or printed, set well discrete from one another, in not quite perfected symmetric relations:

A small octagonal frame surfaced in ivory and black ribbons of thin wicker or of straw, the glass broken out: set in this frame, not filling it, a fading box-camera snapshot: low, gray, dead-looking land stretched back in a deep horizon; twenty yards back, one corner of a tenant house, central at the foreground, two women: Annie Mae's sister Emma as a girl of twelve, in slippers and stockings and a Sunday dress, standing a little shyly with puzzling eyes, self-conscious of her appearance and of her softly clouded sex; and their mother, wide and high, in a Sunday dress still wet from housework, her large hands hung loose and biased in against her thighs, her bearing strong, weary, and noble, her face fainted away almost beyond distinguishing, as if in her death and by some secret touching the image itself of the fine head her husband had cared for so well had softly withered, which even while they stood there had begun its blossoming inheritance in the young daughter at her side.

A calendar, advertising _____'s shoes, depicting a pretty brunette with ornate red lips, in a wide-brimmed red hat, cuddling red flowers. The title is Cherie, and written twice, in pencil, in a schoolgirl's hand: Louise, Louise.

A calendar, advertising easy-payment furniture: a tinted photograph of an immaculate, new-overalled boy of twelve, wearing a wide new straw hat, the brim torn by the artist, fishing. The title is Fishin'.

Slung awry by its chain from a thin nail, an open oval locket, glassed. In one face of this locket, a colored picture of Jesus, his right hand blessing, his red heart exposed in a burst spiky gold halo. In the other face, a picture by the same artist of the Blessed Virgin, in blue, her heart similarly exposed and haloed, and pierced with seven small swords.

Torn from a cheap child's storybook, costume pictures in bright furry colors illustrating, exactly as they would and should be illustrated, these titles:
The Harper was Happier than a King as He Sat by His Own Fireside.
She Took the Little Prince in Her Arms and Kissed Him. ("She" is a goose girl.)
Torn from a tin can, a strip of bright scarlet paper with a large white fish on it and the words:
SALOMAR
EXTRA QUALITY MACKEREL
At the right of the mantel, in whitewash, all its whorlings sharp, the print of a child's hand.

No one will read this description without arriving at a conclusion about the misery of lives lived in these surroundings, but we have the data to arrive at that conclusion ourselves, and at much else besides. We don't need Agee to tell us explicitly. That is the kind of thing massive description can do.

Beyond the Categories: Finding What Doesn't Fit

Description and the "Categories"

What does all that description do for us? Perhaps not the only thing, but a very important one, is that it helps us get around conventional thinking. A major obstacle to proper description and analysis of social phenomena is that we think we know most of the answers already. We take a lot for granted, because we are, after all, competent adult members of our society and know what any competent adult knows. We have, as we say, "common sense." We know, for example, that schools educate children and hospitals cure the sick. "Everyone" knows that. We don't question what everyone knows; it would be silly. But, since what everyone knows is the object of our study, we must question it or at least suspend judgment about it, go look for ourselves to find out what schools and hospitals do, rather than accepting conventional answers.

We bump up against an old philosophical problem here, the problem of "the categories." How can we know and take account in our analyses of the most basic categories constraining our thought, when they are so "normal" to us that we are unaware of them? The exercises of Zen and other meditative practices, as well as creativity training, brainstorming, and similar exercises designed to get people to redefine vague or undefined common subjects, often have as their goal the elimination of the screen that words place between us and reality. Robert Morris, the visual artist, says "Seeing is forgetting the name of the thing we are looking at." John Cage's notorious composition "4′ 33″," which consists of a pianist sitting at a piano, but not playing, for that length of time, calls attention to all the sounds that go on as an audience sits and listens to . . . to what was there to hear all along, but not listened to because it wasn't "music." Names, and the thoughts they imply, prevent us from seeing what is there to see.

You might think that any social scientist would, as a matter of course, expect a social law or general theory to cover all the cases it was supposed to cover, and would, again as a matter of course, systematically investigate the full range of possible applications, taking whatever steps were necessary to do that and to discover every subkind that might exist. You might think the problem of the categories would be an ever-present worry. Social scientists speak of this problem from time to time, but usually dismiss it as a philosophical conundrum ("How can we escape the constraints of our own culture?" "Too bad, looks like it's logically impossible").

In fact, social scientists seldom treat the problem of the categories as a practical research problem you could expect to solve. They usually do just the opposite, concentrating their efforts in any particular field of study on a few cases considered to be archetypal, apparently in the belief that if you can explain those, all the other cases will automatically fall into line. If we are going to investigate revolutions, we study the American, French, Chinese, and Russian (sometimes the English), which is not to say that historians and others ignore the hundreds of other revolutions around the world and throughout history, but rather that these few become what Talcott Parsons, in a felicitously misleading phrase, used to call "type cases," whose study is central to that area of work.

Consider: in the study of work, for quite a long time, people concentrated on investigations of medicine and the law. Though other varieties of work have since been studied intensively, these (and other kinds of work likely to be called professions) are still favorites, far out of proportion to something as simple as the proportion of all work they make up. In the study of deviance, violations of certain criminal laws (the ones usually violated by poorer people) are much more likely to be studied than those committed by business people and other middle-class folks. This disparity persists, even though Edwin Sutherland founded an entire field of study around what he called "white collar crime." (I'll consider these examples at greater length in chapter 4, on concepts.) If we study social movements, we typically study those that succeed rather than those that fail.

One way of avoiding being trapped in our professionalized categories like this is, exactly, massive detailed description of the kind Agee and Perec produced. Careful description of details, unfiltered by our ideas and theories, produces observations that, not fitting those categories, require us to create new ideas and categories into which they can be fitted without forcing. This is one of the "other" sampling questions I spoke of earlier. If we call the choice of things to describe a sampling problem—which, of all the things we can observe about a person or situation or event, will we include in our sample of observations?—then we can see that the general solution of the problem is to confront ourselves with just those things that would jar us out of the conventional categories, the conventional statement of the problem, the conventional solution.

This brings up another paradox, due to Kuhn (1970, 18–22). Science can only make progress when scientists agree on what a problem and its solution look like—when, that is, they use conventionalized categories. If everyone has a different idea about what kinds of entities the world is made up of, what kinds of questions and answers make sense, then everyone is doing something different and it won't add up to anything. This is the situation Kuhn describes as having plenty of scientists, but no science. But scientists can only reach agreement on what to look at and study by ignoring practically all of what the world actually shows them, closing their eyes to almost all the available data. It's best to see this paradox as a tension. It's good to have a common conventionalized way of doing business, but it's also good to do whatever it takes to jar that agreement from time to time.

How do we go about finding cases that don't fit? We can do it by paying attention to all the data we actually have, rather than ignoring what might be inconvenient or otherwise not come to our attention. Or we can see what gets in the way of our finding such cases—whether the obstruction be conventional techniques or conceptual blinders—and, having identified the obstacles, manufacture tricks for getting around them.

Everything Is Possible

The simplest trick of all is just to insist that nothing that can be imagined is impossible, so we should look for the most unlikely things we can think of and incorporate their existence, or the possibility of their existence, into our thinking. How do we imagine these possibilities? I have been insisting on the necessity of choosing carefully, rather than ritualistically, what sort of data to go after, record, and include in our analyses; and on the further necessity of systematically using what we have so far gathered to avoid the traps conventional categories set for us. Random sampling won't help us here, or will help us only at an exorbitant cost. Remember that random sampling is designed to *equalize* the chance of every case, including the odd ones, turning up. The general method for sampling to avoid the effects of conventional thinking is quite different: it consists of *maximizing* the chance of the odd case turning up.

Look at the problem Alfred Lindesmith (1947) confronted when he wanted to test his theory about the genesis of addiction to opiate drugs. The theory, briefly, said that, to begin with, people became addicted to opium or morphine or heroin when they took the drug often enough and in sufficient quantity to develop physical withdrawal. But Lindesmith had observed that people might become habituated to opiates in that way—in a hospital, say, as the sequel to injuries from an auto accident that were painful and took a long time to heal—and yet not develop the typical behavior of a junkie: the compulsive search for drugs at almost any cost. Two other things had to happen: having become habituated, the potential addict now had to stop using drugs and experience the painful withdrawal symptoms that resulted, *and* had to consciously connect withdrawal distress with ceasing drug use, a connection not everyone made. They then had to act on that realization and take more drugs to relieve the symptoms. Those steps, taken together and taken repeatedly, created the compulsive activity that is addiction.

W. A. Robinson, a well-known statistical methodologist of the day, criticized Lindesmith's sample (Robinson 1951). Lindesmith had generalized to a large population (all the addicts in the United States or in the world) from a small and haphazardly drawn sample. Robinson thought Lindesmith should have used random sampling procedures to draw a sample (presumably from populations in prison or identified by having arrest records for narcotics offenses) of adequate size. Lindesmith (1952) replied that the purpose of random sampling was to ensure that every case had a known probability of being drawn for a sample and that researchers use these procedures to permit generalizations about distributions of some phenomenon in a population and in subgroups in a population. So, he argued, the procedures of random sampling were irrelevant to his research on addicts because he was interested not in distributions but in a universal process—how one became an addict. He didn't want to know the probability that any particular case would be chosen for his sample. He wanted to maximize the probability of finding a negative case. (Here he anticipated the procedure Glaser and Strauss [1967] described, years later, as "theoretical sampling.")

The trick, then, is to *identify the case that is likely to upset your thinking and look for it.* Everett Hughes taught me a wonderful trick for doing just that. He liked to quote the hero of Robert Musil's novel, *The Man without Qualities,* saying, "Well, after all, it could have been otherwise." We should never assume that anything is impossible, simply could not happen. Rather, we ought to imagine the wildest possibilities and then wonder why they don't happen. The conventional view is that "unusual" things don't happen unless there is some special reason for them to happen. "How can we account for the breakdown of social norms?" Following Hughes's lead, you take the opposite view, assuming that everything is equally likely to happen and asking why some things apparently don't happen as often as this view suggests. "Of course social norms break down. How can we account for their persistence for more than ten minutes?"

What you invariably learn from such an exercise is that all the weird, unlikely things you can imagine actually have happened and, in fact, continue to happen all the time, so that you needn't imagine them. Oliver Sacks, the neurologist, tells of seeing his first case of Tourette's Syndrome, the neurological disorder that leads people to burst into loud and uncontrollable cursing and dirty talk, in his office and being thrilled at having encountered such a "rare" phenomenon (1987, 93–94). He left his office to go home and, on the way to the subway, saw two or three more people whom he now recognized as Touretters. He concluded that those cases had been there in profusion all along; he just hadn't been ready to see them.

So, though they might not be where you thought they would turn up, if you keep your eyes open you have real cases to investigate. But even cases that come from fiction or science fiction can serve the same theoretical purpose, which is to imagine under what circumstances "unusual events" happen, and what obstacles prevent them from happening all the time.

We might, instead of saying "everything is possible," instruct ourselves to "look at the whole table, not just a few of the cells," or "find the full range of cases, not just the few that are popular at the moment." Each of those names points to another way of talking about this trick that Hughes thought so essential. Let's explore some of the obstacles to seeing the full range of cases and using it to theoretical advantage, and look for some ways of surmounting them. The problems are usually conceptual, arising because we believe something to be true and as a result have not investigated the situation it refers to. If we do investigate it, we will invariably find the odd cases we can use to advance our thinking. But the problems are also social, or sociological, in the sense that our reasons for not seeing the obstacles and doing something about them lies in some feature of the social organization they are embedded in and the social organization of our own work lives.

Other People's Ideas

A world of unlimited possibility is confusing and threatens to overwhelm us with a mass of fact and idea that can't be handled, so we are happy whenever we can persuade ourselves that we already know enough to rule out some of the possibilities the trick of exhaustive description might alert us to. The reasons for that are various, but they invariably involve researchers accepting the ideas other people have about what's important, what's interesting, what's worth studying. But other people have reasons for making those judgments that aren't our reasons. We can respect their opinions, but needn't and shouldn't accept them as the basis for our own decisions about what to include in our samples of cases and data. That's true even when the others involved are our own professional colleagues.

"Everybody Knows That!"

Scientists of every variety want to find something "new," rather than the same old stuff. This can be seen in the persistent misreading of Thomas Kuhn's (1970) idea of a "scientific revolution." Everyone wants to make a scientific revolution in his or her field. Heaven forbid that we just find out something routine, something that fits into the body of social science understanding we already have. Every finding, every tiny development in a field is hyped as a "revolution." That ignores Kuhn's analysis, mentioned above, which tells us that scientific revolutions are rare, that it is only by continuing to work on the same problems that workers in a discipline make any progress on anything.

Most of us, however, do not expect to make a revolution. But we do want, at least, not to study "what is already known," what has already been studied (or so we think). We think we can justify any research topic with the argument that no one has ever studied that particular thing before. Why study restriction of production? Donald Roy had already done that (Roy 1952, 1953, 1954). But Michael Burawoy, undeterred, went to study the same topic again (1979). He pushed understanding of the problem forward by doing so. Quite accidentally, Burawoy went to do his research in the very shop Roy had studied. It was still in the same building, but conditions had changed. No longer independent, the shop was now part of a larger firm. As a result, it no longer had to make its way in a competitive marketplace, because the larger corporation was now an assured market for its products. The shop was now unionized. And so you could study the same problem—how workers bought into management objectives—again. It was the same problem, but now it was occurring under new conditions.

That's a general point. Nothing stays the same. Nothing is the same as anything else. We do not operate in the world of physicists, where we can take a sample of a pure substance off the shelf and know that it is, near enough as makes no difference, the same substance any other scientist in the world will be handling under that name. None of our "substances" are pure anything. They are all historically contingent, geographically influenced combinations of a variety of processes, no two of the combinations alike. So we can never ignore a topic just because someone has already studied it. In fact—this is a useful trick—when you hear yourself or someone else say that we shouldn't study something because it's been done already, that's a good time to get to work on that very thing.

"That's been done" very often does get said to people, however, most often to students searching for a dissertation topic. "No sense doing that, Jones just published an article on it." Such remarks rest on a serious fallacy: that things with the same name are the same. They aren't, at least not in any obvious way, so studying "the same thing" is often not studying the same thing at all, just something people have decided to call by the same name. Just because someone studied the culture of prisoners somewhere doesn't mean you shouldn't study it somewhere else. I will not pursue this thought here, since it's taken up (and the example of prisons gone into at length) in chapter 4, under the heading of "enlarging the reach of a concept."

THE HIERARCHY OF CREDIBILITY

Very often social scientists don't study the full range of phenomena because the people who run the organization we are studying define some of what should be included in our sample of cases and topics as not requiring study. They assure us that if we need to know anything beyond what they've outlined as "the problem," they can tell us all about it and there's no necessity to look further. If we accept that premise, we are letting their ideas dictate the content of our research.

I have elsewhere defined this phenomenon as the "hierarchy of credibility":

> In any system of ranked groups, participants take it as given that members of the highest group have the right to define the way things really are. In any organization, no matter what the rest of the organization chart shows, the arrows indicating the flow of information point up, thus demonstrating (at least formally) that those at the top have access to a more complete picture of what is going on than anyone else. Members of lower groups will have incomplete information, and their view of reality will be partial and distorted in consequence. Therefore, from the point of view of a well socialized participant in the system, any tale told by those at the top intrinsically deserves to be regarded as the most credible account obtainable of the organization's workings. And since, as Sumner pointed out, matters of rank and status are contained in the mores, this belief has a moral quality. We are, if we are proper members of the group, morally bound to accept the definition imposed on reality by a superordinate in preference to the definitions espoused by subordinates. (By analogy, the same argument holds for the social classes of a community.) Thus, credibility and the right to be heard are differentially distributed through the ranks of the system. (Becker 1970, 126–27)

So the presidents and deans of colleges, the managers of businesses, the administrators of hospitals, and the wardens of prisons all think they know more than any of their subordinates about the organizations they run.

That's only a problem for researchers if they accept the idea. If we turn to the leaders of organizations and communities for the final word on what's going on, we will inevitably leave out things those people think unimportant. We think we are being sophisticated and knowledgeable when we accept the ideas suggested by the hierarchy of credibility. It's tempting to accept them, because we are, after all, well-socialized members of our society—we wouldn't have gotten where we are if we weren't—and it feels distinctly odd and unsettling to question so obvious an allocation of respect and interest. Educators, to recur to an example mentioned earlier, think sociologists studying school problems should study students because it's students' failure to work hard enough that makes problems; there's no point, if you talk to them, in studying teachers, let alone administrators, since they can't, by definition, be the problem. And we think to ourselves, "These people run the schools, they must know plenty, why shouldn't I accept their definition of the reality they work in?" Of course, we also know that leaders don't always know everything; that's one reason they let us do research. (They will, however, know if you come up with an answer they don't like.)

The trick for dealing with the hierarchy of credibility is simple enough: *doubt everything anyone in power tells you.* Institutions always put their best foot forward in public. The people who run them, being responsible for their activities and reputations, always lie a little bit, smoothing over rough spots, hiding troubles, denying the existence of problems. What they say may be true, but social organization gives them reasons to lie. A well-socialized participant in society may believe them, but a well-socialized social scientist will suspect the worst and look for it.

One way to make sure you exercise the proper skepticism is to look for "other opinions"—for people placed elsewhere in the organization who will give you another view, for statistics gathered by others than the officials. If you study a school, you will, of course, gather information from the principal and the teachers and the students; but try talking to the janitors and the clerks and secretaries too (and don't forget the people who used to work there).

Another way to get around the hierarchy of credibility is to search for the conflict and discontent whose existence organizational leaders usually deny. Everett Hughes had a wonderful way of doing this. When he interviewed members of an organization, he would ask, with his best innocent Midwestern look, "Are things better or worse around here than they used to be?" It's a wonderful question: almost everyone has an answer to it, it brings up the issues that are salient in the organization, and it prejudges nothing—neither what things might be better or worse, or what the appropriate measure of better and worse might be.

It's Trivial, It's Not a "Real Problem"

This criticism has been made of my work more than once. Just as some people think tragedy is somehow more important than comedy (you can tell I don't), some problems are seen as inherently serious and worthy of grownup attention, others as trivial, flyspecks on the wallpaper of life, attended to only for their shock value or prurient interest, mere exotica. Paying attention to these common ideas is a common reason for social scientists to study less than the full range of social activity that merits their attention.

I must have been immunized against this idea early, because my own research moved back and forth between "serious" and "nonserious" topics without causing me any anxiety. I first studied, for my master's thesis, the musicians who played in small bars and clubs in Chicago neighborhoods, for weddings, bar mitzvahs and other social affairs, and so on. These musicians, of whom I was one, did not belong to so socially worthy a profession as medicine or law. Nor were they workers in major industries, whose behavior (for instance, in restricting production) might have been a source of concern to the managers of those firms. Nobody cared about them, one way or the other. They weren't doing any particular harm (other than smoking marijuana, and no one cared if they damaged themselves that way), they didn't upset anyone powerful, they were just minor cogs in the entertainment industry. Everett Hughes found them interesting precisely because they were social nobodies with no reputation to protect, and so able to voice the conviction that was the major finding of my thesis: that the people they played for were stupid, unworthy clods. Hughes was interested because my finding, extending the range of kinds of work that had been studied, gave him a new hypothesis: that all members of service occupations hated the people they served, but members of high-prestige groups (the doctors and lawyers most people studied) wouldn't say that because it wasn't an appropriate thing for such high-class folks to be saying.

My dissertation research, however, was about the careers of public school teachers. Not a very prestigious group, but engaged in the culturally valuable activity of socializing the young, and respectable enough to satisfy anyone who thought sociology should deal with socially worthy topics. My more conventional friends applauded this choice, though my reason for it was mundane: Hughes paid me a dollar an hour to interview school teachers and I decided I might as well write my dissertation about what I was doing anyway.

This fluctuation continued. I next studied marijuana users, not at the time considered a major problem (this was in 1951, long before dope-smoking became a standard middle-class activity that landed some nice kids in trouble with the police), therefore mere exotica. When it achieved the status of a real "social problem" some years later, my research was redefined as having dealt, after all, with a serious problem.

After a stretch of "serious" topics—studies of medical education and undergraduate collegiate life—Blanche Geer and I then studied trade schools, apprenticeships, and a variety of other educational situations working-class youth often attended. And my friends who thought I had "gone straight" were displeased. But then the federal government declared war on poverty and part of that war was a serious effort to teach more people trades and my research was "relevant" again.

So: recognize that your peers often judge the importance of a research problem by criteria that have no scientific warrant, criteria you might not accept. Knowing that, ignore these common-sense judgments and make up your own mind.

WHY THEM?

The hierarchy of credibility has, as a corollary, that certain people or organizations aren't really worth studying at all. That pervasive bias in the study of higher education at the time Hughes, Blanche Geer, Anselm Strauss, and I did our study of medical students (Becker et al. [1961] 1977) led to researchers studying only the "best places." Robert Merton and his colleagues were then studying medical education at Cornell and Columbia, commonly recognized as two of the "best" medical schools in the country. When we said that we were going to study the medical school of the University of Kansas, knowledgeable experts in research on higher education would ask us, solicitously and as if we perhaps didn't know any better, why we were doing that. "Why not?" "Well," they said, "after all, it's not one of the best schools, is it? I mean, if you're going to go to all the trouble of a big research project, why not study the best? You know, the University of Chicago or Harvard or Stanford or Michigan or some other 'eastern' school?" ("Eastern" was a well-known euphemism for "top-ranked," so that Stanford and Michigan and Chicago became "eastern" schools). Our professional colleagues asked us the same question when we compounded the sin by going on to study undergraduate student culture at the same institution.

Our sampling choice offended an uninspected credo which held that, when you studied one of the major social institutions, you studied a really "good" one so that you could see what made it good. That would make it possible for other institutions of that type to adopt the good practices you had detected, and that would raise the standard of that segment of the organizational world. Such an approach rested on several untested and not particularly believable presumptions. To take just one, such an approach assumed that the supposed difference in quality really existed. No one had demonstrated such a difference, and one major study (Petersen et al. 1956) had shown that it didn't much matter where doctors went to school, because after five years the main determinant of the quality of medical practice (defined as practicing the way medical schools taught you to) was where you were then practicing, not where you had gone to school. If you practiced in a big city hospital, especially one affiliated with a medical school, where a million people looked over your shoulder as you worked, you got a pretty high score on the quality scale. If you practiced alone, in a rural setting, where no one knew what you were doing, your score dropped steeply.

All these reasons lead to people studying a small part of the total range of practices and behaviors Hughes had insisted was our business. Social scientists tended to study successful social movements, the best colleges and hospitals, the most profitable businesses. They might also study spectacular failures, from which of course there is much to learn. But such a sampling strategy means that they pretty much ignored all the organizations that were thought to be so-so, medium, nothing special. And remember that the so-so quality is reputational. So generalizations meant to describe all the organizations of a society have rested on the study of a nonrandomly selected few, with the result that sociology suffered from a huge sampling bias. As Hughes ([1971] 1984, 53) remarked: "We need to give full and comparative attention to the not-yets, the didn't quite-make-its, the not quite respectable, the unremarked and the openly 'anti' goings-on in our society."

To say that we should pay attention to all these marginal cases is by no means a plea for random sampling. I've already suggested that we ought to deliberately seek out extreme cases that are most likely to upset our ideas and predictions. But we ought to choose them for our reasons, not because other people think they are something special.

"Nothing's Happening"

A typical obstacle to finding the odd case arises out of our belief that some situation is "not interesting," contains nothing worth looking into, is dull, boring, and theoretically barren. Though the following example comes from my experiences doing a documentary photographic project, the general point applies to all sorts of social science problems, as I will later make clear.

Some years ago I started photographing the Rock Medicine unit of the Haight-Ashbury Free Clinic in San Francisco, as they attended to the medical needs of people who came to the big outdoor rock concerts impresario Bill Graham put on at the Oakland Coliseum. I knew that what I photographed was what I found interesting, not a function of the intrinsic interest of events and people but rather of my ability to find a reason to be interested in them. Everything could be interesting, was interesting, if I could just get myself interested in it.

But after attending a number of these events (which went on from nine or ten in the morning until well after dark) with the Clinic team, which numbered as many as 125 volunteers (a few doctors and nurses, but mostly civilians), I found myself getting bored. I couldn't find anything to photograph. I felt that I had photographed every single thing that could possibly happen, that nothing interesting was going on most of the time. My finger wouldn't press the shutter button any more.

I finally realized I was picking up and accepting as my own a feeling common among the volunteers of the Rock Medicine unit. They knew what was interesting: something medically serious, maybe even life-threatening. They got excited and felt that "something was happening" when, as in one classic tale they told over and over again, someone fell out of the upper grandstand in the baseball park where the concerts took place, and broke a lot of bones; or when someone experienced a severe adverse drug reaction; or when (another classic event) someone had a baby fifty feet in front of the bandstand. Those events were "something happening," but they were very rare. Most "patients" wanted an aspirin for a headache or a bandaid for a blister, and long periods went by when no one wanted anything at all. Most of the remainder had had too much beer and dope, too much hot afternoon sun, and had passed out, but were not in any real danger. When those things were what was "happening," the volunteers sat around and complained that "nothing was happening." Infected by their mood, I concluded that nothing was happening and therefore that there was nothing to photograph.

One day I realized that it couldn't be true that nothing was happening. Something is always happening, it just doesn't seem worth remarking on. (Just as the John Cage piano piece I mentioned earlier forces us to realize that there is always some sound going on, though we may not identify it as music.) So I set myself the problem of photographing what was happening when nothing was happening. Not surprisingly, a lot was happening when nothing was happening. Specifically, the volunteers, who were mostly in their twenties and early thirties and mostly single, were mostly still looking for Mr. or Ms. Right. Volunteering for this event was like going to a big party with some of your favorite bands playing, free beer, an organic lunch, and a lot of nice-looking young men and women who shared some of your tastes. Once I instructed myself to photograph what was happening when nothing was happening, I found hundreds of images on my contact sheets of these young folks dancing, conversing earnestly, coming on to each other, and otherwise socializing. This added an interesting and important dimension to my sociological analysis and photographic documentation, showing me that there was more to recruiting the medical team than providing some interesting medical experience.

The more general statement of the problem, as I've already suggested, is that we never pay attention to all the things that are going on in the situations we study. Instead, we choose a very small number of those things to look into, most obviously when we do research that measures only a few variables, but just as much when we do fieldwork and think we're paying attention to everything. And, having looked at what we've decided to look at, we pretty much ignore everything else that's going on, which seems routine, irrelevant, boring: "Nothing's happening."

The idea that we should only attend to what is interesting, to what our previous thinking tells us is important, to what our professional world tells us is important, to what the literature tells us is important, is a great pitfall. Social scientists often make great progress exactly by paying attention to what their predecessors thought was boring, trivial, commonplace. Conversation analysis provides a classic example. How, for instance, do people decide who will speak next in a conversation? Conversation analysts suggest that there is a rule, the "turn-taking rule," that requires people to alternate turns and speak only when it is their turn. Well, who cares? Is that worth paying attention to? Harvey Sacks (1972, 342) went on to suggest a major subcategory of this phenomenon: questions. Generally accepted rules governing conversation constrain anyone who asks a question to listen to the answer their question has solicited. Again, so what? Well, that provides an understanding of the annoying habit children have of beginning a conversation with adults by saying "You know what?" Conversation analysis explains this commonplace event as a shrewd exploitation by children of the rule about questions. It is hard to avoid answering "You know what?" with "What?" But once we have asked "What?" we have to listen to the answer, and that was what the child was after all the time, getting our difficult-to-secure adult attention. Suddenly, this "silly result" about turn-taking has explained something about the uses of power, and given us a rule we can take elsewhere, to more adult and "serious" phenomena.

So we can generalize the procedure I used at the rock medicine concerts to cover all the variations of other people's ideas shaping what we choose to study. Researchers pick up, not very consciously, the ideas of the people they're studying and working with. If they think something is trivial, you (as researcher) are likely to think that too. These young people liked the sociability that went with the rock concert. But that wasn't "serious," it wasn't what you especially looked forward to, it wasn't what you included when you wanted to impress someone else about your participation in the event. (The comedian Mort Sahl used to explain that, when he was in college, he got involved in left-wing causes for the same reasons other guys did: he wanted to save the world and meet girls.) Everyone shares these ideas, and it doesn't occur to you to look beyond them. After all, there's plenty to be interested in in the provision of medical services to a young drug-using population, isn't there?

It's not just common sense and the prejudices of our companions that blind us to what's there to see. We often decide what to include and what to leave out on the basis of an imagery and its associated theory that settles all those questions for us a priori. All our theories specify something about what we should look at and, by implication, what we needn't bother with (whatever the theory doesn't bother with). That's the very solid core of feminist complaints that many, if not most, sociological theories are sexist. Those theories aren't openly, or necessarily, male-oriented; they just don't routinely include, in their systematic exposition of topics and problems, some concerns feminists think important, part of what you routinely ought to look for. The male-dominated study of chimpanzee social life, as Donna Haraway has shown, went on and on about dominance and all that boy stuff, without paying attention to the food-gathering and childrearing the females did. There's no good scientific reason for that emphasis and, of course, the males could never have spent all their time trying to push the other guys around if someone wasn't bringing home the bananas and taking care of the kids. The theories that focused on dominance could, in principle, encompass these other matters, but they didn't enjoin researchers to do it in a regular way.

On the Other Hand . . .

I insisted earlier that researchers must learn to question, not accept blindly, what the people whose world they are studying think and believe. Now I have to say that at the same time they should pay attention to just that. After all, people know a lot about the world they live and work in. They have to know a lot to make their way through its complexities. They have to adjust to all its contradictions and conflicts, solve all the problems it throws their way. If they didn't know enough to do that, they wouldn't have lasted there this long. So they know, plenty. And we should, taking advantage of what they know, include in our sample of things to look at and listen to the things the common knowledge and routine practice of those studied make evident.

I don't, however, mean that we should treat "people's" knowledge as better or more valid than ours. Many social scientists, justifiably leery of the contention that we know more about the lives and experience of the people we study than they do themselves, have argued that our work should fully respect the superior knowledge social actors have of their own lives and experience. These researchers want to leave the "data" pretty much as they found it: people's stories in the words in which they were communicated, uncut, unedited, "unimproved" by any knowing social science commentaries and interpretations. Science, these researchers think, really has nothing to add, because people, who know for themselves what they have lived through, are the best source of information about it.

This argument has the kernel of truth suggested in the discussion of imagery: social scientists, who have ordinarily not had the experiences of the people they're learning about, must always rely on the accounts of those people to know what it's like from the inside. (An important exception occurs when the analyst participates in the activities being studied.) But that doesn't make them unconditionally usable for research purposes. Since people ordinarily give us these accounts in a "research situation" that differs substantially from the ones they are describing, the accounts cannot be taken at face value. We, for instance, guarantee our interviewees a confidentiality they could never be sure of in their ordinary lives. This can only make the account of an event something less, and perhaps quite different, than what we might have seen had we been there to see for ourselves.

Social scientists who propose that people necessarily know more than we do about their own lives often add that we must respect the dignity of other people by refusing to appropriate their lives and stories for our own selfish uses, simply presenting, unchanged and uninterpreted, what they have told us. The warrant for this is less obvious: It is not self-evident that everyone social scientists study deserves such respect (the usual counterexamples are Nazis and sadistic police). Further, fully accepting this position might reasonably lead us to conclude that we aren't entitled to make any use at all of the material of other people's lives. Contemporary anthropology is caught up in this dilemma, as are contemporary documentary photography and filmmaking (particularly over the blatantly exploitative nature of many "slumming" documentaries).

I disagree. Sociologists do know some things the people they study don't know. But that's true in a way that makes the claim neither unwarranted nor disrespectful, a way that suggests some sampling tricks we can use. The argument is an extension of one Everett C. Hughes used to make.

Briefly, sociologists and other social scientists do not ordinarily study the life and experience of just one person (even when they focus on one person, in the style of Douglas Harper's study [1987] of a rural jack-of-all-trades, they usually include all the people that central character comes in contact with regularly). Rather, they (at least some of them) study the experiences of a great many people, people whose experiences overlap but aren't exactly the same. Hughes used to say, "I don't know anything that someone in that group doesn't know but, since I know what they all know, I know more than any one of them."

When Blanche Geer, Everett Hughes, and I studied college students (Becker et al. [1968] 1994), we divided our attentions in the field. Geer studied fraternity and sorority members, while I spent most of my time with independents; Hughes studied the faculty. We each learned things that "our" group knew, but others didn't. A "secret" society, dominated by the fraternities, operated a machine that organized campus political life; its leader told Geer all about it and she told me. But the independents I hung out with didn't know about it and I didn't tell them. Conversely, when independents mounted political actions they shared their plans with me and I told Geer, but she didn't tell the fraternity members. So our team, and each of us individually, knew more than any of the participants in campus political life.

Knowing these things didn't mean that we felt superior to the people we studied or that we thought we could find meanings in the events they participated in that were too subtle for them to understand. That would indeed be disrespectful. But it did mean we knew obvious things that the people involved would have understood quite well, had they had access to them. The reason they didn't know them was not that they were stupid or uneducated or lacking in sensibility, but that campus life was organized so as to prevent them from finding out. Saying that does not indicate disrespect for anyone's experience, but rather respect for the reality of the differential distribution of knowledge Simmel described in his essay on secrecy (1950, 307–76).

The message for researchers is plain. When the people studied know what they are doing and tell you about it, listen and pay attention. That doesn't mean to be gullible, because people will tell you things that aren't true from time to time. It does mean to use ordinary channels of organizational communication the way participants do, as a source of information

Jean Peneff makes a specific version of this point when he recommends that researchers do more counting in the field than they ordinarily do. He points out that most areas of social life involve a lot of

> counting, calculating, and enumerating. Factory workers count constantly: how many pieces have I made, how many operations have I done, how long have I worked? Office workers classify, file, count, and inventory. Measurement and calculation are ever-present on hospital services: how many beds are available? How long do I have to wait for a radio? How much time do we have? How many patients are waiting to be treated? How many hours of work do I still have to do? Workers are obsessed with time: the time already passed, the time to make a decision and, of course, how long until we can go home? It is surprising that researchers so seldom use and discuss this incessant preoccupation and evalua-

tion of time, in the form of timekeeping, controls, and planning, even though it is at the center of workers' interactions. (Peneff 1995, 122)

Since people use that sort of information and take it seriously, we should too. Geer, Hughes, and I did when we noticed that undergraduates, preoccupied with grades, spent a great deal of time calculating and recalculating how their grade point averages would vary under differing allocations of effort to different courses. "Let's see, German's a five-hour course, so if I spend time on that my average will go up more than if I study anthropology, which is only three hours." (See the example in Becker, Geer, and Hughes [1968] 1994, 89–90).

So . . . don't ignore things because the people you're studying do. But don't ignore things that they pay attention to either. This may be as good a place as any to remark that it's not as contradictory as it seems to recommend tricks that seem to be at cross purposes, as these last two seem to be. Remember that the point of the tricks is to help you find out more, and that each may work in its own way, pointing you in a direction the other might ignore. Consistency in the midst of the search is no great virtue.

Using Other People's Information

Social scientists very often use information other people and organizations have collected and, as a result, leave out of account whatever those people left out. We don't have the resources of time, money, and personnel available to the United States Census Bureau and have to rely on them for all sorts of information. As a result, we leave things out because the people whose information we're using don't think it's important, even if we do. Or the constraints on their activities prevent them from getting something we want. As Bittner and Garfinkel (1967) explained, people and organizations collect information for their own purposes and under their own system of assessing practicality. They don't gather information so that social scientists can do research with it. So they don't collect all the facts we'd like to have and it's a lot of work for us to do it. Ever since the 1920s, when a lawsuit based on the religious establishment clause of the Constitution put an end to the collection of data on religion by the U.S. Census, estimating membership in various religious groups has been a research nightmare. Much ingenuity and great effort have gone into devising indirect methods of finding out how many Jews or Catholics or Baptists there are, but none of them can approach the breadth and comprehensiveness of the Census. Too bad for us.

Sometimes collecting the data that others haven't collected for us is so expensive and requires so much work that we just don't do it. They don't get it for us, and we don't get it for ourselves, not because it isn't worth having, but because having it is "impractical"—that is, more expensive than the people who pay for such things are willing to pay for.

Following the lead of Bittner and Garfinkel, and of those who have been worried about the inaccuracies of police statistics (a favorite source of data for studies in criminology) and medical records (a favorite source of data for investigators of health problems), a field of sociological research has grown up that deals, exactly, with the sociology of record keeping. This research looks into how records are kept, not as a way of correcting their deficiencies as data sources, but because keeping records is a commonplace activity in most contemporary organizations; to understand how the organizations work you have to know how the records are kept. But knowing that means that you know too much to take them as accurate sources of information for social science purposes. We want full description. What we get is partial description for practical organizational purposes. If we know that police statistics are kept with one eye on how insurance companies will use them to set the price of household theft insurance, and that householders complain to elected officials when their insurance costs more for that reason, we know that police statistics on theft will probably reflect such political contingencies to some degree.

The inaccuracy of every sort of data gathered by others is a very large area of scholarly activity, and I will not try to cover it here. That's another book. Some work deals with the simple fact of inaccuracy: for instance, Morgenstern's (1950) classic dissection of errors in economic statistics. Some of it deals with conceptual problems, as in Garfinkel's questioning of Census data on sex on the basis of his study of a transsexual: how do you classify someone who does not exactly fit into any of the standard categories? Garfinkel, of course, dealt with a rare situation, though he was correct to say that the Census had no idea how many people wouldn't fit into the categories, since they made no independent investigation. Some researchers describe the way the information is not what it ought to be as a result of the work routines of the data gatherers (for instance, Roth 1965, Peneff 1988).

All these investigations of problems with "official" or quasi-official data interest us here because every such problem means that we are losing some information that, if we knew it, would help us recover the cases we need for the complete descriptions that help us get around conventional categories. Since we often rely on such data, no matter what our criticisms and distrust of it (no social scientist can do without the Census, for all its faults), we need a trick for dealing with it. The trick is easy. Ask where the data come from, who gathered it, what their organizational and conceptual constraints are, and how all of that affected what the table I'm looking at displays. It makes rather more work out of consulting a table than you might think necessary, but there is too much trouble built into other people's data to run the risk of not making that effort.

Bastard Institutions

All these obstacles to researchers seeing what is there to see, and using it to enlarge the range of their thinking, can be remedied, and I have suggested a lot of tricks for doing that. The best way of avoiding these errors is to create a more general theoretical understanding of the sociology of making distinctions between what's appropriate and necessary for social scientists to include as they construct their synecdoches. Everett C. Hughes's classic paper on "bastard institutions," a small masterpiece of sociological theorizing (Hughes [1971] 1984, 98–105), shows how conventional choices of appropriate material for sociological analysis rule out a whole range of phenomena that ought to be included in our thinking, and thus make our sample of collective human activity a less accurate synecdoche than it ought to be.

Hughes begins by defining a very general problem of social organization: how institutions define what will and won't be distributed within a given category of service or goods:

> Institutions distribute goods and services; they are the legitimate satisfiers of legitimate human wants. In the course of distributing religion, play, art, education, food and drink, shelter, and other things—they also define in standard ways what it is proper for people to want. The definition of what is to be distributed, although it may be fairly broad and somewhat flexible, seldom if ever completely satisfies all kinds and conditions of men. Institutions also decide, in effect, to serve only a certain range of people, as does a shop that decides not to carry out-sizes and queer styles of shirts. The distribution is never complete and perfect.

Some institutions result from collective protest against these institutionalized definitions—the protest, for instance, that a religious sect makes against the definition of acceptable religion promoted by an official clergy or the protest made by the variety of groups which established new kinds of educational institutions as a reaction to the conception of education established by the classical New England colleges. But there are also:

. . . chronic deviations and protests, some lasting through generations and ages. They may gain a certain stability, although they do not have the support of open legitimacy. They may operate without benefit of the law, although often with the connivance of the legal establishment. They may lie outside the realm of respectability.

Some are the illegitimate distributors of legitimate goods and services; others satisfy wants not considered legitimate. . . . All take on organized forms not unlike those of other institutions. (Hughes [1971] 1984, 98–99)

Hughes suggests calling these *bastard institutions.* They take a variety of forms. Some are not formally legitimate but are not necessarily illegitimate either, though they may be. They are highly conventional and supported by popular opinion, but only within a subcommunity. He has in mind here such informal forms of justice as kangaroo courts in prisons and armies or tong courts in the Chinatowns of another era, but also the institutions Orthodox Jewish communities developed to insure a supply of properly slaughtered kosher meat for their members.

Some are marginal to more legitimate distributors of services. So, right alongside the schools that teach law and accounting are cram schools that teach people how to pass the examinations the state uses to decide who will be allowed to practice those professions. These schools don't pretend to teach law; they teach test-passing. Hughes puts in this category the communities that make available what nearby communities forbid. He loved to point to George Pullman's model community in Chicago, built in the 1880s for the men who worked for him making sleeping cars for railroads. Pullman, who took his version of religion seriously, allowed no taverns in his model town. No problem for the workers. Just across South Michigan Avenue, Pullman's western border, lay Roseland, a mile or so of taverns that provided the cigarettes, whiskey, and wild women unavailable to the east (a specialty that continued into the 1940s, when I occasionally played piano in those same taverns).

In the clearest cases, well-established institutions provide forbidden goods and services for which there is a permanent and substantial market, such as illegal gambling casinos, speakeasies in areas where alcohol cannot be sold legally, and whorehouses of various kinds. Or it might be that there are things that are fine for other people to have, but not available in any appropriate way for people like you. Transvestites who wish to dress in women's clothes find it easy to shop where the clerks expect to sell dresses, pantyhose, and garter belts to six-foot-tall, two-hundred-pound men. As Hughes says of establishments like this:

> They are in direct conflict with accepted definitions and institutional mandates. [They offer] a less than fully respectable alternative or allow one to satisfy some hidden weaknesses or idiosyncratic tastes not provided for, and slightly frowned on, by the established distributors. Still others quite simply offer a way to get something not easily available to people of one's kind in the prevailing institutional system. They are corrections of faults in institutional definition and distribution. ([1971] 1984, 99)

Social scientists have typically studied such phenomena as "deviance" as pathological, abnormal behavior whose special roots have to be uncovered, so that "society" can act effectively to rid itself of the "problem." Hughes, however, wants to include them as "part of the total complex of human activities and enterprises . . . in which we can see the [same] social processes going on . . . that are to be found in the legitimate institutions" ([1971] 1984, 99–100). He connects the legitimate and illegitimate forms of activity this way: "The institutional tendency is to pile up behavior at a modal point by definition of what is proper, by sanctions applied against deviating behavior, and by offering devices for distributing only the standardized opportunities and services to people. But while institutions cluster behavior, they do not completely destroy the deviations."

So, for example, marriage is the modal way of organizing sex and procreation, but some people don't marry and some who do don't confine their sexual activity to legitimate mates. Every society defines a form of marriage (among other things, a device for distributing men among women, and women among men) as involving people whose specific social attributes (for instance, race, class, and ethnicity, but there are others) make them "appropriate mates." But people's ability to take care of mates varies, and the way people move around and often congregate in relative isolation creates situations in which, for many people, there are no suitable marriage mates available. The classic examples are the heroines of Jane

Austen novels, on the one hand, and the men who work in logging camps or ships or mines far removed from the conventional communities in which they might find appropriate mates, on the other. Prostitution and temporary homosexual relationships have been common solutions to the male version of the problem, as the quietly lesbian relationships of middle-class women who "shared an apartment" were at one time for the female version.

So far, the analysis is interesting but not surprising. Other social scientists (e.g., Kingsley Davis 1937) have used similar examples to make similar points. Now Hughes produces a surprise. Deviation moves in two directions, takes two forms, and the social scientist should look at and discuss not only the illegitimate and frowned on deviation (he calls it the direction of the devil) but also the angelic form. Prostitution works to provide scarce women to men, but there is no corresponding device to supply men for women when the imbalance is the other way. So many women who would prefer not to be in that situation have no legitimate male partner (in whatever way legitimacy is defined).

The point, for Hughes, is that the workings of conventional institutions put some people in a position where they are required to be "better" than they want to be or than anyone has a right to expect them to be. "It would be especially important to find out at what points there develops an institutionalizing of adjustments to the position of being better than one wishes" ([1971] 1984, 103).

The institutionalizing of celibacy in the name of religion is the

> realization in institutional form of deviation from marriage in the direction of the angels—a deviation rationalized in the terms of supposedly supreme values, the higher-than-normal ideals of human conduct. For the individual in such an institution the function may be clear; these institutions allow one to live up to some ideal more nearly than is possible out in the world and in marriage. I emphasize the word *allow*, for the world would merely think a person queer to so live without special declaration, without attachment to an ongoing body devoted to this special deviation. . . .
>
> . . . The institutions of celibacy offer a declared, established, and accepted way of not accepting the modal norm of behavior; perhaps a nobler and more satisfying way of accepting the fate that a fault of distribution in existing institutions condemns one to. They may be considered also as institutional provision for those highest lights of idealism that, although engendered by the

established teaching of the virtues, are not provided for in the modal definitions to which institutional machinery is generally geared. Let it be noted, however, that society very often accepts such deviation in an organized institutionalized form, when it would scarcely accept it as isolated individual behavior. . . . The individual deviation may appear as a threat to the whole accepted system; the organized deviations, however, may appear as a special adaptation of the system itself, perhaps as a little special example of what humans are capable of. ([1971] 1984, 103–4)

So, Hughes points out, a classic form of heresy is the demand that everyone live up to some commonly proclaimed virtue:

Society idealizes, in statements and in symbolic representation, degrees of virtue that are not in fact realizable by all people or are not realizable in combination with other virtues and in the circumstances of on-going real life. It appears that society allows some people to approach these levels of one virtue or another in some institutionalized form that will at once provide the spiritual lift and satisfaction of seeing the saintly example before one, without the personal threat that would come from mere individual saintliness offered as something that all of us should seriously emulate and the social threat of a contagious example. ([1971] 1984, 104)

Sociological analysis should then, according to Hughes,

take some matter, some aspect of human life, which is highly institutionalized and is the object of much moral sanctioning, and . . . treat the whole range of behavior with respect to it: the institutionalized norms and the deviations in various directions from the norm. . . . We have seen the norm, the institutionally defined and distributed relations between adult males and females, as a special point in the fuller range of possible and actual behavior, and have at least indicated some possible functional relations between the instituted and the deviation in both the bastard and the angelic directions. ([1971] 1984, 105)

Treating the full range of cases, then, means including what we might otherwise leave out as in some way too weird or raunchy for proper sociologists to consider. It also means using such cases to define and point to the other end of the scale, those activities that are too good to be true, the angelic deviations. In Hughes's hands, this often takes the form of comparisons that seem shocking or highly improper. He liked, for instance, to compare priests, psychiatrists, and prostitutes, noting that members of all three occupations have "guilty knowledge," that they know things about their parishioners, patients, or customers that have to be kept secret. Hughes was interested in a comparative study of the means by which, under the differing conditions in which the members of each profession worked, those secrets were kept.

Leaving cases out because they seem tasteless or politically discomfiting is equally guaranteed to be a mistake. Good taste is a potent form of social control. Nothing is easier than to get someone to stop doing something we don't like by suggesting that it is "cheap" or "not cool" or "gauche" or any of a hundred similar put-downs. The Russian literary critic Bakhtin pointed out that Rabelais told his tales of Gargantua's carryings on in common vulgar language precisely because it was politically offensive to the educated folk who would have preferred a "more elevated" tone. We are likely to be responding to someone's exercise of social control when we unthinkingly accept such criticism, and social scientists often do.

4

CONCEPTS

Having worked on our imagery, and having looked for a proper sample of cases to investigate, a sample that covers the full range of types of the phenomenon we want to learn and think about, we're ready to start the thinking in earnest. That means using concepts, generalized statements about whole classes of phenomena rather than specific statements of fact, statements that apply to people and organizations everywhere rather than just to these people here and now, or there and then. Many social scientists work at these problems deductively, treating concepts as logical constructs that can be developed by the manipulation of a few basic ideas. I'm not very sympathetic to these efforts, which are too divorced from the empirical world to keep my attention. I recognize this as, in some respects, an issue of taste.

A fruitful and more empirical mode of conceptual analysis has been to develop ideal typical models, which consist of "a systematically related set of criteria surrounding a central issue" that is "sufficiently abstract to be applicable to a variety of national and historical circumstances" (Freidson 1994, 32). Using this method, for instance, Freidson solves the thorny problem of defining the concept of "professional power" by creating a model in which "the central issue of professional power lies in the control of work by professional workers themselves, rather than control by consumers in an open market or by the functionaries of a centrally planned and administered state."

But my favorite way of developing concepts is in a continuous dialogue with empirical data. Since concepts are ways of summarizing data, it's important that they be adapted to the data you're going to summarize. The discussion that follows describes tricks for doing that, ways of using your data to create more complex ideas that will help you find more problems worth studying and more things about what you have studied worth thinking about and incorporating into your analysis.

FOUR

Concepts Are Defined

We all work with concepts. All the time. We have no choice, as Herbert Blumer pointed out in a critique of what was called, when he wrote, "operationalism." He noted that you could not have a science without concepts. Without concepts, you don't know where to look, what to look for, or how to recognize what you were looking for when you find it. Psychologists, in their heyday when Blumer wrote, thought they could do without concepts, at least concepts defined in abstract theoretical terms. They thought they could avoid such chronic troubles as arguments over definitions by defining concepts simply, as what they measured by the operations they used to study the phenomenon they were investigating. In the classic example, they said that "intelligence," whose definition was hotly debated then as now, was what intelligence tests measured.

Sociologists equivocated in the same way about the concept of *attitude*. Many researchers assumed that people had thoughts or dispositions or ideas (or something)—summarized as attitudes—inside them, waiting to be released by the appropriate stimulus or situation. What an attitude was wasn't clear. Scientists argued about the definition. But their inability to define an attitude didn't prevent them from inventing attitude measurement, a procedure in which people's answers to a long list of questions produced a number that "measured" their attitude toward movies or foreigners or schools or political parties. The scientists measured the reliability and validity of attitudes, and concocted statistics that described the relations of attitudes to one another and to other facts about people. They thought they could show that people differed with respect to attitudes about this or that, and that those differences correlated with other differences in ways that seemed meaningful.

Critics complained that there was no general understanding of this thing that was being measured. Operationalists evaded those complaints by denying that they had said anything about the actual content or meaning of the measured attitudes: attitudes were just what the tests measured, nothing more. No one believed that. If they had, there would have been much less research on attitudes or intelligence or the other important ideas that were defined operationally. Because, after all, no one really cares about test measurements in themselves—only about intelligence or racial attitudes or propensities to violence or whatever the test is supposed to measure.

A favorite reply to attacks on attitude or intelligence tests was, "You don't want to call it intelligence? Fine! Call it X. OK?" You could deflect this irritating and unsatisfactory riposte by actually referring to the item in question as X. "I see, you've shown that children of different racial groups differ by ten points, on the average, on something called X. So what?" But, of course, no one cares about the differential scores of black and white children on X. Without content, X has no relevance to any question of theory or policy. But people do care about differences in intelligence because, if they really exist, they have serious political and moral consequences of a kind something that is just X could never have. By the third time a critic called X what everyone involved knew was really intelligence, the discussion would get more serious.

This critique may seem quaint and out of date, since few contemporary social scientists would admit to being operationalists of the kind Blumer criticized. But many contemporary researchers act as though they'd accepted a variant of that position. In this sense: they choose, as an "indicator" of the phenomenon they want to talk about, something that has an imperfect, sometimes a highly imperfect, relation to the phenomenon itself, and then treat the indicator as though it were that phenomenon. They ask people their occupation and treat the answer as a measure of social class, by locating the occupation named in a list of jobs whose prestige has been measured or placing it in a Census classification of major occupational groups. They may say that they are measuring what Karl Marx or Max Weber or W. Lloyd Warner or C. Wright Mills meant when they spoke of "social class," but that's neither obvious or particularly believable. People who make such measurements don't insist that a person's occupation *is* social class in the Marxian or Weberian sense, since they haven't demonstrated any relation between the two empirically, but their analyses and discussions implicitly assert the identity. Important as measurement may be, it doesn't do much for our understanding of the concepts we use.

Another way of defining a concept is to collect examples of things we recognize as embodying what the concept refers to, and then look for what the inevitably messy and historically contingent ideas people routinely use have in common. Some common sociological examples of such conceptual work are skill, crime, or profession. We try to formulate a definition that includes all the things we think are alike and leaves out those that are different. We are embarrassed if someone can show that something we didn't think belonged in our collection in fact fits the terms of the definition. Thus, researchers tried to define a "profession" as a special kind of work, different from other occupations. What they wanted to include in the aggregate their definition collected were such highly respected and well-paid occupations as medicine and law. So they framed their definition by listing the traits that characterized those occupations. (Freidson 1994 gives a careful account of these problems, and offers realistic and useful solutions to them.)

Invariably, an industrious and clever critic would find an occupation that fit all the definitional requirements (long years of training, a body of esoteric knowledge, state licensing, and so on) but clearly "didn't fit." Plumbing used to be good for this bit of theoretical skullduggery. Plumbers have the attributes included in standard definitions of a profession: an esoteric body of knowledge (try fixing your own drains), long years of training, state licensing, and the rest. But "everyone knows" that plumbing is not a profession. The seeming paradox arises because the items in the collection the definition is framed to cover have been chosen on the basis of an unacknowledged variable: the social prestige of the occupation. If prestige correlated perfectly with the other criteria, there would be no problem. But it doesn't.

Such problems arise in many areas of sociological work. The theoretical trick that helps solve the problem is to recognize that what goes into the collection the definition has to cover governs the kind of definition we come up with. And collecting the examples is the kind of sampling problem considered in chapter 3. So we look for answers to such questions as: How do we make up those collections? What do we typically leave out? And what harm does it do to be selective in our choice of examples? Definitional problems arise exactly because we have chosen these collections in ways that ignored the injunction of chapter 3 to include the widest possible variety of cases of a phenomenon in our sample. Here are two further examples where the harm is more substantial, or at least more easily seen, than in the case of "profession" (which is, at least on the surface, mainly a conceptual embarrassment, though the policy implications of the definition of that term are quite serious, as Freidson [1994: 149–216] shows).

Skill

Sociologists, economists, and other social scientists rely, implicitly or explicitly, on the idea of "skill." They argue that differences in pay, for instance, result from the scarcity of real skills, so that people who have rare skills get paid more. What would make a skill scarce? One thing would be the differential distribution of natural talent to exercise the skill. People who are tone deaf would find it difficult to learn to play hundreds of songs by ear, as I had to do to hold a job playing the piano in taverns. Some people can manipulate numbers easily and might be especially good at accounting, keeping books, or managing people's money. Some are very skilled with a needle and can sew or knit or crochet excellently. Some have a way with people, know how to ease their fears or make them feel at home. Some have learned decisiveness and are good at it; they can make up their minds in a difficult situation while the rest of us stand around sucking our thumbs.

Another contributor to the scarcity of a skill might be how long you have to work or how much you have to pay to acquire it. People, on this theory, wouldn't invest so much time and energy they might invest elsewhere if it weren't going to pay off. So the number of people willing to acquire the skill will go down if the rewards for selling it are low. If everyone acts in this economically rational way, the number of people in each occupation will reach an equilibrium at a price users will pay for the skill and practitioners will accept.

We can certainly make a long list of skills people have had over the centuries. It's clear, when we inspect such a list, that not all skills are equally rewarded. Skill alone does not produce big rewards. You need a skill that someone else, who can and will pay for it, wants. If you have a very rare skill that very rich people want badly, you will be rewarded handsomely. If, for instance, you are one of the few people who can repair damaged art works owned by wealthy people who prize them highly, you will be paid well to exercise that skill. If you have a skill many other people have—if you are one of the millions who can quickly be taught to cook hamburgers at a fast-food franchise, a group of whom there are more members than anyone needs—you will be paid the lowest legal wage (or less if the bosses think they won't get caught). But even a very rare skill won't do you any good unless people wealthy enough to pay for it at the rate you'd like really want and need it. My ability to play hundreds of tunes wasn't worth much, because the only people who wanted it were band leaders and tavern owners who could, if it got too expensive, manage with pianists who knew a lot less than I did.

The demand for skills varies historically. Temporary conjunctions of circumstances can raise the value of skills ordinarily not worth much.

Hobsbawm (1964) described the unlikely victory of a group of "un-skilled" laborers in the great London gas strike of 1896. London, at that time, was lit largely with natural gas, manufactured by coking coal—that is, by heating coal in large furnaces so that the gas it contained would be released to be captured and piped to households and factories. Running the furnaces—shoveling the coal in and keeping it burning—was unskilled labor. Anyone could do it. It had never required any special training, other than what you got on the job. So, when the laborers who did this work went on strike, conventional wisdom and economic theory alike said it was unlikely they could win.

But they did win the strike, and got a handsome settlement from their employers, who were as greedy as capitalists are supposed to be. How did the workers win? Hobsbawm shows that these unskilled laborers actually had some very important skills and that an unusual conjuncture of circumstances at the time of the strike had made those skills more valuable to the employers than they ordinarily were. Put the question this way: why didn't the employers just go out and hire some other unskilled men to shovel coal into the furnaces? Why didn't they just wait the strike out, manipulating public opinion to make their stubborn employees look responsible for the discomfort householders were suffering and thus bring them to heel?

There were several reasons why employers didn't take these obvious steps. The sellers of gas were facing new competition in the form of electricity. Still a novelty, electricity was potentially just as good a way to light your house and, if a strike went on for a while, customers might be tempted to experiment with the new form of energy. The longer the strike went on, the more customers the purveyors of gas would lose to electricity.

Further, the employers couldn't replace these unskilled laborers as easily as you might have thought. To be sure, what they did required no great schooling. But the machines they tended, while not highly technical and thus not requiring, say, engineering knowledge to run, were old and crotchety. The gas manufacturers had been coasting, collecting their profits and not maintaining the machinery any more than absolutely necessary. So the machines worked but, like all old machines, had to be coaxed. You had to know when to give the furnace a good kick, and where to kick it. These might not be skills in the conventional sense, but if the men who shoveled the coal didn't have them the furnaces didn't work. The bosses could hire other unskilled workers but, lacking that special knowledge, the new men couldn't do the job.

That combination of circumstances gave these unskilled laborers some skills that were at least temporarily valuable, and they used their advantage skillfully to win higher wages. The important lesson for us is that the identical ability may be skilled or unskilled, depending on circumstances. The meaning of the concept of skill depends on which cases you have in mind when you define it.

So skill, if you want to raise your wages by withholding it, must be a skill that someone with money wants. Suppose you have the skills, and they are scarce and people want them, but those potential purchasers of your services would rather not pay you as much as your skills might be worth on the open market. This, I take it, is the point of research and work on what is called "comparable worth." Here's the problem: many people think women have been historically, and still are, discriminated against in the labor market. A great variety of statistical studies show that employers pay women less than men any time they can get away with it. And who can blame them? Capitalism, as Marx said, is a tough system and employers who pay more than they need to for components of their products will soon be driven out of business by shrewder manufacturers who can sell the same product cheaper.

The gas worker example sheds some light on this problem. Suppose the law finally forbids out-and-out discrimination on the basis of gender; women must be paid what men doing the same job are paid. Women will still make less. Now why? Because the distribution of men and women across occupations is skewed. No women play major league baseball and very few nurses are men, and ball players make a lot more than nurses. A disproportionate number of schoolteachers are women; a disproportionate number of corporate executives are men. If you pay all nurses, whatever their gender, the same, and pay all executives, men or women, the same, but pay nurses less than executives, women will end up making less on the average because more of them are in jobs that don't pay as well.

How can that inequity be remedied? Some reformers have attacked the way pay scales are set (it is primarily governmental agencies that are vulnerable to such attacks), noting that salaries are set with reference to the skills allegedly required to do the work, but that skills important in "women's occupations" (that is, occupations most of whose members are women) are either ignored or not valued highly in such evaluations. If technical skills are valued more highly than the skills necessary to deal with complex social situations, and the jobs women are more likely to have—

like nursing and teaching—require fewer technical skills and more "human relations" skills, then women will be paid less even though they are just as highly skilled, although in different areas.

Of course, proponents of the status quo will argue that it can't be shown that the skills are commensurable. But that, of course, is the point. If they aren't, it's because we haven't agreed on how to measure skill. And if that's true, then how do we know that men's skills are worth more? And it's just that judgment that is embodied in the very wage scales being attacked.

I've been a long time getting to the conceptual point, because the point lies in the kind of examples I've given, not in abstract talk. The point is that concepts presuppose that you have inspected the full range of things they cover when you formulate and define them. Now we can see one of the reasons for my earlier emphasis on methods of sampling that produce examples of that range. If you leave some phenomena out because of conventional prejudice or for any of the other reasons I discussed there, your concepts will be flawed. Generalizations of which those concepts are components will contain a lot of noise, random variation that isn't random at all, but rather the result of systematic social biases in the selection of cases you used to define your concepts.

Crime

The same reasoning applies to the well-known phenomenon of white-collar crime. Why did Edwin Sutherland find it necessary to devote his presidential address to the American Sociological Association (1940) to the subject of white-collar crime? Because he wanted to accuse his colleagues of a conceptual error that had a similar basis in inadequate sampling based on conventional, socially approved prejudice. Criminological journals and books, at the time Sutherland delivered his blast, were filled with theories about crime and research on crime. What was crime, this thing all the theories and research were about? Activity that violated the criminal law. That seemed fair enough. The mountains of research that had been done showed that crime was highly correlated with poverty, with broken homes, and all the other conventional indices of what was then called "social pathology." Sutherland asked a simple question: how can that be true when there are crimes being committed by very well-to-do people who do not exhibit the conventional signs of social pathology, and by the largest and most respected corporations in the country, which similarly did not come from broken homes?

The answer to that was simple enough. No one, no conventional criminologists certainly, thought the crimes well-to-do people and corporations committed were, in some fundamental way, "really crimes." Besides, the culprits involved were seldom convicted of criminal violations, because these cases were often settled as civil suits. If there were no criminal convictions, how could there be any criminals? The government was typically more interested in getting the bad guys to stop their mail frauds and security swindles and forcing them to pay off those who had been cheated than in sending anyone to jail. But that was not a natural consequence of the nature of the crimes, which could just as well have been prosecuted under criminal statutes, and occasionally were. It resulted from judgments made by prosecutors, who exercised the discretion the law gave them as to whether to pursue criminal or civil remedies.

Prosecutors had other reasons for not pushing for criminal convictions. As Katz's later (1979) research showed, white-collar crime and crimes of the more conventional kind differ in another important way. In ordinary crime, there's no question that a crime has been committed. Someone has been robbed or assaulted. The question is: who did it? In white-collar crimes, on the other hand, there's no question about who did it. The big grocery chain *did* label meat that weighed 14 ounces as weighing one pound. The question is not who did it but rather is it a crime or not? Such a thing, after all, might have happened because a scale was faulty and the company didn't know about it, or because a crooked butcher was skimming some of the profit for himself, or for any of a number of reasons that would show that the company lacked criminal intent. So, for both sets of reasons, white-collar criminals are convicted of crimes far less often than common criminals.

Sutherland's impeccable reasoning was that if you decided not to include the crimes rich people and corporations committed when you calculated your correlations, you guaranteed the result that crime was correlated with poverty and its accompaniments. Not because it really was, but because you were using a flawed concept, one that pretended to contain all members of a given class, but actually left out a large number of those members on the uninspected grounds of social prestige. You didn't have an empirical finding, you had a definitional artifact.

Defending against Sutherland, conventional criminologists argued, essentially, that "everyone knew" that those rich people and corporations weren't "really criminals." That is, if you accepted the conventional notion of what a criminal was—a tough guy with a mask who jumped out of the bushes, stuck a gun in your ribs and took your money, a guy who made a career of crime, lived a life of crime, shared the culture of crime with others like him (and these criminals were, in conventional thought, male, of course)—then it was clear that the nice people who wore suits and ties and took your money in broad daylight over a desk in a fancy office, and the organizations in whose buildings those offices were situated, didn't look like that at all. They might take your money, but not with a gun; in fact, the way they did it you might not even know you had been robbed unless someone pointed it out to you.

Sutherland arrived at his understanding of white-collar crime by using a trick based on a common feature of organizational life. As I suggested in the discussion of sampling, organizations typically tell lies about themselves. If that's too harsh, we might just say that they like to put their best foot forward, and prefer not to mention things that would make them look bad, especially when those events and activities can plausibly be interpreted as random deviations or character flaws attributable to individuals, things that are in any case beyond what anyone could reasonably expect the organization to guard against. It's the general explanation police departments give when any of their officers get caught misbehaving: "There's a few bad apples in every barrel." This explanation is designed to counter any suggestion that would accept the more sociological hypothesis that the barrel makes the apples rotten—that is, that the department's organization and culture might lead officers who would otherwise be law-abiding into bad ways.

Social scientists will be led astray if they accept the lies organizations tell about themselves. If, instead, they look for places where the stories told don't hold up, for the events and activities those speaking for the organization ignore, cover up, or explain away, they will find a wealth of things to include in the body of material from which they construct their definitions. Sutherland's trick was simple. He looked for facts corporations might not put in their annual reports: the civil suits against them and the settlements they had made of such claims; and the violations of criminal law sociologists did not count because corporations had managed to avoid criminal prosecution, instead settling them as matters of civil law.

When you find events and facts that are not accounted for in the stories conventionally told about a class of organizations, you have usually found a new element or "variable" that needs to be incorporated into the definition of the phenomenon under study. A more general version of Sutherland's trick produces the labeling theory of deviance (see for example Becker 1963). In this way: the conventional story about deviance is that the organizations responsible for dealing with it actually do deal with it effectively. They may not prevent it from happening—police departments may not be able to control every rogue cop—but once it is known to have occurred they find it and punish it. Corporations may not be able to prevent employees from cheating customers, but they track down and punish the cheaters. And so on.

But when you discover that not all deviations are tracked down, and that the selection of which ones to track down is not random, you have good reason to think that you have found another element in the puzzle—namely, a step in the process of detection and punishment that consists of not detecting some people or not punishing some that have been detected. You thus know that "deviance" includes both a possible infraction of a law or rule, and a process of acting in some fashion against whoever might be thought to have committed the infraction. When Sutherland saw that some who committed crimes were not treated the way others were, he knew he was onto something.

Keep in mind that what Sutherland saw was not much of a secret. Every organization enforces the rules it is responsible for in a partial and discretionary way. Sutherland's originality consisted in making that discretion the subject of study. (I'll return to this separation of rule-breaking from the perception and punishment of rule-breaking in chapter 5, when we look into the uses of combinatorial logic for social research.)

All these examples show that concepts that don't cover the full range of cases to which they allegedly apply are flawed. Generalizations that include flawed concepts as terms in the explanatory equation will not explain everything they claim to apply to, as explanations of crime based on juvenile delinquents' activities could not explain the crimes of large corporations. Including the full range of cases forces us to revise our generalizations, make them more complex and more interesting. Then, containing less noise and less unexplained variance, they will explain more of what they are supposed to explain.

The trick here, to repeat, is recognizing that the definitions of concepts rest on what the examples they are based on have in common. However abstract (or "theoretical") the resulting definition is, it bears the marks of that often uninspected selection of cases. That's why I've insisted on the necessity of striving for imagery that enlarges our ideas about what might be present in the world we study. If our imagery is based on a biased sample we will have trouble. If we systematically look for excluded cases, our work will improve.

Defining Concepts: Some Tricks

To review our results to this point: we define concepts (as opposed to discovering their true nature), and our definitions are shaped by the collection of cases we have on hand with which to think about the problem. Suppose we have gathered a good collection of cases and want to proceed with creating a useful concept. How do you do that? It's true that it takes some imagination and some free associating and some consulting of what others have said in the past, but you can do all that and still not know how to create a concept. What do you actually do?

Social scientists ask themselves this question when they begin to gather data without having much sense of what the problem they are studying actually is. That happens more often than we would like to admit. It happens, for instance, when we agree to study a "practical" problem, a problem defined by its importance to the people involved in it. (Since so much research is funded because the problems are practically and politically important, this situation is common.) "Are black students getting a fair shake in education?", however any of those terms is defined, is not a question framed in sociological terms. That's not to say it isn't important or interesting, but rather that when we study it we will have to turn it into a sociological question before we have anything distinctive to say about it. But we don't know what that question will be, not yet. We only know it after we see what kinds of organizations, institutions, and processes are involved in the production of that problem (what kind of a machine is operating to make things happen that way), and only our research will tell us that.

So we find ourselves with a pile of data, trying to figure out what it could be about, sociologically. Students who find themselves in this fix often say they want to "narrow their problem down," a ritual phrase some teacher taught them to say to ward off getting in over their heads. For students, but not only students, that also means finding a way to say something that will be defensible against all attacks; if they make the "problem" narrow enough they can find out all about it, nail it down, and none of the vague enemies they sense around them can get them. (I've discussed those fears in Becker 1986b.)

Students learning to do fieldwork commonly suffer from this disease. They finally get their nerve up to interview someone and then don't know what to ask. When they observe some social situation, they aren't sure what constitutes their "data," which of the things they see and hear they are supposed to write down. That's because they don't know what their problem is, what they're studying. They know they have to do it, so they put anything down. Or so it seems. As a result, their notes are scattered, essentially incoherent; their interviews wander because they don't give the people they are talking to any systematic guidance about what they would like to know.

But there is some order to what they have done, because you can't make the simplest decisions unless you have some idea as to what you are doing. The students' imagery of people and places and situations like the one they're examining has led them to do whatever they did, ask what they did, attend to what they did, ignore what they did. They now have to find out what they had in mind that led them to do all that. The problem is to uncover the imagery that got them into this fix.

My trick here is a version of an old parlor game. In the game someone says, for instance, "Nine Wagner." The object of the game is to imagine the question that is the answer to. In this case, the question that elicits that answer is "Who wrote that piece? Mozart?" And the answer (I took liberties with the spelling) is "Nein! Wagner!" So, trying to figure out what you are doing, you say to yourself, "The data I have here are the answer to a question. What question could I possibly be asking to which what I have written down in my notes is a reasonable answer?" I ask students to reread their notes with this in mind, to pretend that they did everything they did purposefully and have succeeded in doing just what they set out to do. Now they will find out what they did.

The exercise generally makes students unhappy. They see that, whatever vague idea they had in mind when they began their work, they didn't get anywhere near doing it. Unspoken assumptions and unacknowledged imagery—about the problem, but more likely about what they can reasonably expect in the way of cooperation from people—have led them to investigate topics they didn't have in mind and didn't care about, usually very minor and superficial matters whose virtue was that they came to mind during a lull in the conversation. The students wanted to know about patterns of social organization but, under the pressure of performing as knowledgeable researchers when they knew they weren't any such thing, they asked the people they interviewed and participated with about trivia. They want to know about unrest among the factory workers they are observing, but they have only talked to them about the food in the company cafeteria or last night's football game on television. And they know that's not it. They didn't do what they should have done to find out what they wanted to know.

I tell them not to be unhappy. Now they know what they were "actually investigating," what their first attempts actually asked about, and they know that what they learned wasn't what they wanted to know. Knowing that, they can change direction, reformulate their questions, and have something different to put in their notes. Their data are now more likely to be about what they want to be investigating. And, if it appears they may not be able to see something they think it's important to see or ask about something they think it's important to ask about, they can consider alternate ways to get at what interests them.

Their reformulated questions constitute the beginnings of conceptual construction. They see what they aren't interested in and don't want to know about. They usually don't find this very thrilling and think they have just wasted their time on a wrong lead. But they haven't. They can only say that X *doesn't* interest them by having some notion of what *would* interest them. Naming the object of interest is the beginning of conceptualization.

I've made it sound as though this trick could only be done by sociologists who work with qualitative data, unfettered by research designs, able to keep changing their minds as they do their research. In fact, the introduction of microcomputers into everyday sociological life has freed quantitative sociologists from their dependence on mainframe computers, from the long waits those machines inserted between getting an idea, thinking how to test it on your data, and actually getting the results. Freed from the mainframe, quantitative analysis is much more interactive. People run off factor analyses that once took a year of hand calculation in the time it takes to refill their coffee cup. The cost of calculation having been lowered so dramatically, researchers can do analyses just for the hell of it, to see if there is anything to a hunch (Ragin and Becker 1988). And that in turn means

that quantitative researchers too can inspect the answers they have to see
what questions they imply. The same tricks will work for them.

Let the Case Define the Concept

This is a slightly different way of exploiting the recognition that concepts
are defined. Sociologists, concerned to generalize, want to establish that
what they have studied is not the only one of its kind. What good would it
be to get sure knowledge about something when you couldn't apply that
knowledge anywhere else? This concern is enshrined in the well-known
distinction between idiographic and nomothetic sciences. Students especially, I think, want to put their case (the thing they studied) into some conceptual category, for the very good reason that if they can do that then all
the justifications for why you should study such things are ready-made and
easily available to them.

But there's a problem with that. It's not clear that you can say anything
very useful if you focus only on what is common to your case and other
cases with which it shares membership in some class. The more seriously
you take the case, the harder you try to understand it fully so that there's
nothing about it that you have to hide or ignore, the harder it is to see it as
being "just like" any other case it might superficially resemble.

Consider this as a choice between letting the conceptual category define the case and letting the case define the category. We let the category
define the case by saying that what we have studied is a case of *x,* let's say
of bureaucracy or modernization or organization or any of the other
common concepts we use to understand the social world. Doing that
leads us (not necessarily, but often enough in practice) to think that everything that is important about the case is contained in what we know about
the category. Analytically, then, we just have to inspect the case to see that
it has all the attributes a member of that category is supposed to have and
thus is one of the things described by that concept. We check, say, to see
that our case has all the features Max Weber said a bureaucracy should
have. Our analysis is complete when we show that it does have all (or
most) of those things, and have explained why it doesn't have the ones that
aren't there. We ignore those elements of the case whose presence or absence the category description ignores. This strategy helps us develop theory by adding cases to the collection of examples of the type, and
variations to ideas and principles others have developed to explain them.

This is something like the normal science work of articulation described by Kuhn (1970, 27–34).

The more the world, as exemplified in our case, includes just what our concept includes and no more, the better our analysis works. But the world is hardly ever just as we imagined it. In fact, such a rare similarity probably occurs only under some very special circumstances. It occurs, for instance, when we have tailored our concept to fit a particular instance. If I construct a theory of revolution by generalizing from the American or Russian Revolution, then my theory will fit the case I based it on. The world and our concept resemble each other, too, when we have enough control over the world to *make* it exactly fit our categories. Latour explains that science "works," which is to say that its predictions are verified in practice, because scientists change the world until it is just like the setting in which they made their discoveries (1987, 249–50). Louis Pasteur could protect cows from anthrax by vaccinating them only when he could persuade farmers to replicate the essential features of his laboratory on their farms. He says: "Facts and machines are like trains, electricity, packages of computer bytes or frozen vegetables; they can go everywhere as long as the track along which they travel is not interrupted in the slightest" (1987, 250). It is extremely difficult to lay the tracks on which social science can travel. Too many other people have conflicting ideas about how the social world should be arranged to let us arrange it so that our theories will work. So such tracks are best laid in computer simulations and sometimes in laboratory experiments. Unlike Pasteur, social scientists can rarely persuade anyone to turn their real (not simulated) homes or communities into the tracks on which our theories might run.

So the strategy of letting the concept define the case accomplishes a lot, but at a price: we don't see and investigate those aspects of our case that weren't in the description of the category we started with. The things we leave out, however, come back to bother us. Whether we include them in our investigation or not, they are still there and continue to operate in the situation we're studying, almost surely influencing the phenomena we want to understand. It makes sense to include them in our analysis even if our concept doesn't make room for them. Which is the argument for the alternative strategy: letting the case define the category. As in the earlier example, take the American revolution as the model and define a category that has all the attributes (every single one, because we don't know what to leave out) of that case. Anything we find out about the case becomes a crucial part of the concept. What does that accomplish? Can we ever create any generalizations working that way?

Letting the case define the concept lets you define dimensions you might see varying in other cases. You discover that the executives of savings and loan associations sometimes steal money by manipulating banking regulations whose complexity makes it difficult for prosecutors to decide whether what they indisputably did is a crime. That identifies an aspect of "crime" you would not see in cases of assault, where no one doubts that hitting someone with a club is a crime. The generalization that results from your study is that the clarity or ambiguity of an action's criminality, and the things that affect that, are something to include in all future studies of "crime." In a way, the result of working like this is not more answers, but more questions.

Generalizing: Bernie Beck's Trick

I snuck in a move in the above analysis, when I said its outcome was a new aspect of crime to be included in future research—the clarity or ambiguity of an action's criminality. I'll explain what's involved in that move now. Sociologists often know no intermediate stops between the raw facts of the case they studied and the largest, most general categories of social analysis. Thus, they may describe the findings of their research on, say, drinking alcohol, and jump from that to talk about identities or self-conceptions or some other highly abstract aspect of social organization or interaction. As a rule, our research does not have anything very new to say about self-conceptions or identity. Researchers usually use such general ideas to orient their work, to suggest an overall approach and a very general set of questions they might ask. The ideas serve as what Lewontin refers to as "informing and organizing metaphors" whose role is "to bring order into confusion" (1994, 509). What the researchers who use them discover will probably not lead to any reformulation of those general ideas or questions. At worst, the researcher announces triumphantly that what was studied was indeed a case of the development of identity or the adaptive character of social organization. That kind of result isn't useful to anyone. It doesn't add much to whatever warrant the very general theories it is attached to already have. And the general theories don't add much to the specific studies. The advice they offer is too general.

What is useful is the description of something more general than the particular facts we discovered, but less general than notions of identity or social interaction. Something in between, something like what Robert Merton alerted us to as "theories of the middle range." I moved from the savings and loan convictions to the idea of the clarity or ambiguity of an action's criminality, but I didn't explain how I did that. When I teach field-work, I often make that kind of jump in discussing the possible extensions of a student's findings. This is the aspect of what I do that most often pro-vokes the feeling that some kind of magic trick is being performed, that the way I get from A to B isn't something a person can learn to imitate.

During the twenty-five years I taught at Northwestern, my office was always next door to that of Bernard Beck, one of sociology's great teachers and thinkers, whose qualities are less well-known than they ought to be. I learned more from him than I will ever repay, a lot of it from eavesdropping on his conversations with graduate students about their work in progress. None of what I heard has been more useful to me than his trick for getting to this intermediate level of thinking about a research result. Since he has never published this trick, which has the elegance of simplicity, I'm taking the liberty of borrowing it from him.

Beck says to a student who has gathered some data and now is trying to understand what his or her dissertation research is about, "Tell me what you've found out, but without using any of the identifying characteristics of the actual case." I'll use my own dissertation, a study of the careers of schoolteachers in Chicago, as an example (the results are reported in Becker 1970, 137–77). Had I been a student asking Beck for help figuring out what generalization my research could produce, he probably would first have asked me what I had actually found out about Chicago teachers. I could have offered this conclusion:

> These teachers make their careers by moving from school to school within the Chicago school system, rather than trying to rise to higher, better paid positions, or moving to other systems in other cities, and their moves between positions in the school sys-tem can be understood as trying to find a school in which the people they interacted with—students, parents, principals, other teachers—would act more or less the way the teachers expected them to.

Had I told Beck all that, he would, using this trick, have said to me, "Tell me what your research is about, but now you are forbidden to use the words 'teacher,' 'school,' 'pupil,' 'principal,' or 'Chicago.'" To answer such a question, I would have to choose words more general than the specifics of my case, but not so general as to lose the specificity of what I found. If I started talking about "identity" or "rational choice" or similar high-level abstractions, I would lose what I had learned about career movements resulting from choices between more and less comfortable work situations. So I might have answered that my study showed how people in bureaucratic systems choose between potential positions by assessing the way all the other participants will treat them and choosing places where the balance will be best, given whatever they are trying to maximize.

That's how I made the move from the fact that banking executives steal to the statement I made about the clarity or ambiguity of an action's criminality. I restated the assertion that "the executives of savings and loan associations sometimes steal money by manipulating banking regulations whose complexity makes it difficult for prosecutors to decide whether what they indisputably did is a crime" without using any of the specifics. I didn't say "executives" or "savings and loans" or any of the other specifics. I said what class each of those belonged to and so ended up talking about the ambiguity of an action's criminality, a dimension that could be useful in the study of any criminal activity. And I could take another step and talk about something less specific than criminal law—rules in general—and that would let me introduce such interesting cases as whether the ball the pitcher throws is a "ball" or a "strike," the rules for deciding that being as ambiguous as any in the criminal law.

You could argue that, after all, baseball and banking don't have much in common. Right. Every time we make such a comparison and find such a similarity, we will also immediately find such a difference. Both the similarity and the difference give us general categories to think about and use in our analyses. The similarity says, by way of generalizing, "Every set of rules is clear to some degree and ambiguous to another degree." The difference says, by way of a different kind of generalization, "Within the organizations (like baseball and banking) in which rules are made and enforced, there are other things going on, such that those rules will vary along a dimension running from clarity to ambiguity." Making such comparisons reveals further complexities in the creation and application of rules, complexities that can be attended to in future research.

The immediate consequence of that result is that every study can make a theoretical contribution, by contributing something new that needs to be thought about as a dimension of that class of phenomena. The only time that wouldn't be true would be when the two cases studied were identical in every respect—something so unlikely as not to be worth worrying about.

Concepts Are Generalizations

Here's a different approach to the same point. Although we think about them and speculate about them and define them, concepts are not just ideas, or speculations, or matters of definition. In fact, concepts are empirical generalizations, which need to be tested and refined on the basis of empirical research results—that is, of knowledge of the world.

We commonly have difficulty applying concepts to real cases of social phenomena: they sort of fit, but not exactly. That's because we seldom define phenomena by one unambiguous criterion. We don't say "If it has a trunk, it's an elephant, and that's that," or "If people exchange goods on the basis of price, that's a market." If we talked that way, we would know for sure whether a case was or wasn't one of the things we were interested in. (That's something of an exaggeration. We would still have all the problems associated with deciding what a trunk or an exchange on the basis of price is.)

Concepts that interest us, however, usually have multiple criteria. Max Weber didn't define bureaucracy by one criterion. He gave a long list of characteristic features: the existence of written files, jobs defined as careers, decisions made by rules, and so on. Similarly, social scientists usually define culture with multiple criteria: it consists of shared understandings, handed down from one generation to the next; of coherent propositions that embody the basic values of a society, and so on.

In the world we live in, however, phenomena seldom have all the attributes required for them to be, unambiguously, members of a class defined by multiple criteria. An organization has written files, and makes decisions by strict rules, but has no career paths for functionaries. Is it a bureaucracy, or not? An organization has, on paper, all the attributes Weber attributed to a bureaucracy, but is the kind of organization in which such things happen as this incident, reported by Gordon and his colleagues in a study of the public's access to information that was legally supposed to be available from city, county, and state offices in Illinois under various freedom of information laws:

When a professor from the Center for Urban Affairs at Northwestern University sought some voting data in Chicago, for example, he was clearly and repeatedly told, in person, by a clerk with an Irish surname, that those data, while legally public, were not available. While he was arguing to the contrary one day, an Italian surnamed clerk glanced at the professor's name on the written request, and interrupted to say: "Masotti. You Italian?" Dr. Masotti said, "Si," and spoke briefly in Italian to the clerk, who then called to another fellow Italian who labored for 30 minutes to produce a complete set of the initially "unavailable" data. (Gordon et al. 1979, 301)

Even if it has files and rules and all the other Weberian criteria, is that a bureaucracy?

A first reason these quarrels over definitions are important is that the descriptive titles that embody these concepts are seldom neutral, but rather are terms of praise or blame. "Culture," for instance, is almost always a good thing ("bureaucracy," as in the above example, is almost always bad). So we care, beyond technical theoretical considerations, whether we can say that a group has culture or not. We do not wish to reward with the approbation signaled by the honorific title some bunch that doesn't deserve it. Suppose a group's members share understandings, an element I mentioned above as often included in definitions of culture, but invent those understandings on the spot, instead of handing them down from generation to generation. Is that culture, or not? Some social scientists will not want to give a "bad" group that does such things (for instance, a delinquent gang) the honor of having real "culture"; they want to save such a good word for praiseworthy organizations (Kornhauser 1978). (An interesting problem arises here when historians discover that what seemed to be just such handed-down traditions embodying primordial values, etc., were actually invented not so long ago, the way they have discovered that Scottish culture, as embodied in the traditions of the ancient clans and their customary tartans, was invented by woolen merchants with excess stock on hand.)

Another problem can be put more technically. Suppose you have x criteria for an object, and you call objects that have all x criteria O. What do you call the objects that have $x-1$ or $x-2$ or $x-n$ of the criteria? The simple solution is to call them not-O and ignore all the differences among them—that is, treat them as though the only thing that is important about them is what they aren't. But that is often unsatisfactory because hardly any of the objects we study have all the criteria; instead they have varying mixtures of them—what Wittgenstein called "family resemblances." The bureaucracies we study are similar, but they aren't identical the way molecules of copper are. We can, of course, give every combination of possibilities a name. In fact, we seldom do that, because these devices quickly generate a very large number of possibilities we aren't prepared to handle theoretically or practically. (Methods for handling that complexity exist, and I will discuss them in chapter 5.)

So concepts like bureaucracy are really, as we ordinarily use them, generalizations that say: "Look, these x criteria actually do go together, more or less, all the time, enough so that we can pretend that they are all there in every Object O even though almost all Os in fact just have most, not all, of them." That makes a problem because many of your cases don't act as your theory says they will, precisely because they are missing an important attribute that is responsible for that aspect of the behavior of O.

We can often finesse these difficulties, because the number of cases is small or because the objects we collected don't lack attributes that are important for the problem we are pursuing. But when we can't, we should recognize that our "concept" was not just an idea but an empirical generalization that said that all those criteria always went together.

A good example from the world of practical affairs has to do with the concept of "living" somewhere. When the 1960 Census failed to count a large number of young black males, the political consequences forced statisticians and survey researchers to take the problem seriously. The practical question confronting the research committee considering this problem was how to conduct the next Census so as to count the people who had been missed the last time (Parsons 1972, 57–77). The U.S. Census must count people where they live, for purposes of political representation, so the question became a double one: how can we find them *where they live* so that they will fill out our forms, and what does it mean to live somewhere (because if we understand what it means to live somewhere we will know how to reach them)?

The expert committees' discussions revealed a profound ambiguity in the notion of living somewhere. What does it mean to live somewhere? For every criterion proposed, you could imagine a perfectly reasonable exception. You live where you sleep: if I'm on vacation in Mexico do I live in Mexico? It's where you usually sleep: I'm a traveling salesman, I don't usually sleep anywhere in particular. It's where you get your mail: many people get their mail at General Delivery or the City Lights Book Store in San Francisco, but they don't live in those places. It's where you can always be reached: for me, at the moment, that's the Sociology Department at the

University of Washington, but I certainly don't live there. It's where you keep your clothes, it's where. . . .

For most people, most of the time, all those places are the same place. They usually sleep in the place they get their mail, which is also where they have their clothes and can most easily be reached. But for most people sometimes, and for some people all the time, these are different places: they keep their clothes one place and sleep in another. For them the concept is just not adequate and, if we want to take them into account, we have to break the concept down into its component indicators and treat each one separately. In other words, we have to realize that the empirical generalization embodied in the concept is not true: all those criteria don't go together all the time.

You can make this failure of the indices of a concept to stick together as we'd like them to the jumping-off point for expanding and complicating your theory of the world. Marisa Alicea (1989) did that in her study of return migrants to Puerto Rico—people who, having moved to New York or Chicago from San Juan or Ponce, then go back to the island. She showed that, in fact, they move back and forth between their two homes frequently. Thus, it's misleading to think of them as migrants and far more realistic and useful to see them as people who have, as she says, "dual home bases." Taking that result seriously means that another "fact" built into the concept of "living somewhere"—that people can only "live" in one place—has to be seen as simply another possibility that may or may not be true in a given case.

I have sometimes upset listeners with such examples, which seem to entail an extreme constructivism that makes it impossible to do any research at all. They are especially upset if I follow the "living somewhere" example with a mention of how Harold Garfinkel (1967) confounded demographers by describing the case of Agnes, a transsexual who had changed genders socially and then physically, and then asking how the Census could be sure it had correctly classified someone as male or female. Did you have to take down everyone's pants in order to be sure of the classification, he wanted to know? If you couldn't use even so simple an idea as living somewhere or being male or female, how could you observe or count anything?

Alicea's research shows that seeing the concept as an empirical generalization helps you to avoid analytic errors. We conventionally think that migrants live in only one place at a time and, when they move, stop living in

131

the place they used to live in and go to live somewhere else. Well, of course, they do go somewhere else. But they actually have some sort of home (what sort, of course, is the researchable question that makes it worth getting into these complications) in two places, both the mainland U.S. and their home town in Puerto Rico. You can't assume that living in the second place means exactly what it meant when they lived where they used to live before they migrated. Before moving, they might have thought of Home$_1$ as the only home they had. But having acquired Home$_2$, they might decide that they needn't give up the first one, and then might move back and forth between the two the way people with a little more money go to their summer cottages every year. The pathos of the story is that these people may not have, in either place, some of the nice things a "real home" gives you, such as a secure economic base or an affectional base of people who know you and love you. (But having two homes isn't necessarily a deprivation either. Carol Stack's research shows how poor children who can "run away" and live for a while with a neighbor or relative two doors down the street can profit from having multiple homes.)

The trick of seeing concepts as empirical generalizations helps solve the problems created by an unthought-through insistence that all the properties of a concept always go together. Uncoupling them, and treating them as capable of varying independently, turns a technical problem into an opportunity for theoretical growth and articulation.

Concepts Are Relational

I once taught a class called "Classics of Social Research." One of the books we read for the class was Jane Mercer's *Labeling the Mentally Retarded* (1973), a study of the way the label "mentally retarded" was applied in the Riverside, California schools. This study proves, as well as anyone but an ideologue would want it proved, that borderline retardation (as opposed to the "real" retardation that is accompanied by obvious physical handicaps, etc.) is a disease Mexican and Black kids get when they go to school, and are cured of when they leave school.

I was moved in class one day to give a lecture on the idea that all terms describing people are relational—that is, that they only have meaning when they are considered as part of a system of terms. This is not a new idea. I think I first saw it put that way by a Marxist historian (perhaps E. P. Thompson or Eric Hobsbawm) who said that class was a relational term:

terms like "middle class" or "working class" only have meaning in relation to one another or to "upper class," and the meaning is the character of the relationship. "Working class" means that you work for people who are members of the "owner class."

That seems obvious enough. But it's one of those obvious things that people acknowledge and then ignore. How do they ignore it? By imagining that a class, by having a characteristic culture or way of life, would be what it is no matter what system of relations it was embedded in. That's not to say that there aren't class cultures, but rather to insist that such cultures result from some group of people being related to some other group in a way that creates, at least in part, the conditions in which their distinctive way of life develops.

A similar meaning has been attached to the idea of a country being "underdeveloped." In this case it was done by the simple device of treating "underdevelop" as a verb, "to underdevelop," which made it obvious that there were some other countries or organizations that were making that underdevelopment be what it was. In this case, there are obviously two separate things: to be underdeveloped only has meaning in relation to other places that are developed, and the distribution of "development" as a trait is created by the deliberate actions of some of those other organizations.

I took this up in class when one of the students, a clinical psychologist who found Mercer's conclusions hard to accept, insisted that mental retardation was, after all, real, not just a matter of definition or relations. At least, she said, there are some cases in which children are profoundly retarded. I started my reply by asking the students whether they thought I was tall or short. (If you measured me, I would be about 5'10", which, these days, is not particularly tall, but not short either.) They looked confused and waved their hands as if to say that I was medium. I insisted on an answer and, of course, they couldn't give it. I said that I used to be a shorter member of the faculty, when one colleague who measured 6'9" and another one who was 6'6" were around, but that I had gotten taller since they left. I asked a visiting Japanese student if it wasn't true that I would be tall in Japan. She laughed uncomfortably and finally said yes. I said that when I was in high school I would have been a reasonable height to play basketball but not anymore, and went on to point out that height was about as real a fact as you could hope to know about anyone—certainly as real, say, as retardation or intelligence.

The trick here is to place any term that seems to describe a trait of a person or group in the context of the system of relations it belongs to. That shows you that the trait is not just the "physical fact" of whatever-it-is, but rather an interpretation of that fact, a giving of meaning to it, that depends on what else it is connected to. The first thing it is connected to is other traits, which have similarly been given meaning, so that they constitute a system of possibilities. The graded series that runs from "profoundly retarded" to "retarded" to "normal" to "gifted" to "genius" is a good example.

But, the analysis can go on, what else is this system connected to? Why do these distinctions seem "natural" to a no more than ordinarily reasonable person? Why do they seem reasonable enough and important enough to act on? I pointed out that I myself was "profoundly retarded"—in the area of drawing. I could never draw a tree or a dog the way the "good drawers" in my class could. As a result, I had always felt ashamed. This disability had affected my life in nontrivial ways. Another student owned up to being "profoundly retarded" in the area of music, so unable to carry a tune that she had always been told to just mouth the words when her grammar school class sang in assemblies.

Why were these statements ironic, not serious? Because, obviously, these disabilities "don't make any difference." Nothing really bad happens to you if you can't draw or carry a tune. It may be unpleasant and mildly shaming. You may wish you could do these simple things with as little trouble as others. But our world is not so organized as to require us to be able to sing or draw.

Our world, however, *is* so organized that people must be able to do some things that "retarded" people can't do easily or well or at all. To get along, at least at a level some people and institutions define as minimal, you have to be able to read a little, do a little arithmetic, "catch on" to what's going on and pick up various kinds of ideas and skills within a certain length of time, read maps, tell time, understand directions, and so on. Otherwise, you are "slow."

Lewis Dexter (1964), writing about "The Politics of Stupidity," pointed out that all those skills result from our ancestors and contemporaries having built and maintained a world that makes those skills more or less necessary. You could build another kind of world where a similar necessity for physical grace and dexterity would be built into its physical appurtenances. In such a world, it might be necessary, in order to open a door, to perform some rather complex physical movement awkward people would have trouble with; some very awkward people wouldn't be able to open it at all. We might call these people "gawkies" and have special entrances to places built for them, perhaps give them special remedial classes in the hope of reclaiming them for a productive life, although we might have to conclude sadly that their genetic endowment made it impossible.

So there is a great difference between a physical trait and its social importance. We all have all sorts of traits, only a few of which are socially marked as important because of the way they are embedded in a system of relations. They become important when the organization of physical and social arrangements makes them "necessary." Take height. If you are above or below a certain range of height our physical arrangements make it awkward. If you're short your feet won't reach the floor when you sit in standard chairs; if you're tall you'll bump your head on doors if you aren't careful. Our social arrangements are somewhat more forgiving; but still, very tall women and very short men are exposed to troubles finding partners the rest of us don't have.

All this has a historical dimension. Several centuries ago, people's average height was less than it is now—so doorways built in the fifteenth and sixteenth centuries, unless they have been rebuilt, will catch careless contemporary people and bump their heads. Or take the skill of doing simple arithmetic. Anyone, these days, who cannot do addition, subtraction, and other simple arithmetic operations is certainly "slow," maybe even "retarded." But those skills were not always required. Patricia Cline Cohen's *A Calculating People* (1982) showed that it wasn't until well into the nineteenth century that the ordinary American really needed such skills; before that storekeepers and clerks might need them, but not the average person. She calls these skills "numeracy," in analogy to "literacy." The term emphasizes that it is because these are socially valued skills now, built into our everyday operations, that we see them as such important human abilities; at an earlier time such skills might have been interesting cultural ornaments just as singing and playing the flute were, but certainly not "important."

Skills and traits not only become more important, they also become less important. Diana Korzenik's book *Drawn to Art* (1985) describes the changes, back and forth, in the importance of skill in drawing in American society. In the middle and late nineteenth century some important people decided that the reason the United States was falling behind in industrialization was that Americans did not know how to draw. Much invention and adaptation of machinery took place on the floor of industrial shops, where workmen dreamed up improvements and inventions based on their detailed experience of the operations involved. For that to happen efficiently, workmen had to be able to draw plans from which the necessary parts and equipment could be built. But American workmen had not been trained in mechanical drawing and were not as good at it as were, for instance, German workmen. Steps were taken: a movement to have remedial classes for adults, so that workmen could acquire this necessary skill; a push to have drawing taught more systematically in the elementary schools. But that emphasis on drawing was relatively short-lived; other developments made drawing not so important after all, which meant that in the 1930s I could go through elementary school and be thought a bright student even though I couldn't draw (and had, in addition, terrible penmanship, which would have been a severe handicap in the pre-typewriter era).

Who gets to say which traits are important enough to be made the basis for serious and fateful distinctions? Sometimes it is our immediate associates who will decide for themselves whether my inability to draw or your inability to do arithmetic or her inability to carry a tune are serious enough to warrant special negative treatment, or whether my ability to remember and be ready to play one thousand popular songs on the piano or your ability to imitate Cary Grant or Groucho Marx or Judy Garland warrant special rewards. Sometimes, and this is where Mercer's results are so important, the decision is put in the hands of specialized professionals, who possess special esoteric methods for making these determinations. One of Mercer's truly shocking findings is that gross racial and ethnic disproportions in labeled retardation do not appear when teachers recommend children in their classrooms for intelligence testing—the children recommended display the same proportion of Mexicans, Blacks, and Anglos as the general school population. No, the gross overrepresentation of Mexicans appears *only* when intelligence tests are given, when the decision to classify a child as retarded is made by someone who has no experience of the child in the real life of the classroom and cannot interpret the bare test scores in the light of other knowledge of the child. So the professionalization of these decisions, through the development of occupational specialties and monopolies, is another important historical variable affecting how "individual traits" come to be embodied in a set of social relations that make them important.

Politics and power similarly affect how systems of relations make some traits important. If a negative trait is being assigned to people, powerful people can often prevent that from happening to them or theirs. If something good is being passed out, they will do their best to see that they and theirs get it. In the 1980s, the U.S. Congress (presumably trying to give middle-class people something to balance the special resources being allocated to the education of poorer, so-called "underprivileged" children) authorized a program for "gifted and talented" children. I suppose that the distinction mirrors, on the positive side, the distinction between "profoundly" and "mildly" retarded.

This program created a problem for teachers of visual art in the public schools: how do you choose the children who are gifted or talented and thus deserve extra training and opportunities? Even though middle-class parents are, by and large, more interested in other kinds of skills and talents than they are in visual art, still, if it's there to get, they want it. They want it to the degree that the people who decide who gets such special treatment need a scientifically defensible way of making the choices involved. Which is how I ended up at a conference that was labeled as being about "creativity" in the arts but turned out in fact to be about "Can you devise a test of some ability such that I can tell parents that children got into the Gifted and Talented Program on the basis of this test score and please leave me alone, I can't do anything about it if your child's score was low?"

So the teachers' problem became a testers' problem. What do you measure to assess ability in visual art? This was a serious problem because it is much more difficult to agree on a criterion in art than it is in arithmetic or reading. There is, however, one thing that "everyone knows" is important for visual art, and that happens to be the thing I can't do: drawing. Unfortunately, it isn't obvious that the ability to draw, even supposing that it might be relatively easy to test, is closely related to, say, success as a visual artist, any more than such conceptual abilities as ability to visualize spatial relationships or color sense or you name it. Furthermore, it's obvious that if you use a criterion such as success as an artist you might want to include such social and business skills as hustling. Still further, some visual arts, notably photography, don't require any drawing ability at all, so any test based on drawing would necessarily make some gross errors.

What's the point of this lengthy digression about "gifted and talented"? That the power of middle-class parents can affect the way this system of relations is set up and thus make it more or less important, and more or less available to people of different kinds. But their power may not be sufficient to overcome the power of the entrenched professionals into whose hands these determinations have fallen.

A second point to this example is that there are at least two kinds of systems of relations involved. In one, the reputationally desirable position is in the middle, at the mean of whatever is being measured, like height. This recalls Everett Hughes's suggestion, discussed earlier, that we inspect deviations from the average in two directions, looking both for people who have more of whatever it is and people who have less. In his example, one doesn't want to deviate from the modal way of organizing sexual relations, either by being "worse" than others (in ways that produce labels like "rake" or "slut") or by being "better" (being, say, a "goody-goody"). In other relational systems, however, reputations and their results for one's life get "better" the farther you go in one direction, and worse the farther you go in the other direction. Intelligence is like that, as are other traits like artistic ability.

To summarize this set of tricks: Put terms into the full set of relations they imply (as "tall" implies "short" and "gifted" implies "not gifted"). Then look at the way that set of relations is now organized and has been organized at other times and in other places (as in understanding that not knowing arithmetic has a different meaning and different consequences than it did 150 years ago). And, finally, see how things came to be organized the way they are here and now, and what connections to other social arrangements sustain that set of relations.

The Wittgenstein Trick

I've owned a copy of Ludwig Wittgenstein's *Philosophical Investigations* for years, but I read it the way Everett Hughes told me to read the sociological writings of Georg Simmel: not to get a full understanding of what the author might have meant, but rather as a way of generating ideas I could use in my own research and thinking. One of Wittgenstein's ideas has become a standard part of my repertoire. Because it was provoked by a passage in the *Investigations,* I think of it as the Wittgenstein trick.

Discussing the philosophical problems of intention and will in one of the numbered paragraphs that make up the book, Wittgenstein makes this remark: "Let us not forget this: when 'I raise my arm,' my arm goes up. And the problem arises: what is left over if I subtract the fact that my arm goes up from the fact that I raise my arm?" (Wittgenstein 1973, §621). That's the essence of the trick: if I take away from an event or object X some quality Y, what is left?

This trick helps us strip away what is accidentally and contingently part of an idea from what is at its core, helps us separate what's central to our image of a phenomenon from the particular example it is embedded in, as Wittgenstein isolates the core of our intuitive image of intention by separating the contingent physical action from it. Here's an example. I was once part of a panel organized to talk about modern art. One of the other panelists had become a serious, big-money collector of contemporary art three years earlier. When it was his turn to speak, he talked knowledgeably and at length about his "collection," which of course consisted of a large number of paintings, sculptures, and other objects. As I listened to him, I thought, "I have a house full of paintings and other objects, just as he does, but I don't have a collection. Why not?" So I did the Wittgenstein trick. I asked myself: "What is left over if we subtract from the idea of a collection the fact that this collector has a large number of paintings and other art objects in his house?" I turned to my data—the talk the collector was giving—for the answer. He immediately gave me part of the solution to my problem: his collection, as opposed to my mere mass of objects, had, he said, a "direction." It was not just an aimless assortment of stuff, the result of whim and caprice; less pejoratively, it did not represent the untutored application of his own taste. Rather, it resulted from and embodied knowledge and trained sensibility (his own and that of his advisers), and thus had a concrete and explicit aim and structure. Likewise, his collection had a "future." It was headed somewhere. It would be the object of repeated evaluation by knowledgeable experts. It was part of a world of artistic activity and progress, its very accumulation an act of substance in that world. My stuff, in contrast, was just that: stuff I had bought because I liked it, stuff I had traded my photographs for; accumulating it was just a private act that had no significance to anyone but me and mine. (The word "just" is important here, signifying as it often does in philosophical talk "merely" or "no more than.")

In fact, as the collector talked, I realized that having the objects in the house (or the office or any place he actually lived or worked) was not really necessary to his having a collection. Accumulating the objects in one place is not necessary to the *idea* of a collection. Why not? If you are a dealer specializing in new, trendy art (the kind the collector collected), you insist before you sell a piece (the dealer who was the third panelist explained this to me) that the purchaser make the work available for loan to museums for exhibitions. If you, an art dealer, are trying to build an artist's reputation, it does neither you or the artist any good to have an important piece sitting in someone's living room in the Midwest, no matter how much you sold it for. The piece must be where it can be seen by "important people" (that is, people who are important actors in the world in which such paintings are exhibited, bought, and sold) and thus contribute to the development of a career. Many museums have shows that are part of this process, and the purchaser of a work must make the purchase available for them. In fact, I had been in Amsterdam a few months earlier, and had seen, in a show of work by New York artists at the Stedelijk Museum, many pieces by the artists the dealer on the panel represented, some of them in the collector's collection. Truly "with it" collectors thus might not see sizable fractions of their collections for long periods of time. In fact, of course, some people's collections, or portions thereof, are often on more or less permanent loan to museums (which hope to be left those works in the lender's will).

Using the Wittgenstein trick, then, what is left when you take away from "collection" the idea that you have a lot of art stuff in the house? What seemed to be left (in this situation at least, but I think it would be a common view of the problem) was the idea of the collector as a person who has the financial and cultural resources (the latter what Pierre Bourdieu has called "cultural capital") to choose and acquire objects that represent what will eventually turn out to have been major trends in modern art. In his talk, the collector said something like this: "The idea is to find out how to get the best work of an artist who will be historically significant, works that will turn out to be a major part of art history. Your reward is to have your judgment approved by history." On this view, where the objects are is irrelevant, and having objects in itself doesn't make you a collector. The objects are merely the visible symbols of the decisive action the collector has taken by staking big money and a reputation for sagacity and sensibility on the choice of art works, and it's that action that is crucial to understanding what a collection is. (Which is why some members of the art world dispute the characterization of Joseph Hirshhorn, for whom a major art museum in Washington, D.C. is named, as a great collector. Can you, they complain, be a great collector if, as he is said to have often done, you just walk into an artist's studio and after a quick look around buy everything in it? Where's the sagacity and sensibility in that? This, of course, is an art world complaint, not a sociological judgment.) And it's not just the action the collector takes that's important for understanding the idea of a "collection," obviously; it's also the action the rest of the world takes by making what the collector has accumulated significant in art history or not. (I've drawn on Raymonde Moulin's analyses [1967, 1992] of the French and international art markets for some of these ideas. An attentive reader will see, too, that this trick is another way of describing what you've studied without using any of the specifics, which is what the Beck trick does.)

Enlarging a Concept's Reach

The Wittgenstein trick, then, lets us isolate the generic features of a series of cases we think have something in common, the features out of which we can construct the generalization that is a concept. Once we have isolated such a generic feature of some social relation or process and given it a name, and thus created a concept, we can look for the same phenomenon in places other than where we found it. The study of prison cultures furnishes a nice example.

Students of prisons (e.g., Sykes 1958) had demonstrated that the inmates of men's prisons developed an elaborate culture. Inmates created convict governments that took over many of the functions of keeping order in the joint; they developed informal but orderly markets in cigarettes, drugs, tailor-made prison uniforms for the snappily dressed convict, and a variety of personal services; they organized sexual activity; they enforced a strict code of convict behavior emphasizing the necessity of never giving information about other prisoners to prison guards and officials.

Analysts of prison culture attributed these inventions to the deprivations of prison life: deprived of autonomy, prisoners carved out a governmental structure that got some autonomy back for them, and a convict code (of which the prohibition on snitching on other prisoners to prison staff was a major component) that preserved that autonomy; deprived of drugs, sharp clothes, and other goods they were used to in civilian life, they organized markets to provide those things; deprived of sex, they improvised a system of predatory prison-specific homosexual relationships that did not threaten their self-conceptions as macho men. The sociological generalization, a specification of a more general set of ideas that goes back to William Graham Sumner, was that prisoners collectively develop a culture that solves the problems created by the deprivations of prison life.

So far, so good. With this theory in mind, Ward and Kassebaum (1965) studied a women's prison. They found none of the things the theory of prison culture had led them to expect. Quite the opposite. Even the officials of the prison complained about the lack of a convict code: the women were forever snitching on each other in a way that made a lot of trouble for them and thus for the prison staff. No real underground market existed. Sex life was not organized in the predatory style of the men's prison; instead, the women developed pseudo-families, with butches acting as the husbands and fathers of a collection of wives and daughters. (See also Giallombardo 1966.)

Did these differences—the absence of any of the things predicted by the available theory of prison life—invalidate the generalization that the deprivations of prison life lead to the creation of a prison culture? And did that in turn mean that no generalizations about prisons were possible? Not at all. They meant that the generalizations are not about how all prisons are just the same, but about a process, the same no matter where it occurs, in which variations in conditions create variations in results (which is actually a much classier form of generalization anyway).

In this case, the theory wasn't wrong, but you had to put in the right values of the variables, so to speak, to see how it was right. You could still say that the deprivations of prison life led to the creation of prison culture, but that was true only if you understood that these deprivations were different for men and women. Women were not deprived of autonomy because, as they explained to the researchers, they had never been autonomous; they had always lived under the protection of and been subject to the authority of a man: a father, husband, or lover. What prison deprived them of was exactly that kind of protection. So, rather than develop a convict government to replace the autonomy they didn't miss, they developed a system of homosexual relationships in which one woman stood in as the masculine protector.

New women prisoners were especially afraid because, due to variations in the gender distributions of crime, men's prisons have a lot of professional criminals serving time for robbery, burglary, and other less violent crimes, while most women prisoners are in for drugs and prostitution, and for the typically amateur "crime of passion"—that is, murder. Since there are thus more murderers in them, women's prisons sound like very dangerous places to be, even to the murderers who know that they themselves aren't dangerous (they just wanted to kill that one person who done them wrong). So even the murderers are looking for someone to take care of them. Similarly, women's prisons typically allow inmates to buy things they want, like cosmetics and clothes, so there is no need for an underground market.

In short, women prisoners are deprived of different things than men, both because their lives on the outside and, therefore, their needs on the inside, differ, and because the prison is run differently for them. Their culture responds to that difference. The generalization is still true, even though the results are quite different.

The general lesson here, the trick to be applied elsewhere, is not to mistake a specific instance of something for the entire class of phenomena it belongs to. Deprivation probably leads to the collective development of cultural practices designed to relieve it in all sorts of settings, but what constitutes deprivation may vary considerably.

We are most likely to confuse part of a class for the whole in this way when the class has a well-known name that applies to an equally well-known set of instances. That's why people who study "education" almost always study schools. That's where education takes place, isn't it? Everyone knows that. Education, conventionally defined, consists of knowledgeable people teaching people who are less knowledgeable, and typically, not surprisingly, less powerful and less well-placed (children or immigrants, for instance), and doing it in schools. That's what education *is*.

If, however, we think of education and learning as generic social processes, there's no reason to think that those processes take place only in schools. We might try to redefine the subject matter as people learning things, wherever and however that activity happens and whoever does it. Then we could include in our collection of cases the way thieves teach other the latest techniques of their trade, or the way young people teach other to use drugs or engage in sexual activity. But that's just cheap irony, because everyone knows that those activities aren't "education," at least not what any reasonable layperson means by that. Education means schools.

But there's no reason to assume that learning takes place in schools at all, even though that is the story schools tell about themselves and the story well-socialized members of our society believe, or at least pretend to believe so that they won't appear to be nuts. You can study, as an example of learning, how young people learn to use marijuana. You may find, as Schaps and Sanders did in 1970 (and it might be different at another time), that young women typically learn from their boyfriends, while the boyfriends learn from each other. By ignoring the conventional instances that define the concept, you have enlarged its reach. You have discovered new people who do the job of teaching and new relationships in which it is done.

It's quite likely that the process by which boyfriends teach their girlfriends to smoke dope has a lot in common with other activities in which knowledge, skill, and ideas are passed on. It might, for instance, resemble the system described by Gagnon and Simon (1973), in which young women teach their boyfriends to engage in romance, which they have been practicing in solitude for quite a while, while the boyfriends are teaching them to engage in sex, which *they* have similarly been practicing in solitude. If the process works, and each learns what the other knows, they can manage to fall in love in the more or less standard way.

These processes of peer teaching and mutual learning may, in turn, have their counterparts inside schools and other so-called educational institutions. Personal computer users often teach each other how to use their machines, despite or perhaps because of the more conventional standardized instruction available here and there. Students in conventional educational institutions have repeatedly been shown (e.g., Becker, Geer, and Hughes [1968] 1994) to teach each other how to deal with the constraints, requirements, and opportunities those places embody: how much of the assigned work you really have to do, for example.

To take another variation on the standard model of education, some kinds of teaching and learning are, unlike the elementary and secondary education that form the archetypal instances that define the concept, totally voluntary: lessons in piano playing, tennis, and French are all like that. They take place in profit-making establishments, are often if not always individual, and have no fixed term. The students get no credits and no degrees. They just take lessons until they feel they aren't getting anything out of it any more. The distribution of power between student and teacher is so different from the stereotypical school that this is bound to be a somewhat different generic type. (See the discussion in Becker 1986a, 173–90.)

An excellent, perhaps the best, way to enlarge the reach of a concept is to forget the name entirely and concentrate on the kind of collective activity that is taking place. A good example of this strategy is Erving Goffman's analysis (1961) of what places that had the generic features of "total institutions" had in common with respect to the way their inmates (be they nuns, sailors at sea, or mental patients) had to live and the kinds of adjustments they made to living that way. Or his analysis of the characteristic social forms that grew up around people who had stigmas of various kinds (Goffman 1963). The brilliance of these analyses was to show that, in the generic sense he had in mind, everyone had some sort of stigma, not just people who were blind or missing a limb, and every institution was, in some respects, a total institution. Exchanging the conventional contents of a concept for a sense of its meaning as a form of collective action enlarges its reach and our knowledge.

It's time in the next chapter to consider some more formal ways of working with concepts, ways that use the devices of serious formal logic.

5

LOGIC

We have looked in all the places we ought to look to find all the things we ought to find, and in all the places we might not have thought to look if we hadn't used some of the tricks we've already discussed. (We have, for instance, looked in the angelic as well as the diabolic direction for cases on which to base our generalizations, as the chapter on sampling recommended.) And we have found out a lot. We have a lot of cases of a variety of phenomena, and we know a lot about them.

But there's more to do and learn. There are ways to get more out of what we have. There are more things we want to know, and there are ways to get to some of them without getting more data. The tricks that let us do that are more or less purely logical. I don't mean, when I speak of a "logical trick," the application of a strictly syllogistic logic, a simple combining of what is known according to Aristotelian or some other rules (though that's not in itself bad and some of it is involved in what I'm going to describe). I mean, rather, using tricks of logical thinking to see what else might be true *if* the things you already know are true. What can we extract from what we already have that will give us ideas we wouldn't have found otherwise?

That's logic: ways of manipulating what we know according to some set of rules so that the manipulations produce new things, the way you can use the primitive entities and operations of a mathematical system to produce results you would never have imagined those primitives harbored.

We don't derive these new entities just for fun. The possibilities logic gives us tell us there are more things to look for, and more places to look for them, just as the periodic table told physicists that elements they hadn't even imagined possible were out there waiting to be found. Studying society is a process of back and forth, looking in the world, thinking about what you've seen, and going back to have another look at the world. This chapter is mostly about the thinking, but the results of the thinking are clues to where to look next. The two main varieties of logical tricks I'll consider here have to do with looking for the implicit major premises of arguments, and using truth tables to generate lists of possible combinations.

Find the Major Premise

Classical logical arguments consist of syllogisms, the most classical example being the one that explains that all men are mortal, Socrates was a man, therefore Socrates was a mortal. Q.E.D. The standard analysis of such arguments divides what is said into a *major premise,* which states a general truth already agreed to (in this case, that all men are mortal); a *minor premise,* which states a particular fact also agreed to (in this case, that Socrates was a man); and a *conclusion,* a statement that is said to follow from the fact of the minor premise being a special case of, and therefore included in or covered by, the general truth stated in the major premise. Everett Hughes used this classical logical analysis, in a way that can be generalized to many other situations, to understand a problem in race relations in the United States.

Hughes was interested in the way social scientists had, in the 1940s, been led astray, diverted from the real work to be done, by trying to disprove statements of fact made by racists. If someone said that Negroes smelled worse than whites, these misguided do-gooders would set out to prove that, in fact, white people couldn't tell the difference between white and black sweat. And these researchers were positively overjoyed when their data also demonstrated that Chinese Americans found white sweat especially distasteful. Such researchers, Hughes said, allowed themselves to be misled because they did not see the logic of the arguments they were trying to combat. He explained that underlying logic this way:

> Each of these rationalizations brought up in defense of racial and ethnic injustices is part of a syllogism. The minor premise, stating an alleged fact, is expressed; the major premise, a principle, is left out. Instead of driving our opponents and ourselves back to the major premise, we [liberal social scientists, that is] are content to question and disprove the minor premise, the allegation of fact.
> Suppose we take a couple of the common statements: "Jim Crow practices [which mandated separate public facilities, such as theater seats, toilets, eating places, and barber shops, for Negroes] are justified because Negroes smell bad," and "Jews should not be admitted to medical schools because they are aggressive."

He analyzed these statements this way. The argument that Jim Crow practices were justified began with a major premise (neither explicitly stated or empirically demonstrated), the assertion that there should be separate public facilities for people who smell bad. This is followed by an explicitly stated but not empirically demonstrated minor premise, namely, that Negroes in fact smell bad. *If* the premises are both true—needless to say, a very large *if*—then the conclusion that Negroes should have separate facilities inevitably follows.

The second argument, similarly analyzed, would read like this:

> People who are aggressive beyond some determined degree should not be admitted to medical schools. [Major premise]
> Jews are aggressive beyond this degree. [Minor premise]
> Therefore, Jews should not be admitted to medical schools. [Conclusion] (Hughes [1971] 1984, 214)

What interested Hughes was that the major premise of each of these syllogisms was, as he said, suppressed. That is, no one stated the full syllogism as the justification for the injustice being committed because, he suggested, the implied major premises were such that "people of our culture, those who believe in racial and ethnic equality, as well those who use these rationalizations, do not care to bring [them] out in the open":

> We are a people who can be frightened by advertisements which tell us that we will not be promoted to be superintendents of factories and sales-managers of businesses unless we smell nice; and the American woman can be frightened by the threat that she will not get her man or that she may lose him over a matter of a little unpleasant odor of which her best friend can't bring herself to speak. [He refers here to a deodorant slogan of the day that warned, "Even your best friend won't tell you that you suffer from Body Odor."] We are not told at what point in his rise to authority and higher income the man who is about to be lost must begin to make himself pleasant. Nor do we learn whether the man who is about to be lost had so sensitive a nose when he got the girl, or whether he picked up this nicety later. But the reference to the great—and legitimate—American dream of getting ahead is obvious enough. And it is perhaps not difficult to understand why we do not question the main premise behind the alleged fact of Negro odor. ([1971] 1984, 215)

Hughes goes on to examine the similar major premise that lay behind the allegation that the movement of a "lower" social group into a neighborhood lowers property values and that such movement should therefore be prevented. That's a syllogism many groups have found themselves on both ends of in American cities, since the same group can easily be both the people who lower someone's property values by moving in and the people whose values are in turn lowered by yet another group moving in on them. The major premise here asserts that, although people need to act aggressively in their own interest to "get ahead" in America, they had better not let the aggression and naked self-interest show. This too is something people would rather not talk about:

> The thought that I may be one of those whose presence in a neighborhood might—through other people's attitudes toward me—reduce its desirability to them is not a pleasant one to face, especially when combined with my own concern lest some group of people from whom I wish to be dissociated may some day threaten the neighborhood in which I have achieved a social footing and perhaps a dearly bought family house. (215–16)

And that is in turn the major premise no one wants to inspect that underlies the syllogism about Jews and medical schools:

> We Americans do not like to talk about just what degree of aggressiveness is proper; we might find that the amount of this virtue necessary to realize our ambitions is greater than the amount which turns it into a punishable vice. (216)

Hughes's examples may seem somewhat dated now, though the problems he deals with are probably not so much behind us as we would like to think, and his analysis is chiefly concerned with statements of ethnic prejudice and how right-thinking people ought to deal with them. His advice about that is still pretty good.

But what I want to make explicit here is the analytic trick Hughes used to get where he was going. He identified some common racially prejudiced remarks as parts of an incomplete logical argument. Someone states a conclusion and supports it with a statement of fact that serves as the minor premise of a syllogism that is never openly and fully stated. A simple logical exercise then shows you what the major premise must necessarily be to make the minor premise lead to that conclusion. So extracting the hidden major premise is the first trick he teaches us.

Hughes gives us more. He tells us to ask, further, what made the argument, stated in this incomplete form, seem so compelling and unanswerable. It needn't always be true that the major premise causes such ambivalence as the examples Hughes used. What will always be the case, his analysis leads us to think, is that the major premise will be so rooted in people's daily experience as not to require demonstration or argument. So the second part of the analysis is more *socio*logical than logical, aimed at finding the patterns of daily life that produce that kind of common-sense certainty among people who share the characteristic problems, constraints, and opportunities of a social situation.

Seen in this more general light, the trick helps solve several common research problems. The people we study often do things that seem strange, hard to understand. We can usually understand those activities better when we extract and make explicit the major premises that have been left unstated, and see how they arise out of and are supported by the experience of daily life. For example, we see and hear people make distinctions between categories of things and people, but we seldom hear them explain why those lines are the right ones to draw. Further, our own theoretical reasoning often (I might better say usually or always) leaves something important out, something that can be discovered by logical analysis. By bringing the left-out something back into our analysis, we can add new dimensions to our thinking and understanding. Better yet, if we look to what in our own experience as social scientists led us to leave that something out, we will learn an important lesson about how we work that might stand us in good stead in solving other research problems.

Understanding Strange Talk

When we gather data—in interviews, through observation, or by reading documents generated by the people and organizations we study—we often hear or read language that draws a line, separating things into categories. We hear people make distinctions, between "us" and "them," a common distinction well known to be sociologically significant, and between "this" and "that," which is the more general form. You can treat these distinctions as diagnostic of that organization, those people, their situations, their careers. When your notes record such distinction-making and line-drawing, you know that this is something to follow up, to find out more about. Who is drawing the line? What are they distinguishing between by doing it? What do they think they will accomplish by making that distinction, drawing the line there?

Drawing the Line: Crocks

One kind of line-drawing consists of stating that "There's *this kind* and there's *that kind*." For years I've entertained my fieldwork class (I hope I've entertained them) with the story of the word "crock," as that term is used by medical students, using it as an illustration of how you can use the trick of uncovering people's unstated assumptions in the field to find out what questions you should be pursuing, as a way of solving the mundane research problem of what you should do today, who you should talk to or observe in order to find out what. As we'll see, the trick takes you far beyond simply uncovering an ideological contradiction, takes you right to the heart of how a complex social activity is organized and carried out. (The lengthy account that follows, originally written for other purposes, can also be read as a real-life example of what people actually do when they "do fieldwork.")

In the fall of 1955, I moved to Kansas City to begin fieldwork at the University of Kansas Medical School, on the study of medical education I've mentioned earlier in this book (Becker et al. [1961] 1977). When I showed up at the school that fall, I knew I was supposed to study medical students and medical education; but, to be truthful, I had very little idea of what I was going to do beyond "hanging around with the students," going to classes and whatever else presented itself.

I had even less idea what our "problem" was, what specifically we were going to investigate. Social scientists had constructed a field called "socialization" at the intersection of sociology and social psychology, and Robert Merton and his collaborators had been studying the socialization of medical students to the role of doctor. Maybe that was it, but I wasn't comfortable with that way of describing what I was going to do. My dissertation, a study of schoolteachers' careers, could have been said to be in the "sociology of education," but that didn't seem to be the best way to study medical students either. The farthest I had gone in conceptualizing my problem was to say to myself that these kids entered the school at one end and four years later came out the other end, and something certainly must happen to them in between.

In any event, I was more concerned with our family's move from Urbana (what a relief to get out of there!) to Kansas City (which I hoped, and this turned out to be true, would provide a better place to practice my other trade, piano playing), and with getting to know my way around what seemed to me the enormous buildings that were the University of Kansas Medical Center.

I knew next to nothing about the organization of medical education, and consoled myself about my ignorance with the "wisdom" that told me that therefore I would have no prejudices either. How scientific! I didn't even know, and had to be told, that the first two years of the four-year medical course were mostly academic, while during the last two "clinical" years students actually worked on hospital wards, attending to patients.

Fortunately, the Dean of the school took me in hand and decided that I should begin my investigations with a group of third-year students in the Internal Medicine Department. There were two third-year student groups, superintended by different faculty members, and he took care that I ended up with the one run by the "benign" doctor. I learned soon enough that the other was one of those legendary terrors whose temper cowed students, house staff, and most of his patients.

I didn't know what internal medicine was but learned quickly enough that it had to do with everything that wasn't surgery or pediatrics or ob-stetrics or any of a lot of other named specialties. I soon learned too that the people who practiced internal medicine considered themselves, and were considered by others, to be the intellectuals of the medical business, as opposed to the surgeons, who were thought to be money-grubbing brutes, or the psychiatrists, who were thought to be crazy themselves.

With no problem to orient myself to, no theoretically defined puzzle I was trying to solve, I concentrated on finding out what the hell was going on, who all these people were, what they were doing, what they were talk-ing about, finding my way around, and most of all getting to know the six students with whom I was going to spend the next six weeks. I was a Jew-ish smart aleck from the University of Chicago and they were several vari-eties of small town and larger city Kansans and Missourians, but we got on well from the start. They were interested in what I was doing and curious about my work and job ("How much do they pay you to do this?" they wanted to know). They thought it was nice that I got paid to study them, and did not doubt that they were worth the trouble.

None of us were sure what I was "allowed" to do or which things they did were "private," while others were OK for me to follow along on. Clearly I could go to class with them, or make rounds of the patients with them and the attending physician. But the first time one of the students got up and said, "Well, I have to go examine a patient now," I could see that I had to take matters into my own hands and set the right precedent.

Neither the Dean nor anyone else had said I could watch while students examined patients. On the other hand, no one had said I couldn't do that. My presence during a physical examination might have been construed as a violation of patient privacy, except that it would be a joke to raise that matter in a medical school, where such intimate procedures as rectal and vaginal exams were often carried out before a sizable audience. The student, being new at examining patients, wasn't too eager to have me watch him fumble. But if I let the situation get defined as "The sociologist can't watch us examine patients" I'd be cut off from one of the major things students did. So I said, with a confidence I didn't feel, "OK. I'll come with you." He must have thought I knew something he didn't, and didn't argue the point.

Making rounds worked like this. The physician whose group I was working with had a "service," a number of beds occupied by his patients. A resident or two and an intern worked on the service, and six students were assigned to it. Every patient was assigned to a student, who was responsible for doing a physical examination, taking a history, ordering diagnostic tests, making a diagnosis, and planning a course of treatment. Mind you, all that work was done again by an intern, a resident, and the physician, and the treatment the physician decided on was the one that was carried out.

Every morning the whole group assembled and walked around to see all the patients on the service; that was making rounds. At each bed, the physician talked to the patient, asked the house staff about any developments since yesterday, and then made that patient the occasion for an informal quiz of the student to whom he or she had been assigned. The quiz could be about anything, and students were nervous about what might come up.

During my first week in the school, while I followed the students and others through the ritual of making rounds, I made a big discovery. It wasn't the breakthrough "Aha!" that researchers often report. Rather, it was a piece of detective work that took me, and several of the students, most of the next week. Its ramifications occupied me and my colleagues for the duration of the project.

One morning, as we made rounds, we saw a very talkative patient, who had multiple complaints to tell the doctor about, all sorts of aches, pains, and unusual events. I could see that no one was taking her very seriously and, on the way out, one of the students said, "Boy, she's really a crock!" I understood this, in part, as shorthand for "crock of shit." It was obviously invidious. But what was he talking about? What was wrong with her having all those complaints? Wasn't that interesting? (By the way, this first patient was in fact a woman and the noncrock that followed a man, which "confirmed" for everyone involved the medical stereotypes that said crocks were overwhelmingly women.)

As I've already said, my discovery of what the word "crock" meant was not a lightning bolt of intuition. On the contrary, it was a version of the trick of extracting an unstated premise or premises that was guided by sociological theorizing every step of the way. Like this. When I heard Chet call the patient a crock, I engaged in a quick but deep theoretical analysis. I had a piece of theory ready to put to work here. To put it most pretentiously: When members of one status category make invidious distinctions among the members of another status category with whom they regularly interact, the distinction will reflect the interests of the members of the first category in the relationship. More specifically, and perhaps less forbiddingly, the invidious distinctions students made between classes of patients would show what interests they were trying to maximize in that relationship, what they hoped to get out of it. To make the connection to major and minor premises clear, we could say that when they made this distinction, they reasoned from some premise they found it unnecessary to make explicit, something so obvious to them as not to require saying or even thinking explicitly.

So, when Chet called the patient a crock, I made this theoretical analysis in a flash and then came up with a profoundly theoretical question: "What's a crock?" He looked at me as if to say that any damn fool would know that. So I said, "Seriously, when you called her a crock, what did you mean?" He looked a little confused. He had known what he meant when he said it, but wasn't sure he could explain it. After fumbling for a while, he said it referred to someone with psychosomatic illness. That let him off the hook for the moment by partially satisfying my curiosity, though I still wanted to know what interest of his as a student was violated by a patient with psychosomatic illness.

But, as a good scientist, I wanted to check my finding out further, so I held my tongue. The next patient we saw, as it turned out, had a gastric ulcer, and the attending physician made him the occasion for a short lecture on psychosomatic illness, with ulcer the example at hand. It was quite interesting, and when we left the room I tried out my new knowledge and said to Chet, "Crock, huh?" He looked at me as though I were a fool, and

said, "No, he's not a crock." I said, "Why not? He has psychosomatic disease, doesn't he? Didn't you just tell me that's what a crock is? Didn't we just
spend ten minutes discussing it?" He looked more confused than before
and another student, eavesdropping on our discussion, undertook to clear
it up: "No, he's not a crock. He really has an ulcer."

I don't remember all the details of what followed. What I do remember
is that I got all the students interested in the question and, between us, with
me asking a lot of questions, and applying the results to succeeding cases,
we ended up defining a crock as a patient who had multiple complaints but
no discernible physical pathology. That definition was robust, and held up
under many further tests.

But my problem was only half solved. I knew that students thought
crocks were bad, but I still didn't know why . What interest of theirs was
compromised by a patient with many complaints and no pathology? What
were they not saying that made that reasonable? When I asked them, students said that you couldn't learn anything from crocks that would be useful in your future medical practice. That told me that what students wanted
to maximize in school, not surprisingly, was the chance to learn things that
would be useful when they entered practice. But if that were true, then it
seemed contradictory to devalue crocks, because there were many such
patients. In fact, their teachers, the attending physicians, liked to point out
that most of the patients a physician saw in an ordinary practice would be
like that. So a crock ought to provide excellent training for practice.

When I pursued that paradox, students told me that you might have a lot
of patients like that later on, but you couldn't learn anything from seeing
them here in school. Not what they wanted to learn, anyway. Which was
what? They explained that all their teachers ever said about what to do
with crocks was that you should talk to them, that talking made crocks feel
better. The students felt they had learned that with the first one. Succeeding crocks did not add to their knowledge of crockdom, its differential diagnosis, or its treatment. A crock presented no medical puzzles to be
solved.

What they wanted to learn, students said, was a certain kind of knowledge that could not be learned from books. They studied their books duti-
fully, preparing for the quizzes that punctuated rounds and other such
events, but believed that the most important knowledge they would acquire in school was not in those books. What was most worth learning was
what my colleagues and I eventually summarized as "clinical experience,"

the sights, sounds, and smells of disease in a living person: what a heart murmur really sounded like when you had your stethoscope against a patient's chest as opposed to its sound on a recording, how patients whose hearts sounded that way looked and talked about how they felt, what a diabetic or a person who had just suffered a heart attack looked, even smelled like.

You could only learn those things from people who had real physical pathologies. You learn nothing about cardiac disease from a patient who is sure he's having heart attacks every day but has no murmurs to listen to, no unusual EKG findings, no heart disease. So crocks disappointed students by having no pathology you could observe firsthand. That showed me an important and characteristic feature of contemporary medical practice: the preference for personal experience over scientific publications as a source of the wisdom you used in guiding your practice. We eventually called this the "clinical experience" perspective, and found its traces everywhere. Perhaps most importantly, even faculty who themselves published scientific papers would say, in response to a student's question about something reported in a medical journal, "I know that's what people have found but I've tried that procedure and it didn't work for me, so I don't care what the journals say."

Crocks had other irritating characteristics, which students eventually explained under my barrage of questions. Students, perpetually overworked, always had new patients to work up, classes to go to, books and articles to read, notes to record in patient charts. Examining patients always took time, but examining crocks took forever. Crocks had dozens of symptoms to describe and were sure that every detail was important. They wanted to describe their many previous illnesses in similar detail. Many of them had been able to persuade physicians (who, the students thought, should have been less pliable) to perform multiple surgeries, which they also wanted to describe fully. (I remember a patient who had had so many abdominal surgeries that her navel had been completely obliterated. That made a deep impression on all of us.)

So crocks took much more of your time than other patients and gave you much less of anything you wanted for your trouble. That showed me another important feature of medical school life: everything was a tradeoff of time, the scarcest commodity for a student or house officer, for other valuable things. We found the traces of that proposition everywhere too. For instance, students often traded patients with each other. Why? Well, if

I've had three patients with myocardial infarcts (as I learned, with the students, to call a heart attack) and you've had three patients with diabetes, it's obviously mutually advantageous for us to trade, so that neither of us wastes our time learning the same facts and having the same experiences three times while missing another equally useful set of facts and experiences altogether.

Students disliked crocks, I eventually learned, for still a third reason. Like their teachers, students hoped to perform medical miracles, and heal the sick, if not actually raise the dead. They knew that wasn't easy to do, and that they wouldn't always be successful, but one of the real payoffs of medical practice for them was to "do something" and watch a sick person get well. But you can't perform a medical miracle on someone who was never sick in the first place. Since crocks, in the student view, weren't "really sick," they were useless as the raw material of medical miracles.

We eventually called this attitude the "medical responsibility" perspective, and saw its traces everywhere too. Perhaps its most bizarre (to a layperson) outcropping was the idea that you weren't fully operating as a doctor unless what you did could, if done wrong, kill people. This was enshrined in a put-down of the specialty of dermatology we heard several times: "You can't kill anybody and you can't cure anybody." A more accurate rendition of the general principle involved would have been "You can't cure anyone *unless* you can kill them."

Learning what a crock was was thus a matter of carefully unraveling the multiple meanings built into that simple word, and especially of working out the logic of what was being told to us, finding the major premises on which student (and staff, for that matter) activities were based. The trick here is not dazzling and requires plenty of work, consisting as it does of following out the uses and meanings of terms that seem, when we first hear them, strange and even unintelligible. Making people explain what we don't understand, and checking it against what we see and hear, produces the missing premises in the arguments they routinely make to explain and justify what they do.

This may seem obvious, but sometimes the distinctions people make seem so mundane, so trivial, that we don't pay much attention to them, and thereby lose some analytic grasp we could have had. Some other examples are intraracial terms, the terms Samuel Strong (1946) described in his analysis of social types in the black community in the 1930s ("race man" or "Uncle Tom," etc.); such sex role terms as "sissy," "tom boy," and "tease," some of which Barrie Thorne (1993, 112–19) analyzed in her study of kids in school and on the playground; and the kinds of intra-occupational distinctions found wherever an occupation deals with the public (as doctors, just like the students they once were, distinguish between routine and interesting cases, or janitors distinguish tenants who treat them with respect from those who don't).

"It Isn't (Whatever)"

Researchers often hear people say that something *isn't* something: "That isn't photography"; "That isn't science"; "That isn't Jewish." Those are three obvious and common kinds of "that isn'ts": artistic, epistemological, and ethnic. This formulation, when you hear it, is a good diagnostic sign of someone trying to preserve a privilege, something they have and want to keep and don't want to share with anyone else. You find these statements in writing as well as speech, because they are often made quasi-officially, by the (perhaps self-appointed) representative of some group whose interests seem to be threatened. To understand the sociological import of such a statement, you ask what the situation is in which it is being made, what problems the group whose statement it is are having, what the statement's authors are trying to prevent someone else (whose identity is also to be discovered) from having. One thing you *don't* do is try to decide what it really is, whatever "it" is. That's not a social scientist's business, although many social scientists have thought it was; our business is to watch others try to enforce the ban of something from some prized category, not to decide whether the ban is justified.

This can be understood as an example of George Herbert Mead's notion of objects (at least as expounded in Blumer 1969, 61–77). An object is constituted by the way people are prepared to act toward it; that includes social objects (people, not to be coy about it). So giving names, saying that something is or isn't something, is a way of saying how that thing ought to be acted toward or, if the name sticks, will be acted toward.

I'll explicate one such statement as an example. "That isn't photography" (there are hundreds of examples, historical and contemporary) is typically uttered by conventional art photographers when someone shows them a photograph that seems to "work," successfully communicate something, but is not in a style or mode they use, feel comfortable or identify with, or can do at all. If people in the photographic art world accept this style, what these photographers do, now the conventional norm, will be overthrown or, at least, will have to share whatever there is to share with this new thing. Specifically, a contemporary art photographer who says of some new form of making or exhibiting photographs—such as, let's say, exhibiting photographs in a computer—"That isn't photography" means "I don't want people who do work like that to be able to get a job teaching in a department of photography in a university or art school, I don't want them to be eligible for grants from the Photographic Division of the National Endowment for the Arts, I don't want their work to be exhibited in the places I exhibit or published in the places I publish." This could be labeled as "turf talk," but that doesn't convey the full import of making such a distinction, because what is involved is also a conception of reality. People who say "That isn't photography" have organized their lives, or some part of their lives, around thinking that certain ways of doing and seeing are the "right" ones. It's how they see the world, so someone who does things differently doesn't just interfere with their livelihood, but also challenges their hold on reality, which is what lies behind some of the animus in such remarks (Becker 1982, 305–6).

A special and important version of this kind of line-drawing, and one in which the hold-on-reality element is very strong, is epistemological, as conveyed in "That isn't science." Science, for many academics and intellectuals, refers to something special. To speak of science as distinct from other forms of knowing is to announce as real the possibility of arriving at warranted knowledge of the world that is independent of anyone's beliefs and temperament. The existence of that method is a safeguard against the irrational, which forever threatens to burst out and destroy civilization as we know it today. When scientists denounce a version of their field that threatens them (when, say, there is something like a Kuhnian Revolution, a paradigm shift, going on), they may say that it isn't science. Bruno Latour (1987, 179–213) has analyzed this matter at length in his discussions, following Goody (1977), of the Great Divide, of the supposed gulf between the way "they" (the savages, the nonscientists) think and the way "we" (the civilized, rational, scientific folks) think.

Another version of such line-drawing occurs when someone wants to say that something or someone *isn't* something, in order to prevent it from being treated in a way they don't want it treated. Marijuana, accordingly, is or isn't a narcotic, depending on how you think the government ought to treat it. Marijuana smokers are or aren't addicts, for the same reason.

All of these cases embody the same trick: look for the premise, basic to the argument someone is making, that isn't being stated. Odd words said and odd lines drawn are two clues to the presence of those unstated premises. When you find the unstated premise, ask what in the lives of the people involved makes it necessary or useful for them to make the argument they make, and to keep its major premise to themselves.

OR ELSE WHAT?

A special case of the above trick is useful when the person not stating the full argument is a social scientist. This happens more often than you might think, frequently in association with what is often called "functionalist" analysis. In this kind of theorizing, the researcher looks for how society meets certain invariant and ineluctable physical and, more importantly, social needs. The establishment of a need, and a corresponding social function that therefore must be carried out, looks like a scientific enterprise similar to establishing the need for biological systems to do things like provide nourishment, get rid of waste, and reproduce the organism, and to finding the structures that do those things and explaining their existence by the fact that they do them.

Everett Hughes explained what was wrong with that approach in an essay on "going concerns," a term he used where others might have said "institution" or "organization":

> [T]he dichotomizing of events and circumstances as functional and dysfunctional for systems is likely to be of limited use in the long run; in part, because it may carry the assumption that someone knows what is functional—that is, good for the system; in part, because these are value terms based upon the assumption that there is one right and known purpose for which the system (going concern) exists, and the actions and circumstances which appear to interfere with the achievement of this one purpose are dysfunctional. Argument over purposes, goods, and functions is one of the commonest forms of human discourse and many are the going concerns that thrive upon it, although it is both conceivable and likely that some survive such disputes and actual shifts of purposes better than others. It is quite common to have an annual meeting to decide on the purpose for the year to come. Do we play basketball for the glory of God this year, or destroy communism? I am certainly not suggesting that either purposes

or functions be left out of consideration in study of going concerns; on the contrary, I am suggesting that discovery of them and
their relations to going concerns is another of our chief businesses. ([1971] 1984, 55)

One of the distinctive marks of the approach Hughes was criticizing is
the use of the imperative voice. Social scientists often use the imperative—
locutions like "must" or "will have to"—when they talk about the neces-
sities that shape organized social activity: "every social organization must
take care to limit its boundaries" or "every social organization must control
deviance" or . . . fill in the blank. Using the imperative asserts inevitability.
If an organization or society "must" do something, well, it just "must,"
that's all, nothing to discuss. The implication (sometimes made explicit in
the sterner functionalist tracts) is that otherwise the organization or society will simply cease to exist. An even stronger version of that implication
is that the necessity is a matter of logic, almost a matter of definition. If the
society or organization doesn't do or have the required thing, it won't even
be a real society or organization.

It's a useful trick, when you read or hear those telltale imperative
phrases, to ask this simple question: "Or else what"? Because the source of
the necessity is never as obvious or impervious to questioning as those
statements assume.

Asking "Or else what?" smokes out the conditions under which the
necessity holds. Nothing is ever *that* necessary. It is just necessary if certain
other things are to happen. "An organization must attend to its boundaries." Or else what? "Or else it will get confused with other organizations." All right, organizations sometimes get confused with other
organizations. So what? The world won't come to an end, will it? "If it gets
confused with other organizations, it won't be able to do its work efficiently." I see. Who said it had to do that work? That's the issue Hughes
raised above, speaking of the setting of goals as one form of organizational
activity, not the inexorable working of a law of nature. And who set the
criterion of efficiency by which the work should be evaluated? Those are
serious and, neither incidentally nor trivially, researchable questions. "Not
only that, but its confusion about borders will infect all its neighbors too
and, eventually, the whole society, which will thus not operate efficiently."
OK. Who says the society has to be efficient and that its parts should be
easily distinguished from one another? "If those tasks aren't accomplished,

the society will perish. Look what happened to Rome!" Well, what happened to Rome? Did it disappear? No, it changed. Is that so terrible? "What are you, some kind of a nut?"

The statements of necessity social scientists make are perhaps better understood as ways of focusing on something the authors want everyone to see as a problem. But social problems do not exist independent of a definitional process (Spector and Kitsuse 1977). They are not social problems because it's in their nature to be problems. They are problems because someone, somewhere, experiences and defines them as problems. And it's someone in particular who does that, not some generalized who-knows-who-it-is.

When I say an organization must punish deviance or its norms will cease to be effective, that is, in one sense, just another way of saying that some organizations will have ineffective norms. That statement is by no means equivalent to the proposition—and far less does it constitute a proof of it—that organizations in that condition can't continue to exist. But it is a way of making the problem of the development of ineffective norms seem like something that has to be dealt with, a real *social problem*. Problems, after all, by definition have to be solved. Stating the factual proposition that an organization has ineffective norms or, to put the same requirement in different words, saying that the punishment of deviance is a necessity, makes taking the problem of avoiding a breakdown of norms a given, a precondition of the inquiry. Nothing in the empirical science of sociology, however, requires us to treat the breakdown of norms as something to be avoided at all costs. That's a moral or political commitment that many social scientists might wish to make. Many have made it. It's easy enough, however, to see how other political or moral commitments would lead to the conclusion that strong norms are bad, rather than good. An anarchist, committed to individual freedom, might well conclude just that. In fact, most reform organizations operate on such premises, insisting that something other people think is just dandy and necessary is in fact evil and needs to be done away with.

Theoretically, focusing on one possible outcome—like the breakdown of norms—out of the full range of possibilities makes the rest of that whole range (which we have been at pains to extend and complicate in our consideration of sampling problems) a residual category. If I say that organizations must punish deviance in order to be effective I treat any outcome other than the society being fully effective as a residual category not worth going into. It divides the possibilities into being effective and . . . who cares what else, it doesn't make any difference, it's not effective, therefore it's no good. Q.E.D. But the other possibilities are worth analysis because, after all, many interesting states, worthy of our attention, lie between perfect organizational efficiency and chaos.

Nor is effectiveness, to stick with the example, the only dimension along which we might find it interesting to classify organizations. When analysts choose which outcomes to be interested in they are making a po- litical, not a scientific choice. We needn't be interested in bureaucracies whose functionaries act like minor servants in a feudal barony (the way the men behind the counter at the Cook County Election Commission treated the researcher described in chapter 4), but that lack of interest is not dictated by the requirements of sociology as a science. The political impli- cation of relegating social phenomena to residual categories is that what gets lumped together as "other" isn't worth bothering with. That implica- tion is what has led, for example, people of mixed racial heritage to want to be counted in the U.S. Census not as black or white or Hispanic, but as whatever mixture they happen to be, and certainly not to be set aside as "other." (The Census, as we have already seen, is a place where problems that look strictly methodological reveal their political character, as when the undercount of young black males artificially elevates their "crime rate" by reducing the number of people who belong in the denominator of that fraction.)

Definitional forms of the gambit create similar difficulties. Sometimes analysts using the imperative will say, and may mean, that the point is not that you can't have some other form than perfect efficiency, or survival, but rather that they want to define organizations that are perfectly efficient or that survive as the subject of study. Anything that doesn't have that charac- ter just doesn't interest them. That position is subject to the same com- plaint. Why shouldn't we be interested in a full range of possibilities? Asking that question is not the same as saying that you have to be interested in everything, which is always dismissed as counseling unreachable perfec- tion. It's just saying that you want to deal with the question already raised more completely. "More completely" means adding possibilities so that you can find out more of what goes into the making of a situation or phe- nomenon. The next section describes methods for discovering and adding dimensions to an analysis by the logical manipulation of what we've already learned.

Truth Tables, Combinations, and Types

I've earlier described tricks designed to generate a wealth of varieties and versions of social phenomena. I insisted that the imagery that informs our work be broad enough to recognize all sorts of features of social life, and be constructed in a way that increases the number and variety of features the researcher knows about. It followed that sampling ought to be conducted so as to maximize the possibility of finding what you hadn't even thought to look for. Allowing for this kind of diversity in the features or dimensions we consider is not at all the same as recognizing that some phenomenon varies along a given dimension. Variation and diversity are two different things. I've hinted at, but not really explained, why maximizing diversity is a good thing to do. Now I want to consider the good uses to which you can put the variety of stuff such an approach produces.

But first we have to see why, though some good may come of having all this stuff, managing it is such a problem for social scientists. Lazarsfeld and Barton, authors of one of the solutions to this problem we're going to consider, describe it this way:

> Sometimes the analysis of qualitative observations confronts a mass of particular facts of such great number and variety that it seems quite unworkable to treat them individually as descriptive attributes or in terms of their specific interrelationships. In such a situation the analyst will often come up with a descriptive concept on a higher level which manages to embrace and sum up a great wealth of particular observations in a single formula. . . .
>
> In a study of a village of unemployed in Austria, the researchers made use of a collection of separate "surprising observations." Although they now had more time, the people read fewer library books. Although subject to economic suffering, their political activity decreased. Those totally unemployed showed less effort to look for work in other towns than those who still had some kind of work. The children of unemployed workers had more limited aspirations for jobs and for Christmas presents than the children of employed people. The researchers faced all kinds of practical difficulties because people often came late or failed to appear altogether for interviews. People walked slowly, arrangements for definite appointments were hard to make, "nothing seemed to work any more in the village." (Boudon 1993, 212)

They also describe a familiar solution to this problem that many social scientists have used: the combination of this welter of fact into a summary statement, a type:

> Out of all these observations there finally arose the over-all characterization of the village as "The Tired Community." This formula seemed clearly to express the characteristics which permeated every sphere of behavior: although the people had nothing to do, they acted tired—they seemed to suffer from a kind of general paralysis of mental energies. (Boudon 1993, 212–13)

Charles Ragin, author of another of the solutions to the problem, explains the usefulness of typologies more generally:

> Empirical typologies are valuable because they are formed from interpretable combinations of values of theoretically or substantively relevant variables which characterize the members of a general class. The different combinations of values are seen as representing types of the general phenomenon. . . . Empirical typologies are best understood as a form of social scientific shorthand. A single typology can replace an entire system of variables and interrelations. The relevant variables together compose a multidimensional attribute space [a Lazarsfeldian notion to be discussed shortly]; an empirical typology pinpoints specific locations within this space where cases cluster. The ultimate test of an empirical typology is the degree to which it helps social scientists (and, by implication, their audiences) comprehend the diversity that exists within a general class of phenomena. (Ragin 1987, 149)

The methods I want to consider here complicate and systematize the simple procedure of making types, which fundamentally consists of nothing more than giving a name to a lot of stuff, the name suggesting the proposition that all that stuff goes together in some frequent, perhaps even necessary way (that's what I was talking about earlier in speaking of concepts as empirical generalizations). These methods, which seem superficially quite different, can be seen as versions of one basic procedure, designed to manage and make maximal use of such empirical variety. Each method emphasizes a different part of that procedure, and uses different descriptive language and terms consistent with the different settings in which it arose, but all three work by combining a small number of relevant attributes into a type. The mathematical version is called "combinatorics," the logical version is usually discussed with the help of "truth tables," and social scientists are probably most familiar with the procedure as the "cross-classification of qualitative variables," prototypically the creation of four-fold tables. In whatever form, the idea is to combine what we know in logical ways that tell us more than we knew before.

The social science methods I'll discuss are property space analysis (as described by Paul Lazarsfeld and Allen Barton, singly and jointly), qualitative comparative analysis (the "Boolean Algorithm" introduced to social science by Charles Ragin), and analytic induction (associated with the work of Alfred Lindesmith, Donald Cressey, and others). I'll give some examples of each, with just enough discussion of history and context to make clear how and why their emphases differ. Comparison of the three styles of sociological work suggests that what underlies all three is the use of the classical logical device logicians call a truth table, which exhibits all the possible combinations of some set of properties, to create types.

Art Works and Truth Tables

There are many places to find an explanation of the relatively simple ideas and procedures associated with truth tables. I'll start with the discussion Arthur Danto, the philosopher and art critic, gave of some features of an art world (1964). Danto proposed a form of logical analysis designed for quite different uses than the social science ones we're interested in (or, for that matter, the aesthetic ones he was considering), but which can be adapted to our purposes. Two features of his analysis appeal to me. On the one hand, what he does is philosophically technical; none of the operations, which can seem so straightforward and commonsensical in other descriptions, are, inspected closely, simple at all. That's why his definitions are so prickly. On the other hand, this isn't logic for the fun of it. He went through these operations in order to get to some tough empirical points about judgments of art works. The operations he engages in, in various forms, show us how to squeeze more out of our data, and find more things to study. I'm going to quote him at some length, explaining what's going on in each paragraph as I go along.

Danto begins by talking about "predicates," things you can say about an object ("predicate" of them) that could, in principle, be shown to be true or false. He says that if objects are of a certain kind—eggs, let's say—there will be pairs of these terms (or predicates) such that one of each pair must be true of any egg and both members of the pair can't be true of the same egg. If the object is an egg it is either, we can say, raw or cooked and it can't be both; if it's neither (as a frying pan, for example, would be neither), then, whatever else it might be, it can't be an egg, because all eggs are one or the other. He applies this idea to art works: an object is an art work if at least one of each such relevant pair of opposite properties (which he will get to but hasn't yet, since he is just laying groundwork here) is true of it. There will be many objects of which neither member of such a pair is true, and those objects aren't art works. He says it this way (which will give you a taste of the technical philosophical talk he uses to make his argument):

> I shall now think of pairs of predicates related to each other as "opposites," conceding straight off the vagueness of this *demodé* term. Contradictory predicates are not opposites, since each of them must apply to every object in the universe, and neither of a pair of opposites need apply to some objects in the universe. An object must first be of a certain kind before either of a pair of opposites applies to it, and then at most one and at least one of the opposites must apply to it. So opposites are not contraries, for contraries may both be false of some objects in the universe, but opposites cannot both be false; for of some objects, neither of a pair of opposites *sensibly* applies, unless the object is of the right sort. Then, if the object is of the required kind, the opposites behave as contradictories. If F and non-F are opposites, an object o must be of a certain kind K before either of these sensibly applies; but if o is a member of K, then o either is F or non-F to the exclusion of the other. The class of pairs of opposites that sensibly apply to the (δ) Ko I shall designate as the class of K-*relevant predicates*. And a necessary condition for an object to be of a kind K is that at least one pair of K-relevant opposites be sensibly applicable to it. But, in fact, if an object is of kind K, at least and at most one of each K-relevant pair of opposites applies to it.

This careful and technical way of putting things avoids linguistic traps my looser formulation might fall into; but the loose one is good enough for our purposes here.

Danto then considers the interesting possibility that there are pairs of such opposite terms—he calls them "K-relevant predicates for the class K of artworks"—that no one has ever thought to apply to art works, but that could reasonably be applied to them, and the equally interesting possibility that there are perhaps other pairs of opposite terms of which the people involved in dealing with these works only know one. In that case, not knowing that the opposites of the terms even existed, these people might conclude that the presence of these single attributes were defining characteristics of an art work; they were what made it art. In the first case, no one knows the attribute exists; in the second, everyone knows about it, but can't imagine that an art work might not have it.

> [L]et F and non-F be an opposite pair of such predicates. Now it might happen that, throughout an entire period of time, every artwork is non-F. But since nothing thus far is both an artwork and F, it might never occur to anyone that non-F is an artistically relevant predicate. The non-F-ness of works goes unmarked. By contrast, all works up to a given time might be G, it never occurring to anyone until that time that something might both be an artwork and non-G; indeed, it might have been thought that G was a *defining trait* of artworks when in fact something might first have to be an artwork before G is sensibly predicable of it—in which case non-G might also be predicable of artworks, and G itself could then not have been a defining trait of this class.

This is pretty abstract, and he now puts some art historical meat on the logical bones:

> Let G be "is representational" and let F be "is expressionist." At a given time, these and their opposites are perhaps the only art-relevant predicates in critical use.

"Representational"—the accurate representation of a person or object or landscape—exemplifies something that everyone all along thought so necessary to a work of art that a work that didn't have it wasn't art at all. And "expressionist"—the quality an art work might have of expressing the subjective experience of the artist—exemplifies something no one had until then considered in connection with art works, something that really didn't exist as a possible thought about art works until someone came along and made it important.

> Now letting "$+$" stand for a given predicate P and "$-$" stand for its opposite non-P, we may construct a style matrix more or less as follows:

What he calls a "style matrix" is what I earlier called a truth table: a device that displays the logically possible combinations of the two characteristics "expressionist" and "representational."

Expressionist (F)	Representational (G)
+	+
+	−
−	+
−	−

So a work can have both properties, one or the other, or neither. That exhausts the possible ways of combining the two. These combinations aren't just logical curiosities. Danto created them because they correspond to recognizable artistic styles:

> The rows determine available styles, given the active critical vocabulary: representational expressionist (e.g., Fauvism); representational nonexpressionist (Ingres); nonrepresentational expressionist (Abstract expressionism); nonrepresentational nonexpressionist (hard-edge abstraction). Plainly, as we add art-relevant predicates, we increase the number of available styles at the rate of 2^n.

That is, if we add a third thing an art work can have—say, conceptual content—we add four more possible combinations, because $2^3 = 8$.

Logic doesn't dictate what critical terms can be added to the ensemble. That's up to the inhabitants of the art world. Logic simply says that when you add a new term (or predicate)—a new something that can be said of an art work—you double the number of conceivable types of art works.

> It is, of course, not easy to see in advance which predicates are going to be added or replaced by their opposites, but suppose an artist determines that H shall henceforth be artistically relevant for his paintings. Then, in fact, both H and non-H become artistically relevant for *all* painting, and if his is the first and only painting that is H, every other painting in existence becomes non-H, and the entire community of paintings is enriched, together with a doubling of the available style opportunities. It is this retroactive enrichment of the entities in the art world that makes it possible to discuss Raphael and De Kooning together, or Lichtenstein and Michelangelo. The greater the variety of artistically relevant predicates, the more complex the individual members of the artworld become; and the more one knows of the entire population of the artworld, the richer one's experience with any of its members.

The somewhat surprising result of this analysis is that, when these new predicates or attributes are added by the addition of innovative art works, previous art works acquire properties they never had before.

In this regard, notice that, if there are m artistically relevant predicates, there is always a bottom row with m minuses. This row is apt to be occupied by purists. Having scoured their canvases clear of what they regard as inessential, they credit themselves with having distilled out the essence of art. But this is just their fallacy: exactly as many artistically relevant predicates stand true of their square monochromes as stand true of any member of the Artworld, and they can *exist* as artworks only insofar as "impure" paintings exist. Strictly speaking, a black square by [Ad] Reinhardt is artistically as rich as Titian's *Sacred and Profane Love;* this explains how less is more.

Keep in mind, Danto reminds us, that the absence of some property is not nothing, it's an absence that is a real property of the object that lacks it.

Fashion, as it happens, favors certain rows of the style matrix; museums, connoisseurs, and others are makeweights in the Artworld. To insist, or seek to, that all artists become representational, perhaps to gain entry into a specially prestigious exhibition, cuts the available style matrix in half: there are then $2^n/2$ ways of satisfying the requirement, and museums can then exhibit all these "approaches" to the topic they have set. But this is a matter of almost purely sociological interest: one row in the matrix is as legitimate as another. An artistic breakthrough consists, I suppose, in adding the possibility of a column to the matrix.

Danto ends by tossing off the "almost purely sociological" thought that, whenever the guardians of art world institutions insist on restricting the definition of art by only recognizing one of some set of such alternatives, the number of possible styles the institutions can accommodate is cut by half. That's an interesting, and not obvious, result, and it's the fruit of purely logical operations.

Danto did not produce this analysis just for the joy of making philosophical distinctions. What he describes in abstract language is precisely what happened to art critics and aestheticians when Marcel Duchamp (and his followers and colleagues) appeared in the art world. These artists made works which had none of the qualities by which art works were then known (e.g., they were neither representational or impressionistic), but which yet were accepted by important participants in the contemporary art world as the real thing. The classic instance was Duchamp's snow shovel; he bought a snow shovel at the hardware store and signed it, and so made it into an art work (on the theory that, since he was an artist, anything he signed would be a work of art). Many people thought otherwise, but collectors bought these works, they were exhibited in major museums, and critics wrote serious articles about them. So, in a practical sense, they *were* art. The aestheticians could argue, but the art world had decided. So the crisis for aesthetics was to account for these objects being art when they had none of the things that, to that point, could make something a work of art: no *F,* no *G.* What they had was *H,* a conceptual quality that from then on had to be seen as an essential feature (or predicate) of any art work, whether it was present or absent.

The three methods I'm going to analyze can be expressed in Dantoese. Here's the core of his method. We identify an object as having some characteristic, like height or weight (or being representational or expressive). This leads us to see that all objects (of the relevant kind) have some value of that characteristic, even if it is zero. We never know all the characteristics a thing could have, but only become aware of them when we find an object that has the particular characteristic in some way that differs enough from the way others have it to get our attention. Once we know the characteristic exists, we can see, from then on, that other objects exhibit this trait, although in a different version or degree (at the extreme, in its absence).

The methods I'm going to discuss rest on just such a conception of objects belonging to a common class, each one characterized by some combination of the presence or absence of relevant traits. The class might be Lazarsfeld's analysis of the property space of authoritarian character types, in which the characteristics are the ways authority was exercised and accepted by family members. It might be a class of individuals, studied by Ragin and his colleagues, whose members experience varying degrees of mobility in a government bureaucracy, and the traits of age, seniority, education, and so forth that are associated with those varying outcomes; or a class of strikes, some of which were successful, other not, the traits being the presence of a booming product market, the threat of sympathy strikes, and the existence of a large strike fund; those are examples of Boolean methods. Or it could be, as in Lindesmith's classic study of addiction (1947), one of the examples of analytic induction I'll use, the class of people addicted to opiate drugs, and the traits might be prior experiences that, when present in the right combination, lead to them being in that state. In each case, a truth table generates all the possibilities, which are then combined to make the types the analyst works with.

Each of these methods is a family of tricks for dealing with the complexities produced by the emphasis on finding as much variety as possible and systematically looking for out-of-the-way phenomena. I'll devote most attention to explicating the logic of these methods. The tricks that flow from them are nothing more than the application of these methods in the specific circumstances of a particular research project, so they don't have any special names other than the names of the methods. Don't be fooled; they are still useful tricks, among the most useful we have.

Property Space Analysis (PSA)

Survey researchers get their data by having "respondents" fill out questionnaires, or by having interviewers talk to them and fill the questionnaires out for them. The researchers then know a great many discrete facts about a lot of people: their age, their income, their schooling, their opinions on a variety of subjects. Paul Lazarsfeld and his colleagues routinely used surveys as the basis for their sociological conclusions, in studies of such varied phenomena as the use of radio campaigns to sell U.S. Treasury bonds (Merton 1946), the way voters decided which presidential candidate to vote for (Lazarsfeld, Berelson, and Gaudet 1948), and the organization of the U.S. Army (Stouffer et al. 1949). They so often solved the problem of describing such complex phenomena by constructing typologies that combined or implied many dimensions that Lazarsfeld thought it worthwhile to explore the logic of that operation. He, and others working with him, developed a family of related methods and concepts for the construction of categories, dimensions, and types.

Lazarsfeld saw that characterizations containing so much complexity could leave crucial ambiguities unresolved, so that the resulting analyses were confused and confusing. He also saw, perhaps more importantly for the job of pushing research on to new discoveries, that the logical possibilities implicit in a typology were usually not fully explored, and so left useful hints for continuing empirical work buried.

He adapted the systematic procedures of truth table construction to the solution of the problem of combining separate attributes into types. He defined a way of combining logical possibilities to bring them into a sensible alignment with empirical realities—an operation he called "reduction"—and, conversely, for extracting from ad hoc typologies the attributes out of which the types had been constructed—an operation to which he gave the ungainly label "substruction." To do this, he made use of the idea of a "property space" (which he also referred to as an "attribute space"). We can call the whole scheme and its associated operations "property space analysis" (PSA), although Lazarsfeld himself, as far as I know, never used that term.

PROPERTY SPACES

Lazarsfeld described the basic idea of property spaces in a number of places, often using the same language and giving the same examples (whose unthinking sexism now makes them a little embarrassing):

> Suppose that for a number of objects, several attributes are taken into consideration. Let it be these three: size, beauty, and the possession of a college degree. It is possible to visualize something very similar to the frame of reference in analytic geometry. The X-axis, for instance, may correspond to size; in this direction, the object can really be measured in inches. The Y-axis may correspond to beauty; in this direction the objects can be arranged in a serial order, so that each object gets a rank designation, rank No. 1 being the most beautiful. The Z-axis may correspond to the academic degree; here each object has or has not a degree. The two possibilities shall be designated by plus and minus, and shall be represented arbitrarily by two points on the Z-axis on the two opposite sides of the center of the system. Each object is then represented by a certain point in this attribute space, for instance, by the following symbolism: (66"; 87%; plus). If the objects to be grouped are women in a certain sample, then this particular woman would be 5½ feet tall, would rank rather low in a beauty contest, and would have a college degree. To each individual would correspond a certain point in the space (though not every point would correspond to an individual) . . . each space will, of course, have as many dimensions as there are attributes in the classifying scheme. (Boudon 1993, 212)

In this example, you place each case in a three-dimensional property space. The first property, size, is what is called a continuous variable, one that can be measured numerically. The second, beauty, also measures a variable quality, but one it's not easy to attach a real number to; you just place the cases in an order dictated by how much of that quality they have, and the result is called an ordinal variable. The third, having a college degree, is a simple yes-or-no, what's called a dichotomy. With three dimensions, it's easy to visualize the property space being talked about as a real physical space in which every case would occupy a particular physical spot. Computer programs generate graphic distributions of cases in three-dimensional space in seconds and further the spatial illusion by letting you "rotate" the resulting picture so that you can "see" clusters of similar cases.

It's easy to manipulate cases in the ways Lazarsfeld thought useful when they belong to one of a few categories (in the limiting case, just two), the way the characteristics of art forms did in Danto's analysis; when they are, like beauty or having a college degree in the above example, ordinal variables or dichotomies. Then the property space can easily be represented as a table constructed by cross-classifying those "variables." The cells contain cases characterized by some combination of the variables that make up the analysis. (Continuous and ordinal variables like height or income are usually incorporated into such an analysis by dividing them into a few groups, so that people whose exact income you knew, for instance, might be divided, for convenience, into rich, poor, and in between. These are "categorical" variables. It is always possible to use statistical techniques like correlation, which do not occasion such a loss of information, with such data.)

Robert Merton made this operation (which we might, in his honor, call the four-fold table trick) famous, generating all sorts of types by cross-classifying characteristics divided into a few categories. I used the simplest form myself, in an example that will perhaps be familiar, to construct a typology of deviance. By considering the possible combinations of people who did or did not break some set of rules, and who were or were not perceived as having done so (two dichotomous variables, note), I generated this simple table:

Types of Deviant Behavior

	Obedient behavior	Rule-breaking behavior
Perceived as deviant	Falsely accused	Pure deviant
Not perceived as deviant	Conforming	Secret deviant

I created this typology by laying out the possible combinations of two characteristics, each conceived as having only two possible states, in tabular form.

More generally, the trick is to identify the characteristics you want to use to describe your cases; divide them in whatever way seems appropriate (e.g., more or less, by non-numerical differences like eye or hair color, or by the simple presence or absence of something); and then make a table in which the categories of one characteristic are the headings of the table's rows and the categories of the other are the headings of its columns. Each cell then contains a type logically distinct from those in the other cells. Taken together, the cell entries constitute all the types that can logically exist.

(I could also have represented these ideas as Danto did his, in truth table form:

Follows Rules	Perceived as Deviant
+	+
+	−
−	+
−	−

The top row is the falsely accused type who follows the rules and is accused of not doing so; the second row is the conformist who follows them and is so seen by others; the third row displays the pure deviant, who does not follow the rules and who is so seen by others; and the last row contains the secret deviant, who breaks the rules without anyone knowing it.)

So constructing a table is logically the same as making a truth table in which the types are characterized by pluses and minuses. The tabular method of creating types has some advantages. It provides a physical space in which you can put the names of the types you have generated, as I did for the types of deviance. Better yet, the cells can hold the absolute number of cases that consist of that combination of characteristics, or such information as the percentage of such cases that had some other characteristic; this lets you exhibit three variables in a space made for two. Then the numbers in the cells can be compared and hypotheses evaluated. If I had had the information, I could have compared the percentage of men and women, or blacks and whites, or people over 25 years old or who lived in large cities, in each of the types of deviance, and thus made an interesting test of the idea that there were gender or racial differences in the processes that put people in those cells. This is the kind of analysis survey researchers prefer. That is probably why Lazarsfeld (who was well aware of truth tables and, in fact, even used the device once in the material I'm quoting from) preferred the tabular form.

The great advantage of the procedure, whichever form you use, is that the logic guarantees that there are not and cannot be any types other than those it defines. You might be empirically wrong about what ought to be included in the analysis, in which case your typology would not correspond to anything in the real world. But, if you only considered what you had defined as relevant, the boxes in the table or the rows in the truth table would be all there was.

But since graphical devices are not simple windows on reality any more than words are, there are disadvantages too. Like every form of representing data and ideas, they make some things clear only by obscuring others. The tabular form Lazarsfeld favored makes it hard to put on paper the property space generated by combining continuous variables. Furthermore, though the extension of property space logic to more than three variables is straightforward, the mechanics of the layout quickly get awkward (despite the computer graphic possibilities I mentioned above). One of Lazarsfeld's favorite examples, which involves the three variables of race, education, and nativity treated as simple dichotomies (the kind of data often gathered in a survey), makes this clear. An eight-cell table shows all the possible combinations of these three items, and also illustrates the complexity (still not overwhelming) of the visual representation:

	Native American		Foreign-born	
	White	Nonwhite	White	Nonwhite
College degree				
No degree				

We might want to add, as a fourth variable, urban or rural residence. Lazarsfeld did that in two ways. You can represent that additional variable by putting into each cell, as I've already noted, the proportion of its occupants who lived in cities. Or you can make two tables like the one above, one for urban residents and one for rural. Beyond four variables, such tables are, practically speaking, unreadable. That is, they do not allow readers to do easily what I earlier quoted John Tukey describing as the basic statistical operation: comparing two numbers to see if they are the same or if, on the other hand, one is larger than the other. So the giant tables produced by an analysis that uses several variables are just not analytically useful. (Barton's discussion [1955, 55–56] gives some good examples.)

As we have seen, we can easily convert tables into truth tables, and vice versa. Here is the same set of combinations, this time expressed by Lazarsfeld as a truth table, exhibiting all the possible combinations of the three items, numbered for later discussion, as simple yes-or-nos:

Combination Number	College Degree	White	Native American
1	+	+	+
2	+	+	−
3	+	−	+
4	+	−	−
5	−	+	+
6	−	+	−
7	−	−	+
8	−	−	−

Whether boxes in a conventional table or rows in a truth table, these logically created combinations are the types you can use in further analysis, sure that there cannot be any other types not accounted for (unless, as in Danto's example, a new characteristic is introduced). Notice that, as Danto remarked, every time a new characteristic enters the analysis the number of types doubles, assuming that the new characteristics are all dichotomies; it gets worse if they have more divisions. Conversely, every time you get rid of an attribute, you reduce the number of types by half.

Reduction

Lazarsfeld recognized that generating so many types by cross-classifying variables created difficulties, for which he had a solution. The operation he called "reduction" collapses the different combinations from such a table into one class. Here's how you do it.

Suppose we have generated the above truth table and the typology it embodies. Now we have more types than we think we need (what we need them for is, of course, an important question). Lazarsfeld asks us to consider the three variables outlined above—race, nativity, and education—as three factors that generate varying amounts of social advantage. Since being black (he treats "black" and "nonwhite" as identical, which of course they aren't) is such an enormous and overriding social disadvantage, we can combine all four categories containing the variable "black" (categories 3, 4, 7, and 8) into one class without losing any information. That is, whenever the people assigned to a cell in this table are black, we know (from knowledge we bring to the study from previous experience) that it won't matter that they are native-born rather than foreign-born, nor will it matter what their education is; they will all suffer substantial social disadvantage, no matter how they rank on those variables. We will not lose any information (or, some might say, any predictive value) about social advantage if we combine the four cells containing black people. We can combine the two categories of foreign-born whites (2 and 6) in the same way, and on the same grounds: that being foreign-born is a substantial disadvantage that will make differences in education unimportant as far as social advantage goes. Native-born whites can be usefully distinguished by education, which presumably makes a difference in their social advantage, so we retain combinations 1 and 5 as separate classes. (The example is hypothetical, invented to show off the method; Lazarsfeld knew as well as we do that things are more complicated than that.)

Combining all these categories in this common-sense way reduces eight categories to four classes. We have reduced the number of things to keep track of and lost nothing needed for the analysis we have planned. We have a more manageable typology, but one that still has implicit in it the full set of possibilities the dimensions could produce if we hadn't made the reduction. Lazarsfeld describes three ways of reducing the number of types we have to work with. Although each one makes some difficulties, each is a useful trick for reducing clutter.

Functional Reduction. Some reductions make use of what we already know on some empirical basis, as in the above example.

> In a functional reduction there exists an actual relationship between two of the attributes which reduces the number of combinations. If, for instance, Negroes cannot acquire college degrees [e.g., by law] . . . certain combinations of variables will not occur in actuality. In this way, the system of combinations can be reduced. The elimination of combinations can either be complete or these combinations may occur so infrequently that no special class need be established for them. (Boudon 1993, 161)

So functional reduction involves eliminating two kinds of combinations: those that are not possible, either logically or socially, and those that, occurring infrequently, are irrelevant.

Functional reduction is thus an empirical matter. We decide what cells to combine by seeing how infrequently the combinations in them occur. No sense making room for what isn't there to take it up. But making the list of possible combinations should remind researchers that whether or not there are cases of a particular combination really *is* an empirical question, so they should check out the actual frequencies rather than ignore some combinations on the basis of "what everyone knows." Looking for un-likely cases (of the kind chapter 3 recommended we pursue), a skeptical fieldworker might, via a property space analysis, generate all the logically possible combinations of attributes, and then look especially hard for the combinations common sense says don't happen, those that might be seen as likely candidates for a functional reduction. The combinations might actually exist but be socially "invisible," not socially accepted or recog-nized. In the social system of the Old South embodied in Natchez, Missis-sippi (described in Davis, Gardner, and Gardner 1941), for instance, everyone belonged to one of two color castes, between which there was no legitimate form of mobility (if you were black you couldn't become white, the way a working-class person could become middle-class) or marriage (no child could legitimately be born from cross-caste sexual rela-tions). But a consideration of all the possible racial combinations of parents would alert the investigator to what just nosing around would also have shown: that there are such children, no matter what social logic says. Knowing that might lead a researcher to investigate how real people deal with the social logic of the racial caste system, and what rules they follow in classifying such socially "impossible" offspring.

Arbitrary Reduction.   Arbitrary reduction refers to the assignment of in-dex numbers to different combinations of attributes, usually in order to treat a variety of different specific empirical conditions as equivalent. For instance, in an analysis of housing conditions,

> [s]everal items, such as plumbing, central heating, refrigeration, etc., are selected as especially indicative [of the "quality" of hous-ing], and each is given a certain weight. Central heating and ownership of a refrigerator, without plumbing, might be equiv-alent to plumbing without the other two items, and therefore both cases get the same index number.

In other words, the members of the type have in common an underly-ing abstract quality, like "bad housing," for which you have no immediate and concrete measure. You can arbitrarily invent a score by giving people a point for the presence of a refrigerator or central heating or any other item you think a good indicator of the quality of housing, and then let the resulting scores define your types, even though the actual characteristics of the cases combined in the cell differ. This procedure reduces the number of possible combinations by treating specific items of household equipment as the same. It's "arbitrary" because the items you count are only related to the underlying attribute by a chain of somewhat shaky inferences, and because you could have chosen other items and thereby equalized different combinations of items.

Pragmatic Reduction.   Lazarsfeld cites the example of race, nativity, and education given earlier as an example of a pragmatic reduction, one made in light of the research purpose—in that case, to study social advantage. There might be many good reasons not to lump all blacks together in a sociological analysis, but when it comes to social advantage you might as well. Since being black is, in the analytic terms proposed by Everett Hughes ([1971] 1984, 141–50), a "master status trait" that will override anything else in any other situation, it is decisive for one's social disadvantage. (To repeat, such statements are typically made to provide simple examples for didactic purposes; don't take them as statements about how the world is. James Baldwin once wrote that the only thing worse than being black in America was being poor in Paris.) So, for this particular purpose, you can combine them.

A second example of pragmatic reduction involves combinations of two variables that could affect "marital success." Imagine two attributes, each divided into three ranks (e.g., wife's attitude toward husband and husband's economic success, however those might be measured). Combined in a property space, these produce nine types (that is, there are nine cells in the resulting table, or nine rows in the truth table). Lazarsfeld says:

> Suppose . . . we find that if the wife's attitude toward the husband is favorable, then the economic success will not affect marital relations, whereas, if the wife has a medium attitude toward him, he needs at least medium success to make the marriage a success, and only great success can save the marriage if the wife's attitude is altogether unfavorable. If the problem is to classify all the marriages into two groups—one for which the attitude-success combinations are favorable for good marital relations, and one for which the combinations are unfavorable—the [following] diagram of a reduction would ensue. (Boudon 1993, 161–62)

Six of the nine cells in the table that accompanies this example are shaded to indicate favorable combinations, and three (low success and medium or low attitude, and medium success and low attitude) are shaded to indicate unfavorable combinations. Nine possible combinations of men's success and women's responses to it have been pragmatically turned into two.

Reduction tricks, of whatever variety, turn more categories into fewer, and do so by putting logically distinct combinations into the same class, giving them the same name for analytic purposes.

SUBSTRUCTION

The trick to which Lazarsfeld gave the awkward name "substruction" is the logical converse of reduction. Reduction puts combinations together, in the interest of simplicity. Substruction takes them apart, in the interest of discovery.

Social scientists love to make typologies, but seldom make them logically and so don't always exploit the full richness of what they have made. But remember that typologies and property spaces are logically connected: a typology is a set of names for the cells in a table made by cross-classifying variables, and the cells in such a table are a typology. Lazarsfeld used that logical connection to create a method for finding the dimensions that underlie any ad hoc typology, claiming that "once a system of types has been established by a research expert, it can always be proved that, in its logical structure, it could be the result of the reduction of an attribute space" (Lazarsfeld and Barton 1951, 162). Most typologies were, he thought, probably incomplete; a complex property space had been reduced by combining some of the cells in its table in one of the ways we've just discussed, although the typologist may not have understood that that's what had been done. The resulting typology doesn't name or acknowledge the existence of all of its implicit possibilities. So Lazarsfeld, having explained how you could reduce a set of types, devised a way of undoing the reduction and recovering the full property space and the dimensions that had produced it:

> The procedure of finding, for a given system of types, the attribute space in which it belongs and the reduction which has been implicitly used is of such practical importance that it should have a special name; the term *substruction* is suggested.
>
> When substructing to a given system of types the attribute space from which and the reduction through which it could be

deduced, it is never assumed that the creator of the types really had such a procedure in mind. It is only claimed that, no matter how he actually found the types, he could have found them logically by such a substruction.

Lazarsfeld insisted, correctly, on the practical importance of this trick. It's a wonderful way of milking ideas and insights that were not arrived at logically (so few are) for the rest of what they contain. Using it, a researcher "would see whether he has overlooked certain cases; he could make sure that some of his types are not overlapping; and he would probably make the classification more useful for actual empirical research" (163). He gives, as an example of the utility of substruction, a study of the structure of authority in the family conducted by Erich Fromm.

Fromm distinguished four kinds of authority situations: complete authority, simple authority, lack of authority, and rebellion. Lazarsfeld used items from questions asked of both parents and children to reconstruct the full array of combinations implied in Fromm's ad hoc types. First, he reduced a number of possible combinations of the use of corporal punishment and interference in the children's activities (the measures used as indices of the parental exercise of authority) to three: parents did both, neither, or one or the other (the two being treated as equivalent). He similarly reduced children's acceptance of what parents did to three types, collapsing categories of whether they reported conflict with their parents and whether they had confidence in them. A 3 × 3 table laid out the nine logically possible combinations of exercise and acceptance:

Parent's Exercise   Children's Acceptance

	High	Medium	Low
Strong	1	2	3
Moderate	4	5	6
Weak	7	8	9

Seven of the nine combinations have a clear relationship to Fromm's four types: 1 and 2 are complete authority, 4 and 5 are simple authority, 8 is lack of authority, and 3 and 6 are rebellion. Combinations 7 and 9, however, aren't accounted for in Fromm's typology, and at least one (7) suggests a possibility he apparently hadn't thought of: that some children whose parents didn't exercise much authority wished that they would. Logic suggests the possibility; research sees if it is a reality. That's how you use the trick of substruction.

(Is there only one attribute space and one reduction behind every typology? Probably not, Lazarsfeld says. Since typologies are usually vague and impressionistic, therefore ambiguous, you can usually extract more than one set of dimensions from them. Different attribute spaces originating from the same typology can be transformed into one another; this is the logic of "interpreting a result," his well-known procedure for finding the "meaning" of a relationship between two variables by introducing a third one that increases the relationship between the first two. "Such an interpretation consists logically of substructing to a system of types an attribute space different from the one in which it was derived by reduction, and of looking for the reductions that would lead to the system of types in this new space. This is what transformation means" (167). I won't pursue these possibilities here, but there are some interesting things to be found out.)

Lazarsfeld's use of truth tables and their transformation into tables as a way of creating types, and the close attention he gave to the operations of reduction and substruction as ways of varying the number of types the analyst works with, show the marks of his attachment to survey interviews and questionnaires as the way to gather data. He created typologies, and made them more complicated, using the tricks of tabular construction, reduction, and substruction, in order to discover the relationships between variables measured in a survey. What did living in a Republican neighborhood do to an Irish Catholic worker's propensity to vote for Democrats? If your brothers and sisters voted for Democrats but your fellow workers voted for Republicans, what would you, subjected to such "cross-pressures," do on election day? He found types useful primarily as a way of defining categories that could then be used to get at the relationships between variables. The answers that satisfied him gave "the average effect of a cause in a theoretically defined set of observations" (Ragin 1987, 63). Which is something a lot of social scientists are looking for.

Qualitative Comparative Analysis (QCA)

A lot of other social scientists, however, are looking for something different, and using the analytic procedures associated with conventional survey methods makes problems for them. Charles Ragin developed qualitative comparative analysis (sometimes referred to as "Boolean analysis" for reasons that will become clear) to deal with just such intractable problems in conventional methods of analysis in (a) the handling of large bodies of data that contained relatively few facts about a large number of cases (the typical kind of data produced by surveys and statistics gathered for administrative purposes), and (b) the analysis of a small number of historical cases, especially those involving the history of specific countries and the explanation of specific events in those histories (e.g., under what circumstances did riots occur in countries that receive aid from the International Monetary Fund?).

In the first case, that of data on large numbers, conventional analytic methods produced chronic problems, shrugged off by practitioners as the price of getting any scientific results at all. The typical way of formulating and solving problems depended on developing a statistic that allowed the analyst to estimate something called the "contribution" of a specific independent variable or variables to variation in a dependent variable by a number that varied between 0 and 1. Thus, we might say, to take an example Ragin has used (Ragin, Meyer, and Drass 1984), that race "contributed" x percent to a person's chances of promotion in the federal bureaucracy he and his colleagues studied, while education "accounted for" y percent and seniority z percent (and so on, for the several variables on which data were available),

But these numbers are not intuitively understandable, which is why I put those expressions in quotation marks. To say that education accounts for y percent of promotion says nothing about how this "accounting for" occurs. Should we understand that in y percent of the cases considered for promotion, the decision maker makes education the criterion? Or that the decision maker adds up points—so much for race, so much for education, so much for seniority, and so on—the way teachers give so many points for tests, so many for papers, so many for class participation, and promotes the person if the score is high enough, the points due to education being its "contribution" to the result? Or that there is a complex procedure by which, say, the decision maker first decides whether the candidate meets some criterion on education, and then decides among those who do on the basis of a similar criterion for seniority, and among those remaining on the basis of race, and so on until all the variables have been taken into account? The "accounting for" is purely statistical. Translating the numbers into socially meaningful actions by real people is an imaginative exercise in constructing imagery not often constrained by any serious acquaintance with the situations under study.

Further, the questions these analyses answer are often not the ones people want answers to. Knowing the contribution of particular variables to a distribution of promotions doesn't tell us what combinations of age, gender, race, and other attributes lead to people getting the promotions bureaucratic rules entitle them to, which is what students of ethnic discrimination, for instance, want to know. In such cases, we're looking for configurations of phenomena rather than their individual "contributions" to some result.

In the case of historical analyses, the methods designed for the analysis of large numbers of cases do not work, and often cannot work. There are just not enough countries to produce sufficient cases to satisfy conventional rules of thumb about how many cases must be in a cell before a statistical analysis is acceptable. Nor is it likely, no matter how many countries the former Soviet Union eventually turns into, that there will ever be enough countries for such analyses. The typical solution is to redefine the problem in a more general way that produces sufficient cases but loses the specificity of the original question. (Here and elsewhere in this section I have relied heavily on the arguments and examples in Ragin 1987 and Ragin, Meyer, and Drass 1984.)

Furthermore, historical analyses are often concerned with understanding specific events, usually events about which prior historical research has already uncovered a great many facts: the Russian Revolution, the Great Depression of 1929, the influence of Protestantism on the development of science. Many of sociology's classical problems take this form. The full detailed knowledge of these events that is already available is an embarrassment for conventional analytic techniques, because there are no good methods for handling so many variables, time sequences, and the like. What we want are techniques that let us use the full knowledge we have.

More fundamentally, the methods of qualitative comparative analysis embody a way of thinking about the work of social science that differs substantially from what Ragin calls "variable oriented" methods of analysis, which treat theories, as I've explained, as statements about the relative importance of variables as explanations of some result we want to account for. The explanations are meant to be universal, sociological laws of great generality, the variables exerting their influence independently of social or historical context. In this view, you do research by creating a "data contest" in which the rival interpretations of a social phenomenon, represented by their favorite variables, slug it out, the winner being the one (or ones) that account for most of the variation in the thing to be explained. Perhaps most importantly, these approaches look for one answer to the explanatory problem when the events to be accounted for may in fact arise from any of several combinations of causal conditions. Ragin says:

> Instead of asking questions about relatively narrow classes of phenomena (about types of national revolts, for instance), they [social scientists] tend to reformulate their questions so that they apply to wider categories (such as questions about cross-national variation in levels of political instability). Instead of trying to determine the different contexts in which a cause influences a certain outcome, they tend to assess a cause's average influence across a variety (preferably a diverse sample) of settings. (Ragin 1987, vii)

Ragin did not want to do away with conventional multivariate statistical analysis, but he did want to provide alternatives better suited to some of the problems social scientists want to solve. He found the tools for constructing those alternatives in the algebra of sets and logic, often referred to as Boolean algebra (after George Boole, the nineteenth-century British mathematician and logician who developed it). Constructing truth tables of the kind we have already discussed is fundamental to this algebra; in fact, it's from this algebra that they originated. I will give only the sketchiest version of these matters, just enough to make the underlying logic of the method clear enough to be compared to the others we're considering. Ragin's writings contain several descriptions of the method and a number of examples of its applications. He and his colleagues have used it to study, among other things, riots in Third World countries (Walton and Ragin 1990), patterns of discrimination in employment (Ragin, Meyer, and Drass 1984), and the politics of ethnicity (Ragin and Hein 1993). The material is just technical enough that a good way to get a thorough understanding is to work through one or more of the examples yourself. Of the three methods we're considering in this section, this is the most clearly "logical."

The method preserves the complexity of the situations underlying phenomena of interest while simplifying them as much as possible. It does that by discovering the smallest number of combinations of variables (remember that a combination of variables is a type) that produce (occur in conjunction with) the outcomes to be explained. As a result,

> the relations between the parts of a whole are understood within the context of the whole, not within the context of general patterns of covariation between variables characterizing the members of a population of comparable units. . . . [C]ausation is understood conjuncturally. Outcomes are analyzed in terms of intersections of conditions, and it is usually assumed that any of several combinations of conditions might produce a certain outcome. . . . Multivariate statistical techniques start with simplifying assumptions about causes and their interrelation as variables. The method of qualitative comparison, by contrast, starts by assuming maximum causal complexity and then mounts an assault on that complexity. (1987, x)

Boolean methods resemble property space analysis in interesting ways, though they are quite different from it, and I will occasionally comment on similarities and differences between the two.

Procedures

The basic steps of a Boolean analysis are simple (I'll give a brief example shortly):

1. Decide what outcomes you want to investigate, and what "variables" you will use to "explain" them.
2. Define each variable or outcome as a categorical variable, typically as the presence or absence of some element. You can treat them as simple dichotomies (e.g., white or nonwhite) or treat each of several possibilities as a presence or absence of one of the categories of the variable (white or nonwhite, black or nonblack, Asian or non-Asian, etc.). (There are ways of transforming continuous numerical data into such categories, which are not unique to this method.)
3. Make a data matrix, a table whose rows and columns provide cells for all the combinations of those variables. This form, standard for quantitative data, is easily adapted to qualitative data.
4. Reformat the data matrix as a truth table that lists all the possible combinations of the presence or absence of these attributes.

5.   Differences between two situations that do not affect the outcome to be explained can't be the reason the situations differ, so we needn't worry about them. An example: if some labor unions whose membership is predominantly of one race conduct successful strikes and other unions whose membership is substantially multiracial also conduct successful strikes, whether the union's membership is uni- or multiracial can't be a cause of a strike's success. This being the case, an analyst can "minimize" the truth table, using the following rule: "If two Boolean expressions [i.e., combinations of values of the variables and outcomes] differ in only one causal condition yet produce the same outcome, then the causal condition that distinguishes the two expressions can be considered irrelevant and can be removed to create a simpler combined expression."

6.   Use a systematic procedure (an algorithm) described in Ragin's text to find the "prime implicants," the smallest number of combinations of variables necessary in order to construct an adequate explanation of the outcomes, removing those that aren't logically necessary. I won't describe the technique here; it's fully described in Ragin's book and elsewhere, and he and his colleagues have written a computer program that does the job for you. It's only necessary to understand that the result is an algebraic expression that lists the combinations of presence or absence of variables that will "cover" (explain) the outcomes you're interested in.

7.   Interpret the resulting equation, which is quite easy: for example, Outcome X occurs when variables A and B and either variable C or D are present, or some similar expression of the several combinations of variables or their absence that accompany the outcome of interest. (Among other things, as Ragin explains [1987, 99–101], the equation makes it easy to identify and distinguish the necessary and sufficient causes of what you're interested in.)

Ragin gives a hypothetical example (for details see 1987, 96ff.) of a study in which the analyst considers three causes of successful strikes: a booming market for the industry's product, represented by $A;$ a serious threat of sympathy strikes by other unions, represented by $B;$ and a large union strike fund, represented by $C.$ He codes strikes as successful (S) or not. (The absence of a condition is denoted by a lower-case letter, so an unsuccessful strike is coded as *s* and the absence of a large union strike fund, for example, is coded as *c*.) Of the eight possible combinations of the presence or absence of the three causes (Abc, aBc, abC, ABc, AbC, aBC, abc, ABC), only four (in this hypothetical example) lead to successful strikes (AbC, aBc, ABc, ABC). That is, to give these abstractions back their names, strikes are successful when there is a booming market and a large strike fund but no threat of sympathy strikes, when there is neither a booming market nor a large strike fund but there is a threat of sympathy strikes, and . . . work out the other two yourself, it's good for you.

The algebra allows a simplification of the solution. Without going into the mathematical details, the equation can be reduced to three situations (AC, AB, and Bc). Those can in turn be further reduced algebraically to S = AC + Bc, which means that successful strikes occur when there is a booming market and a large strike fund *or* (plus does not mean addition in Boolean notation, but rather the logical operator OR) when there is a threat of sympathy strikes and a low strike fund. Another manipulation, which I won't go into, allows you to specify the conditions under which strikes fail.

This may all seem pretty abstract and frighteningly mathematical, but the algebra is in fact simple, easy enough for me to follow and therefore nothing for anyone to be afraid of, and the applications to real data are easy; Ragin gives many examples (which, as with anything mathematical, it pays to work out for yourself). The things that might seem difficult—what do you do when cases that share a combination of causes have different outcomes? what do you do when the world does not produce real-life examples of some of the combinations?—have workable solutions (for which I again refer you to the book).

A Different Way of Thinking

QCA shares so many features (like the use of truth tables and their analogs) with PSA that the two might seem to be only slightly different versions of the same thing. Not so. As Ragin points out repeatedly, the methods look for different results, and have a different image of the goals of social science, of the kinds of answers being looked for. In some (but not all) ways, it's a different paradigm.

Causes. Boolean research views causality in a markedly different way than conventional quantitative research, in which researchers look for a variable's effect on other variables across a wide variety of situations. A successful conventional project produces an equation that explains how much of a strike's successful outcome is due, respectively, to the three variables of booming market, threat of sympathy strikes, and large strike fund. The researchers don't expect that equation to vary from strike to strike. If the variables' effects vary across situations, they are undependable and the researcher doesn't have a result.

Boolean researchers, on the other hand, do not expect causes to operate independently of one another in that way; rather, they expect to see their effects vary, depending on the presence or absence of other factors, on the context they are at work in. Explanations are typically "multiply conjunctural": conjunctural in that causes are understood as combinations of factors, and multiple in that many such combinations might produce the same result. Boolean researchers expect to find more than one major causal pathway, more than one set of conditions under which the outcome to be explained occurs. Different factors may well combine in different, sometimes contradictory ways to produce similar outcomes. Since you may not have investigated all the conditions necessary for a complete explanation, your explanation may not account for all the cases.

Consider the problem of opiate addiction. It is a common finding in late-twentieth-century American cities that opiate addicts (in the late twentieth century, of course, the opiate is heroin) are male, young, black or Hispanic, and urban dwellers. These relatively stable findings are cited as evidence of a connection between addicts' age, sex, ethnicity, and habitat, considered as causes, and their addiction, taken as the consequence. The connections are explained in a way consistent with the imagery of the lives of such people held by researchers—an imagery, remember, with no grounding in experience and based largely on the fantasies of middle-class researchers about lower-class life. That imagery suggests that, in the desperate circumstances of such lives, people eager for the "escape" drugs provide follow an inexorable path to addiction.

Alfred Lindesmith (1965) found a major problem with that theory: in the latter half of the nineteenth century, addiction correlated with a very different set of demographic characteristics. Addicts then were typically white women, often from small towns or farms, and middle aged. The difference is easily explained as a consequence of what kinds of people found drugs easily available to them. At that period in American history, the government exercised little control over the distribution of opiate drugs. Patent medicines, and especially those concocted for "women's complaints," the then common euphemism for the difficulties sometimes associated with menopause, often contained hefty doses of opium, and anyone could buy them at the corner drugstore. Women did buy them and take them. Some took enough, often enough, to become addicted.

In 1911, the U.S. government passed the Harrison Narcotics Act, which effectively removed opiate-containing medications from the legal market. Women who could no longer buy their medicine at the corner store sometimes found an accommodating doctor to write a prescription; more often they just suffered the troubles of withdrawal, attributing them to the menopausal problems that had led them to take opiates in the first place.

Over the years following the passage of the Harrison Act, an underground market developed and found its natural home in neighborhoods that could not defend themselves against the intrusion of the narcotics business. Not surprisingly, those were usually neighborhoods in which blacks and Hispanics lived. Since the drug traffic was illegal, the people who engaged in its distribution end were likely to be males in their late teens and early twenties—not old enough to be middle managers, but just the age at which criminality most often occurs. And, if you are in distribution, or if the distribution is occurring in the streets and apartments all around you, you have easy access to drugs and can indulge whatever curiosity what you see might provoke in you, and that is a crucial step in the process of addiction.

So such "causes" of drug addiction as age, sex, race, ethnicity, and urban dwelling are highly variable in their effects, considered historically, and depend for their causal impact on being one element in a conjuncture of factors. It's the combination, the conjuncture, that's causal, not the individual factors each adding its little push to your score on addiction-proneness. It's being a woman of menopausal age in the United States *when* anyone could buy that "medicine" easily; or being a young, black man *in* a very poor neighborhood *when* the laws had turned the distribution of drugs into an illegal business in which you or your neighbors might find a job. These quite different conjunctures can produce the same result: addiction. Put more generally, and in slightly different language, different conditions may satisfy the same causal requirement. Alternatively, you could say that some more general characteristic—like availability—lay beneath the superficial demographic ones that didn't, after all, explain the variations in addiction.

Ragin describes such problems as involving "illusory differences":

[I]dentification of underlying commonalities often does not involve a simple tabulation and analysis of common characteristics. Investigators must allow for the possibility that characteristics which appear different (such as qualitatively different systems of [availability]) have the same consequence. They are causally equivalent at a more abstract level . . . but not at a directly observable level. Thus, there may be an "illusory difference" between two objects that is actually an underlying common cause when considered at a more abstract level. (1987, 47)

Deviant Cases.   QCA and PSA also differ in the way they deal with "deviant cases." A deviant case (an expression that plays a prominent part in the discussion of analytic induction below) is one that doesn't do what the analyst thought and predicted it would, and thus challenges the conclusions he or she would like to make. You do your research, gather your data, and most of the cases "come out right," but a few don't and they cast doubt on the conclusion all the other cases support. In the typical survey analysis, the kind out of which and for which PSA was developed, when a theory links two variables as cause and effect, the cells in the table that contain the combinations of values specified by the theory should contain all the cases, while the cells with the other combinations are empty. (Because of the way tables are set up, the predicted and expected cases are said to "lie on the main diagonal;" in a truth table they would be described by those rows the researchers expected to contain all the cases.) Conventional quantitative researchers accept such deviant (or "negative") cases as an expectable consequence of the random variation characteristic of the world, or of an inevitably less than perfect measurement of their variables, or as due to the action of variables that weren't included in the analysis because no one knew how to measure them or because no one knew they existed or played any part in the problem. Searching for missing variables (along with attempts at improved measurement) is what researchers in this tradition do in later phases of their research. But they do not expect all the deviant cases to ever disappear, and they are perfectly content with probabilistic statements that say, for instance, that children from broken homes are more likely, to such-and-such a degree, to be delinquent than children from intact families. That some children from intact families are delinquent and some from broken homes are nondelinquent doesn't disconfirm the basic proposition relating the two variables, as long as most of the children exhibit the combination the analyst's theory specifies.

Boolean analysts, on the other hand, work toward the discovery of relationships in which the same conjunctures of factors always produce the
same result, relationships to which there are no exceptions, no deviant
cases. They intend eventually (well, one of these days) to account for, have
an explanation of, every case of the phenomenon under study. In their attempt to uncover these invariant relationships, they hope and expect,
along the way, to find "deviant cases," which will constitute the growing
edge of the analysis. Boolean investigators focus on the theoretically unexpected case, because they expect it to lead them to some new, as yet un-
foreseen, pattern of causes and consequences. The result they look for is
what we might call patterned diversity: a complex of related types growing
out of a network of causes operating in different ways in different situations. (A good example is the network of causes, conditions, and consequences of culture in men's and women's prisons, discussed in chapter 4.)
They look for more conditions to add to the explanatory formula, and
more kinds of outcomes to add to the list of what's to be explained.

As a result, they often do something strictly forbidden to serious survey
researchers (although often done in practice): they decide that the deviant
case they have discovered is not an exception to their theory, but a hitherto
unsuspected phenomenon that deserves and will get its own category.
(We'll see this move again when we consider analytic induction.) Researchers often realize, in the course of their work, that some of the things
they thought belonged in the category they wanted to explain don't belong there. They differ from the other things in that category in some important way. Prompted by an unexpected term that has turned up in their
Boolean equation, they decide that perhaps all successful strikes are not
alike. Conventional researchers are likely to insist that when such a thing
happens, it's just too bad, you cannot recategorize the offending cases and
restate the hypothesis so that it works. These ascetics insist that, confronted
with such results, you must gather new data from a new sample before you
can take advantage of your insight. Such an unrealistic requirement would,
of course, put an end to qualitative historical research, because there is no
gathering a new sample, and would make studies like Lindesmith's, based
on interviews with hard-to-find addicts, impossible in any practical sense.
More to the point, it treats as a sin what is actually a major scientific virtue:
the willingness to revise your thinking in the light of experience, the dialogue of evidence and ideas Ragin (1987, 164–71) puts such emphasis on.

Another consequence of the attempt to model the complexity of social life: Boolean analysts don't worry much about the numbers of cases in the different cells of the table. If the theory says young black men should be addicts and some aren't, while some middle-aged white women were, it makes no difference how many of each you've found. One is as good as a hundred for demonstrating that a theory has not taken account of some important possibility. Thus, Ragin points out,

> notions of sampling and sampling distributions are less relevant to this approach because it is not concerned with the relative distributions of cases with different patterns of causes and effects. More important than relative frequency is the *variety* of meaningful patterns of causes and effects that exist. (Ragin 1987, 52)

For its full effect, then, this approach requires the kind of sampling for the fullest variety of cases we discussed in chapter 3.

Analytic Induction (AI)

Many researchers do not aim to explain such a wide range of potential outcomes as PSA and QCA try to explain. They are interested not in all the byways and possibilities, but in one particular result they consider, for theoretical or practical reasons, the only really interesting outcome. Put in the language we've been using, that means the researcher really only cares about a few rows of the truth table (in the limiting case, and often enough in practice, just one row). They put the other combinations truth table analysis sensitizes you to in a residual category of "what we aren't interested in." Researchers and theorists often do this when they see the phenomenon to be explained as an "important problem," either because it is something everyone in the society cares about or ought to, or because it has a special theoretical priority. Drug addiction satisfies both these requirements. It is both a long-standing "social problem" and an interesting example of something people persist in doing in the face of considerable hardship and strong penal sanctions. So it is an affront both to the mores of the society and to all the theories according to which addicts should have long ago quit.

The method some sociologists have used to deal with questions like that is called "analytic induction," and it's no accident, as people like to say, that the canonical example of AI concerns that topic. AI is usually seen as antithetical rather than complementary to the other methods we've just considered. It isn't ordinarily understood as involving truth tables. But it in fact resembles PSA and QCA in ways that will become clear when we lay out its logic in truth table terms. (A major exception to the conventional view is Charles Ragin's analysis [1994, 93–98] of Jack Katz's [1982] study of the careers of "poverty lawyers." Ragin and I think alike on these matters, and you should consult his analysis in conjunction with this section.)

Robert Cooley Angell (1936) is sometimes credited with the first use of AI in sociological research, but the genealogy of the method extends back to John Stuart Mill and his method of agreement and indirect method of difference (you'll find a simple explanation of these in Ragin 1987, 36–42). The more immediate ancestors are George Herbert Mead and his interpreter Herbert Blumer, both of whom emphasized the importance of the negative case, the instance that falsifies your hypothesis, as the key to advancing scientific knowledge. The essential argument is that finding out that your ideas are wrong is the best way to learn something new. (See Mead 1917; Lindesmith 1947, 12.)

"Classical" analytic induction is exemplified in Alfred Lindesmith's (1947) study of opiate addiction, which I've already talked about elsewhere in this book. Cressey (1953) and Becker (1963) used his example as the model for their studies of embezzling and marijuana use. Each of these three studies explains the one specific outcome of interest—opiate addiction, the criminal violation of financial trust, using marijuana for pleasure—by describing the steps of a process that produces that result. The explanation of the outcome is, just as in QCA, invariant: it applies to every case that fits the definition of the phenomenon to be explained.

When you do analytic induction, you develop and test your theory case by case. You formulate an explanation for the first case as soon as you have gathered data on it. You apply that theory to the second case when you get data on it. If the theory explains that case adequately, thus confirming the theory, no problem; you go on to the third case. When you hit a "negative case," one your explanatory hypothesis doesn't explain, you change the explanation of what you're trying to explain, by incorporating into it whatever new elements the facts of this troublesome case suggest to you, or else you change the definition of what you're going to explain so as to exclude the recalcitrant case from the universe of things to be explained. Researchers usually rule out many cases this way and, once they have redefined them as not the kind of thing the theory is trying to explain, more or less ignore them. These two possibilities are the same ones Ragin suggests are available to users of Boolean methods.

The method, in the form I've just described, works very well in the kind of research exemplified by the three canonical examples I mentioned, in which the researcher studies some form of behavior conventionally labeled as deviant by interviewing, one at a time, people thought to have behaved that way. You can see the connection if you imagine trying to use this method with survey interviews. In a survey, you gather your data all at once, or nearly so, and you cannot vary what you ask and how you ask about it without losing the comparability of cases gathering them simultaneously makes possible. Gathering data an interview at a time, on the other hand, makes it easy and natural to discover new variables (which, in this style of research, more often appear as "steps in a process" than as "variables"), explore their import, and look for their operation in successive cases. It similarly makes it easy to deal with those variations in the phenomenon itself that merit being treated as separate theoretical entities requiring their own explanation.

The strong point of PSA is as a method for creating and analyzing types by manipulating logical possibilities. The strong point of QCA is its emphasis on conjunctural explanation, the search for combinations of elements that produce unique and invariant results. The strong point of AI is as a method for discovering what has to be added to or subtracted from an explanation so that it will work.

Researchers seldom use AI in its classical form, because it seems to be suitable only for this very limited class of research questions relating to processes of deviance. You could say that for those problems it is the method of choice. But saying that makes the method seem useless for anything other than these specialized cases. In fact, in slightly less "rigorous" and single-minded versions, it is widely used, especially by researchers who want to describe and analyze such processes as the breakup of couples (Vaughan 1986) and researchers who want to study the complexes of organized activity, which have been variously called "institutions" or "organizations" or (Everett Hughes's version) "going concerns." Ethnographers commonly use the basic logic of AI to develop descriptions of parts of organized activities and their interconnections. In this less rigorous form, AI is ideally suited to answering "How?" questions, as in "How do these people do X?" The X to be explained might be a system of land tenure in an agricultural community, a system of work relations in a factory, the organization of a school, or any of the other problems students of social organization concern themselves with.

Rigorous Analytic Induction

Opiate Addiction. Alfred Lindesmith, a student of Herbert Blumer (whose views on research I discussed in chapter 2) and Edwin Sutherland (the criminologist whose invention of the concept of white-collar crime I also discussed), created the model later practitioners of AI imitated. In his dissertation, eventually published as a book titled *Opiate Addiction* (1947), Lindesmith analyzed his interviews with "from sixty to seventy [morphine and heroin] addicts" with whom he worked over a number of years. He relied as well on cases and materials from the published literature on drug addiction. He aimed

> to understand and provide a rational theoretical account of the behavior of opiate addicts, and to avoid making moral or ethical judgments concerning the conduct of the addict. The central theoretical problem of the investigation is posed by the fact that some persons who are exposed to addiction and experience the effects of morphine or heroin become addicted, while others under what appear to be the same conditions escape addiction. The attempt to account for this differential reaction leads, as will be seen, to a consideration of the essential characteristics of addiction as well as of the conditions of its origin. (Lindesmith 1947, 5)

He developed his theory in response to (in dialogue with, Ragin would say) what he learned from the people he interviewed, and he revised it every time something in his case materials showed him it was incorrect or incomplete.

Lindesmith's theory of addiction asserts that people become addicts by going through a three-step process (I discussed this theory briefly in chapter 3). They first take a large enough amount of some opiate drug over a long enough time to develop physiological habituation—that is, until their bodies have adapted to the continued presence of the drug so that its presence is necessary for the person to function normally. Then, for whatever reason (lack of availability or a decrease in their interest in the experience, for instance), they stop taking the drug and quickly develop withdrawal distress, a characteristic combination of symptoms running from unpleasant (runny nose and other flu-like symptoms) to severely upsetting (muscle cramps, inability to concentrate), though seldom as dramatic as the version Frank Sinatra made famous in the movie version of

Nelson Algren's "The Man With The Golden Arm." (Lindesmith [1947, 26–28] summarizes these effects.) Finally, they interpret their withdrawal symptoms as due to not having taken drugs, and they interpret themselves as having become addicts, which they understand to mean that from now on they will require routine injections of drugs to be in a normal physical and psychological state. Then they act on this new understanding of themselves by taking another shot and thus relieving their symptoms. At this point they begin to engage in the "normal" behavior of an addict, which is to do whatever their situation makes necessary to guarantee that they are never without a supply of drugs sufficient to keep them from experiencing withdrawal again. They don't always succeed—they often do go through withdrawal—but they certainly try.

Lindesmith's theory says that anyone who goes through those three steps will be an addict, and no one will be an addict who has not gone through them. All his cases support the theory, and in his book and throughout his life he challenged critics to produce a negative case that would force further revision of the theory. No one ever produced such a case (it's not clear that his critics ever tried very hard to do that), even though the theory was widely contested and criticized.

The final theory was different in some respects from the one he started with. His research did not simply consist of checking out his ideas against the facts and seeing if he was right or not. Interviewees sometimes turned themselves into "negative cases" by telling Lindesmith something that showed that the current version of his theory was wrong. For example:

> [T]he second hypothesis of the investigation was that persons become addicts when they recognize or perceive the significance of withdrawal distress which they are experiencing, and that if they do not recognize withdrawal distress they do not become addicts regardless of any other conditions.
>
> This formulation . . . did not stand the test of evidence and had to be revised when cases were found in which individuals who had experienced withdrawal distress, though not in its severest form, did not use the drug to alleviate the distress and never became addicts. (Lindesmith 1947, 8)

When he found such negative cases, Lindesmith either changed the theory (as in the above instance) or, more controversially, redefined what he was trying to explain. That meant that, as he did the research, he sometimes discarded negative cases by deciding that they were not, after all, cases of addiction as he was coming to understand it. There was an intimate and continuing dialogue between what he was finding out and how he defined what he wanted to explain.

Lindesmith also tested his theory by checking implications you could logically derive from it against data in the literature. His theory, for example, assigns a crucial role to consciousness and the ability to engage in causal reasoning. The prospective addict must be able to reason that his distress is caused by lack of the drug. If you don't understand the concept of causality and so can't make if-then connections, you can't make a causal inference like that. Therefore, he reasoned, children too young to engage in causal reasoning (according to Piaget, for instance) and animals (who, we suppose, also can't reason causally, though this is less clear) should not be capable of becoming addicts. His reading of the literature in psychology and medicine showed him that children (for example, infants born to addicted mothers) and animals (who were the subjects of laboratory experiments on addiction) did become physically habituated. But children and chimpanzees never become addicts who engage in the kind of conduct human addicts do.

Lindesmith's theory of addiction was politically controversial (as he later explained—see Lindesmith 1965). The Federal Bureau of Narcotics and physicians from the Public Health Service hospital for addicts in Lexington, Kentucky thought it was wrong, since it seemed to suggest that addiction was not the product of a weak or criminal personality but rather could happen to anyone. That in turn could lead what they thought of as an ignorant and unwary public to the conclusion that the best way to deal with the "problem" of addiction would be to let physicians prescribe drugs for addicts, and the federal agencies were adamantly opposed to that, pretty much on moral grounds (Lindesmith 1965).

Politically controversial conclusions are often attacked on methodological grounds. I won't repeat the earlier discussion of the criticisms of Lindesmith's work based on sampling considerations. What's relevant to our topic here are criticisms of how he defined the object of his study. How does a researcher do that? Is it OK to change, in midstream, the definition of what you're studying and what constitutes a case of what you are going to explain? Conventional practice says no, you can't do that.

Lindesmith thought you not only could, but should. He thought, when he began his research, that the then current idea of an addict was ill defined, arbitrary, and not based on real knowledge of the process of addiction or the world of addicts. He therefore saw his research problem as not merely to understand *how* people became addicts or what "caused" addiction, but also to sharpen the definition of what an addict and addiction *were*. If that meant changing his mind about what he was studying while he was studying it, fine. In both its classic and later versions, AI always involves just such a mutual clarification of the conceptual solution to a research problem (e.g., how do people get to be addicts) and the definition of what constitutes the problem and its embodiment in real life (e.g., how to define an addict and addiction).

This is the same dialogue of data and image, you will recognize, that Ragin (1994, 93–100) insists on as essential to Boolean methods, in which researchers simultaneously redefine what is being studied while refining their understanding of its explanation. You can see the similarity between the two in Ragin's descriptions of them. He says that "analytic induction is used both to construct images and to seek out contrary evidence because it sees such evidence as the best raw material for improving initial images" (94) and similarly describes how, when we use Boolean methods, "Evidence-based images emerge from the simplification of truth tables in the form of configurations of conditions that differentiate subsets of cases" (130).

Let's put what Lindesmith did in truth table terms. When you change the theory you are using to explain the outcome of interest, you add a new factor or variable or step-in-the-process to the list of causes. That, in turn, means that you add a new column, which can contain a plus or minus, to the truth table. That doubles the number of rows in the table, the number of possible combinations of all those factors. And that means that every case—both the new one that caused the change and all those that came before—now has to be seen as having some value of that quality. When some addicts told him they had had withdrawal symptoms but had not taken another injection to relieve them, he added a column, labeled "took a shot for relief," in which every case could have a plus or minus.

When you get rid of a case, or class of cases, on the other hand, you do two things. You add a new variable to the list that describes outcomes of the process, which has the same consequence as adding a new possibility to the list of causes: a new column in which to put pluses or minuses to describe each case. And then, having defined this new column, you get rid of every combination that has a plus in it. You've defined your negative case out of the universe of what you're obliged to explain.

The basic procedure of AI, then, is to reduce the truth table to one row, which contains all the cases of the outcome to be explained and has pluses in all the columns. All the other combinations are considered irrelevant and uninteresting. Not because they aren't interesting from some point of view, but if what you want to do is explain one particular outcome, like opiate addiction, the others aren't worth going into. Or, at least, it can seem that way. In fact, a lot of other material is necessary to make that row intelligible, and that's where problems arise for a strict version of AI.

Lindesmith's work displayed those problems. He found the explanation he was looking for, a universal theory of opiate addiction, and it is true that it has never been successfully challenged. But he paid a price. He was expert on many other aspects of addiction, especially the interplay of legal and cultural definitions of the drug on the one hand and the correlates of addiction on the other. But his rigorous and exclusive adherence to the procedures of AI meant that he had no way of talking, in the logically compelling way he had dealt with the addiction process, about many things he knew a lot about. The truth table kind of logic that worked for that process wouldn't handle the more complex network of collective activity that was the world of drugs and law enforcement. And that's a problem for this way of working: how to preserve the virtues of the logic while giving full weight to the complexities of social organization?

Embezzling.   Donald Cressey, a student of Lindesmith and Sutherland at Indiana University after World War II, was another early advocate of AI. His dissertation, later published as *Other People's Money* (1953), is a study of embezzling. Perhaps it's better to say that he intended to investigate "embezzling," but soon ran into serious data collection problems that caused him to redefine what he was studying. Those problems, and his solutions, give us another view of the uses of truth table analysis in its AI form.

Drug addiction, Lindesmith's topic, is very much a group activity. The world of addicts includes friendship circles, markets, and systems of mutual help. Junkies know one another, and can introduce a researcher they take a liking to to other people who can be interviewed. Embezzling, however, is a solitary, secret activity. Neither a commonly indulged vice nor a professional form of crime, it creates no social world of peers and colleagues, so the embezzler you find and interview doesn't know any other embezzlers to refer you to. Finding one addict (or, say, one professional thief) opens the door to finding many more; when you find one embezzler, that's all you've found, and the hunt has to begin anew.

So the only way Cressey could find embezzlers to interview was to go to jails and interview people who had been convicted of that crime. That didn't create as serious a sampling problem as it would have in the case of some other crimes. There's reason to think that, say, burglars who are in jail are not a random selection from the pool of all burglars, but rather consist of the people who aren't so good at the job, or who did not make appropriate arrangements with a professional fixer (see Conwell and Sutherland 1937)—in other words, they aren't the same as the ones who never went to jail, and that means that the causal story leading up to their crime may be very different from the amateur's story. Almost all embezzlers, however, end up in jail. The auditors always show up, find that some money is missing, and can easily figure out who caused the shortage. By then it's too late to do anything but leave the country (which, of course, embezzlers sometimes do). So the embezzlers in jail are probably pretty much like the ones who aren't there yet.

But there's a more substantial difficulty with the sample you find in jail. It goes to the heart of the definitional problem that causes practitioners of AI to throw cases out of their sample. There shouldn't be a definitional problem, because everyone knows what embezzlement is, don't they? Certainly. Embezzling is when someone can get their hands on the company's money and take it without resorting to force or firearms, using some sort of financial trickery instead. But people who embezzle from their employers in a way that more or less coincides with that folk definition are not always convicted of and put in jail for the crime of embezzlement. The legal definitions of the crime set out certain requirements the prosecutor must meet in order to make that charge stick. But the prosecutor, even though he knows that the person he has in custody stole the money, may still not be able to meet those legal requirements. He might, however, be able to meet the requirements for another, similar charge. As a result, people who have committed what would conventionally be thought of as embezzlement can end up in jail for committing crimes called "larceny by bailee," "confidence game," or forgery. Cressey explains:

> the legal category [of embezzlement] did not describe a homo-
> geneous class of criminal behavior. Persons whose behavior was
> not adequately described by the definition of embezzlement
> were found to have been imprisoned for that offense, and persons
> whose behavior was adequately described by the definition were
> confined for some other offense. (Cressey 1951)

So the offense for which an embezzler is convicted reflects the prosecutor's ability to make a winning case rather than a routine and unchanging definitional response to a set of facts.

Cressey thus had to inspect all the cases falling under those other headings to make sure he was getting the people whose stories he wanted. In truth table terms, he had to get rid of the column labeled "convicted of embezzling" and insert some new ones in which to record the presence or absence of some other criterion or criteria that would distinguish the cases of interest to him. Choosing who to interview (from people in the several criminal categories) by applying the common-sense definition I recited in the last paragraph, he had still another problem. The people that definition captured differed in such obvious ways that it was unlikely that a single invariant explanation existed for their behavior (even though their behavior was all "the same," in that they had all, after all, helped themselves to their employer's money). Some of the people in jail conformed to the conventional stereotype of a well-meaning person who took a job in good faith, but then got into some difficulty and stole money with the intention of putting it back, but got caught. Other jailed embezzlers, however, were professional criminals who somehow managed to get a job in a bank (or some other position of financial trust). They had every intention of stealing. You needed different explanations for these two situations. Cressey was only interested in the first type, the person who didn't intend to steal but then did. The second type could be explained easily enough as the intentional application of professional skills, the way you would explain a surgeon performing operations. That seemed a less interesting theoretical problem to him, perhaps because it had already been studied by others (as his mentor Sutherland had analyzed the professional behavior of thieves [Conwell and Sutherland 1937]).

So Cressey redefined the subject of his study as the criminal violation of a position of financial trust that had been taken in good faith, ignoring the official name of the crime the person had been convicted of, and threw out cases that did not meet that definition (in other words, got rid of all rows in the truth table that had a plus in the column headed "took the job intending to steal"). It's not really necessary to the argument here that you know the explanation for these people's violation of trust, but it would be cruel not to tell. Cressey explained that their activity went through three stages. First, the embezzler-to-be developed nonshareable financial problems, problems that might not be as damaging to someone else but were poison

for a person in a trusted financial position. It's all right for a college professor to play the horses and lose, but it's not all right when a bank teller does
it. So the bank teller can't tell anyone that he or she needs some extra cash
and thus get the money in a legitimate way. Or, at least, they don't think
they can do that. Although what was nonshareable might vary, the non-
shareability was the point, not the specific activity. Then they learned the
techniques required for successful theft. That wasn't too hard because they
were usually the same techniques you needed to do the job in the first
place, and you learned them as you learned the job itself. Finally, now well
on their way to doing it, they developed a rationale, an explanation of why
it was all right after all for them to do something they would once have regarded as forbidden and criminal. They might, for instance, tell themselves
that "It's a big company and they cheat too."

Marijuana Use. I read Lindesmith's book when it came out and was
greatly taken with his use of AI. I thought it would be a good way to approach a subject about which I had enough prior knowledge, through my
work as a dance musician and through personal experience, to think that it
would provoke an interesting variation on Lindesmith's theory: marijuana
use. (The study I'm discussing appears in Becker 1963, 42–78.)

Unlike opiates, marijuana does not produce addiction. People use it
much more casually, sometimes a lot, sometimes not at all. I didn't think
that pattern of use could be explained by the standard physiological or psychological theories Lindesmith had already, in my view, demolished for the
case of opiate drugs. But neither could marijuana use be explained by invoking a Lindesmith-like process based on adaptation to withdrawal distress, because users of marijuana didn't suffer withdrawal. What had to be
explained was not the obsessive behavior of addiction, but the voluntary
action I described as "the use of marijuana for pleasure." My explanation,
too, had three steps, three stages of an educational process: learning to in-
gest marijuana so physiological effects could occur; learning to recognize
those effects (since they were relatively subtle and easily ignored or attributable to "normal" circumstances, as thirst might be) and attribute them to
having taken the drug; and learning to enjoy the symptoms, which were
not "obviously" enjoyable (it's not necessarily a lot of fun to have your
mouth dry up or to be dizzy).

I found negative cases requiring reformulations of the theory and re-
definitions of the phenomenon. The most interesting and important one

arose when I interviewed a musician I had worked with in various bands, who confided that he had never gotten high and had no idea what people were talking about when they used that expression. I asked him why on earth he bothered to continue to smoke dope, considering the possible legal sanctions. He explained that everyone else did and he didn't want to look like a square. I decided that cases like his (another one showed up later in the research) were not what I was talking about; they would have been interesting for a study of, say, peer pressure, but that wasn't what I wanted to explain. So I dropped the case from my sample, describing it as a case "in which marijuana is used for its prestige value only, as a symbol that one is a certain kind of person, with no pleasure at all being derived from its use" (Becker 1963, 44). That is, I removed from my truth table all the rows in which a person had a plus for prestige as a motive combined with a lack of the ability to get high. Rows (cases) which contained prestige *and* ability to get high remained.

I used AI the same way Lindesmith and Cressey had. I was as interested as they were in the development of self-conceptions and individual lines of activity, which meant I wanted to understand how people came to see marijuana as pleasure-giving and themselves as people who knew how to use it to get and enjoy that pleasure. But I also insisted, more than either of them had, on introducing the social context of the activity into my explanation, emphasizing that people typically (though not necessarily) learned what they had to learn by being taught by more experienced users.

And (the most important difference between my work and that of Lindesmith and Cressey) I didn't content myself with one process. My analysis also incorporated a theory about social control, based on my observation that marijuana use typically did not interrupt users' conventional lives. To avoid such interruptions, users had to find ways to avoid the consequences of the legal prohibition of marijuana use, and of the belief of many people they had regular contact with (parents, employers, associates, and so on) that it was a bad thing to be doing. These problems introduced another necessary adaptation, this time to the forces of social control.

So I described a second process, more or less in the AI style, concluding that people would only begin and continue to use marijuana when they successfully dealt with the problems associated with the definition of the practice as deviant. For example, since possession and sale of marijuana were illegal, it was difficult to get, and if you couldn't get it, you couldn't smoke it. Similarly, users had to find ways to keep their use hidden from law enforcement officers, relatives, employers, and others who might punish them in some way if their use was discovered. And users had to convince themselves that smoking marijuana did not have the bad effects sometimes attributed to it. If any of these conditions were not met, use would not continue.

Had I incorporated the two processes into one model, I would have had a six- rather than a three-step process. The six steps, combined, constituted the columns of a truth table. The combinations of pluses and minuses in those columns described the situations in which use occurred and those in which it didn't—because, unlike Lindesmith's interviewees, who stopped use only when some external force interfered, the people I talked to did stop and start all the time. I dealt with the combinations that led to stopping and starting up again casually. I can see now that, had I understood the possibility, I could have constructed a truth table, QCA style, that would have systematized that analysis. I would have had a much more complex set of rows and columns than the ones Cressey and Lindesmith created, one that showed that the possibilities of AI were greater than the earlier studies had suggested. (Ragin's [1994, 94–98] analysis of Katz's [1982] study of the careers of poverty lawyers is a well worked out example of what's possible.)

I had a reason for keeping the two problems of learning to get high and of adapting to systems of social control separate. The two processes, while connected, did not affect how much and how often people smoked in the same way. Learning to enjoy the drug's effects was something that would have to occur no matter what the legal situation of marijuana in the society. Getting high is getting high, no matter the legal status of the activity. The process of dealing with the negative definitions of use, on the other hand, was historically contingent. An analyst only had to deal with that set of constraints on marijuana use when such social controls were operating. And, historically, matters did change to some extent in the years following this research, so that some of the contingencies operative in the second process were no longer present, at least for some people and at some times.

These three examples of classic AI are rigorous, to the point of obsession, in the way they apply the method. They consider one major hypothesis, designed to explain one specific outcome, and rigorously exclude other, "extraneous" outcomes as not being cases of the phenomenon to be explained. Thus, I ignored the people who continued to smoke marijuana even though they never learned to enjoy it, because I didn't think it was interesting to explain the behavior of this group. I didn't pursue that phenomenon, though I might have; it wasn't an "uninteresting" outcome, as contemporary interest in "peer pressure" suggests. Similarly, Cressey excluded cases of professional criminals who took positions of financial trust exactly so that they *could* violate them. He wasn't interested in that outcome. Someone interested in the operation of banks as social organizations might well wish to consider both types of violation and develop parallel explanations of the two similar, but not identical, outcomes.

I don't intend what I've just said as criticism of Lindesmith, Cressey, or myself for making those choices. But we should recognize that these choices are dictated not by scientific considerations, but by the problems we wanted to solve. We could as easily have chosen to solve a wider range of problems by investigating a wider range of outcomes. Researchers who are interested in simultaneously investigating a variety of outcomes have used superficially different, but in fact quite similar, methods and logic. These methods can be seen as variants and extensions of AI.

Not-So-Rigorous Analytic Induction

Weird Cases and Comparisons.   Some sociologists (I'm one and Everett Hughes was another) annoy their colleagues, and especially students who are trying to simplify their theses and therefore their lives, by countering every seemingly reasonable generalization anyone proposes with a contradictory example. I mentioned, in chapter 4, the meeting I attended at which people tried to devise a test of artistic talent and wanted to use drawing as the ability one would measure. That didn't seem unreasonable on its face, but I immediately spoiled everything by asking whether the other participants considered photography a visual art and, if they did (and, of course, they did), how an ability to draw could measure someone's potential as a maker of artistic photographs. I made the same theoretical move when, after medical students had told me that a crock was someone with psychosomatic disease, I confronted them with the patient with an ulcer; they "knew" that the ulcer had a psychosomatic origin (as it happens, the cause of ulcer is now thought to be a microbe rather than the psyche), but knew just as securely that the patient who had it wasn't a crock.

I didn't raise those exceptions to the generalizations my companions were making about drawing or crocks just to be annoying, although it was fun and I am mischievous. I did it to explore the ideas of artistic talent and patient misbehavior that were implicit in the talk I was listening to. If I could so easily think of an activity everyone knew was artistic that did not have the feature they had just attributed to all artistic activity, then that feature couldn't be a defining characteristic of visual art. If I could so easily find a patient with psychosomatic disease who wasn't a crock, then that wasn't what defined a crock. In both cases, I was using these negative cases (because that's what they were) just the way someone doing analytic induction does: to find new variables, new aspects of the thing being analyzed. Insisting that the generalization has to cover this inconveniently negative example adds columns to the truth table whenever you find cases that aren't explained by the combinations already there.

You don't actually have to see negative cases in order to use them for this purpose. It's enough to be able to think of one, if what you're going to do is use it to look for more dimensions and elements in a situation or process you're interested in. If you're wrong, and the imaginary case produces elements that turn out to be of no empirical relevance, that's no tragedy. Better to have thought of it and then found out you're wrong than never to have thought of it at all. That's why Hughes and others read fiction so avidly. It's not because inventors of fictions have superior insight denied to the rest of us. But they might describe something carefully enough that we could extract a negative instance of some theory of ours from it. Since there are so many more novels and novelists than there are social scientists and empirical studies, they are bound to cover a greater variety of situations than we do, and thus describe possibilities we wouldn't otherwise know about.

Ethnographic Practice.   Plucking weird cases and comparisons out of novels or the air is just me trying to think up new ideas, to make conversation, to help students out of a rut they've gotten into in their thinking, to help myself out of a similar rut. But, in fact, the conventional practices of ethnographic fieldwork often involve the same trick, although I have to give some background before I explain how that's so. Ethnographers are seldom so single-mindedly interested in finding a unique solution to one specific problem as Lindesmith or Cressey were. Instead, they are typically interested in developing an interlocking set of generalizations about many different aspects of the organization or community they are studying, and much of the force of an ethnographic description comes from seeing how the various generalizations support each other.

So Hughes, describing the experience of a Canadian town undergoing industrialization, tells a complicated story about how vocations for the priesthood arise in its French-speaking families:

> The child is reared in a homogeneous community, where he shares the respected status of a farm-owning family. But within the bosom of each family all must be ordered toward future diversity of fate for the several children. One will be a farm proprietor and will carry on the family in the native parish. The others, even while at work on the farm, are to be turned into potential priests, nuns, doctors, teachers, businessmen, artisans, colonists, or simply into grist for the mills of industry. The adult proprietors [of farms] are of one class; their children are destined for dispersion among the various estates of an urban and industrial civilization. The remarkable thing is, not that family solidarity keeps the several individuals at work, without conscious or unconscious sabotage, but rather that they do this in the face of the fact that most of the children will have no part or parcel of the farm and will be able to call it "home" only in reminiscence. (1943, 8)

> Nearly all of the priests of Cantonville [the town Hughes studied] are farmer's sons who, at an early age, were sent off, at their family's expense, to a *collège* and then to a seminary. (171)

> [A] key factor in the [religious] vocation is its function for the family and the kind of family effort which brings it to fruition. The testimony of priests in general is that the urban working class does not produce priests. The few cases of vocation which came to our attention in the community were those of sons of smaller businessmen, fairly successful in their enterprises, but not of the first rank in their social position. None of the distinctly high-ranking families, new or old, has produced a priest in the memory of any of the older residents. One may suggest, although the data are not adequate for proof, that the deeper piety of the rural people and lower-middle classes or urban people, along with the family solidarity engendered by maintenance of a family enterprise, is the condition most favorable to directing sons toward the priesthood. Gaining a living from individual wages and salaries is not favorable; nor is the more secular spirit, expressed in a more sophisticated set of social ambitions, of the middle and upper classes favorable to vocations, even though such families may conduct successful enterprises. (185)

So there is a system of inheritance (in the French style) that gives the farm to the eldest son but provides some equivalent living for the other children; until they reach the age of independence, the children provide the labor for the farm; one of the ways of providing for a son or daughter (though in this patriarchal society more attention is given to the son's fate) is to have them become religious functionaries; and the piety of rural life, particularly, provides an appropriate setting for the development of such feelings. The book gives detailed verification, arrived at through painstaking and systematic analysis of a mass of facts gathered in the field (a family-by-family census of occupations of fathers and sons, for example), of this collection of strong empirical statements about the society. The analyses are buttressed with tables containing information on all the families of specific classes and geographical locations. A composite portrait of the whole system of religion, land tenure, and economic development is constructed from interlocking generalizations about these different parts or aspects.

As an ethnographer like Hughes pursues such generalizations, he uses procedures that parallel AI. He states provisional hypotheses about a particular phenomenon, like the relation between family status and religious vocations. He looks for disconfirming cases, rethinks the generalization so that these cases are no longer disconfirming, and continues the search for negative cases in places where they would be likely to occur. It's what I did as I pursued the meaning of the word "crock." The goal of this search for disconfirming evidence is to refine the portrait of the whole—to offer, in the end, a convincing representation of its complexity and diversity.

But ethnographers don't create their data by requiring people to do something special for them—fill out a questionnaire or participate in an interview or focus group. They are, instead, usually at the mercy of "the moment," and have to wait for events that would be theoretically important to them to happen while they're doing their research. And they have a lot of generalizations to test in their effort to construct a portrait of the whole, as Hughes did. So ethnographers can't realistically pursue any single generalization in the strict, single-minded way characteristic of the classic AI studies. Nor should they. The similarity to AI lies elsewhere: in their refusal to write disconfirming evidence off as some sort of dismissable variation, in their insistence on instead addressing it as evidence that has to be theoretically accounted for and included as part of the story.

Ethnographers can, however, apply the trick of looking for negative evidence. When Blanche Geer and I studied campus life at the University of Kansas (Becker, Geer, and Hughes [1968] 1994), we did that with respect to the question of campus leaders. We had established a division of labor in

our field work. She studied fraternities and sororities, I studied independents. One day she interviewed the head of the Interfraternity Council
and asked how he had arrived at that position. The answer took an hour,
and included a lengthy account of political deals and machinations that began as soon as he had arrived on campus as a freshman. We thought it would
be interesting to see if that was the way it worked in general, and for
women as well as men.

So we made a list of the twenty or so most important positions in campus organizations held by men and women, and set out to interview them.
She continued to interview the men, all of whose stories resembled that of
the IFC president. I interviewed the women, and had a great surprise.
When I asked the IFC president's opposite number, the head of the Pan-
hellenic organization, how she had come to occupy that position, she
shocked me by saying "I don't know." I said, "What do you mean you don't
know? How can you not know that?" And then she explained that she
found out she was president when the Dean of Women called her to con-
gratulate her. She thought, but wasn't sure, that it was her sorority's turn to
have the presidency, and that perhaps the president of her sorority had
nominated her, or maybe the Dean had just decided to choose her. There
were no stories of deals, no plots, no political machinations. It just happened. And that turned out to be a stable finding, a real difference between
the way men and women were treated by the college administration, and
consequently a real difference in the experiences men and women had in
college.

I have spoken here of ethnographic practice, but it is clear that similar
strategies are appropriate for people who work with historical data, or with
combinations of statistical data taken from available records. A useful exercise would be, to cite just one example, to see how Lieberson (1980) handled the search for negative and complicating information in his analysis of
the causes of the economic and social situation of present-day American
blacks.

The systematic search for negative cases shows up in a procedure used by
many or most ethnographers in analyzing and sorting through their data
(see the description in Becker, Gordon, and LeBailly 1984). Briefly, analysts in this style typically assemble all the data that bear on a given topic and
see what statement they can make that will take account of all that material, what generalization best encompasses what is there. If some data do not
support a generalization, the analyst tries to reframe the generalization,

complicating it to take account of the stubborn fact; alternatively, the analyst tries to create a new class of phenomena that differs from the one the datum was originally assigned to, which can have its own explanatory generalization. Thus, in handling the fragments of data out of which an ethnographic analysis is constructed, the analyst mimics the operations of AI.

The Underlying Logic of Combinations

The big trick of combinatorial thinking is: Think combinations! (As opposed to the most common alternative, which is: Think Variables!) Propose some elements or, better yet, let the world propose them to you through the data you collect or through less formally gathered impressions. See what the cases that interest you are made up of. Work out the possible combinations. See which ones turn out which way, why some exist and others don't.

The three combinatorial methods I've discussed at such length—property space analysis, qualitative comparative analysis, and analytic induction—seem to differ considerably. But, as my scattered remarks to this point were meant to suggest, beneath the superficial differences lies a common logic and method, in varying forms designed to take account of the differing problems each was devised to solve. The three methods have in common the intention of milking a set of ideas or categories for all they're worth. They rely on a basically similar notion of extracting all the possibilities inherent in such a set for explicit consideration.

The way each does that is its special trick, and each of them is a trick (or, better, a family of related tricks) you can learn and use. The three groups of tricks are best understood by seeing them as differing ways of working with a truth table, in which the rows are the cases being studied and the columns the properties attributed to cases. Once you set up the columns, you can describe every case your research turns up by some combination of the presence or absence of each feature specified in them.

Better yet, you can incorporate the complexity of the social world into your thinking by working out every possible combination of those presences and absences. That lets you recognize the possibility of cases you haven't discovered empirically. You might never actually find them, because they might not exist—not where you're looking or not at all. But you know that they could exist, at least logically—like the possibilities laid out for physical scientists in the periodic table of elements—and you know what to look for. You know that, if you don't find them, there is something wrong with your table or, more likely, that their absence requires an explanation, which will most likely be created by adding still more elements to the analysis, more columns to the truth table. Adding those columns will, in turn, create more potential types to be looked for. In this way, truth table analysis is a way of being more formal about the requirement to sample for the full range of possibilities.

Property space analysis's trick for multiplying possibilities is simple, easily understood, and well known to social scientists: make a table in which the rows are the varieties of one variable and the columns the varieties of another. The cells created by the intersection of the two define the possible combinations, the types. That's not as good a way of laying out possibilities as a truth table, because it's hard to accommodate more than a few properties without generating a bewildering number of headings, subheadings, and cells and thus making the result visually incomprehensible. But such a table has the advantage of providing a physical space in which you can put numbers: the numbers of cases that have that combination of characteristics, or the percentage of cases of that combination that have some other characteristic you want to emphasize. A key feature of much social science analysis, especially work based on survey data or its analogs, consists exactly in the comparison of such numbers in order to evaluate the relative effects of one variable on another. PSA was invented to deal with such data, and shows that in its emphases. It does that job well.

PSA's two subsidiary tricks, which Lazarsfeld and Barton call "reduction" and "substruction," are complementary ways of manipulating truth table columns, making fewer of them by combining those that can be combined without violence to common sense, making more of them by ferreting out the principles on which ad hoc typologies have been constructed.

Qualitative comparative analysis is not much concerned with numbers or percentages of cases, or with evaluating the influence of variables considered separately. It was created to do a different job: to find explanations of historical events about which we know too much to swallow any simple answers. It is pointed toward the description of combinations of elements considered as wholes, toward conjunctures of things, people, characteristics, and events. Its trick is the truth table trick in its pure form, as a tool of Boolean algebra. It multiplies possibilities by adding new elements to the table, in the form of new columns that will contain pluses and minuses, as new elements come to the analyst's attention. It compares combinations, rather than numbers, seeing which combinations of elements produce which combinations of outcomes. It's prepared to find new causes, and also new effects, new outcomes. QCA reduces all that complexity through the operation called minimization: seeing which elements play no role in the phenomenon to be explained and can thus be dropped from the analysis, which reduces the columns of the table and thus the number of combinations that have to be dealt with. Like all mathematically based ideas, these Boolean methods bring with them a variety of subtricks that have already been worked out and verified. If, for instance, you know the combinations of elements that produce the outcome of interest to you, purely logical manipulations give you the combinations that produce the obverse of that combination.

Analytic induction's single-minded insistence on one outcome, and one set of causes that produce that outcome, which are its tricks, reduce complexity very successfully. That emphasis makes sense in light of AI's development as a way of explaining deviant activities. Students of those research problems don't care about the whole logical tree of possible outcomes, only about the one node out at the end that is the thing they want to explain: the addict or the embezzler. So it's natural that AI doesn't, on the surface, seem to be very good at multiplying possibilities. But it actually does create more types. When analysts discover a negative case, they search for a new condition that accounts for its existence. That new condition is, of course, a new column in the truth table, and so doubles the number of possible combinations. AI's great trick is to dismiss all those possibilities, except the one that is of central interest, from further consideration. It redefines those combinations as irrelevant. So, when I discovered someone who continued to smoke marijuana even though he wasn't having any fun, I refocused the analysis to explain the behavior of people who used it for pleasure, and ignored all the possible combinations of events whose outcome was using for social prestige.

AI's less rigorous form, widely used in ethnographic and historical research, consists in focusing on things that don't fit the picture you're developing. It simply counsels the researcher to look for trouble, look for exceptions, look for things that don't fit, and when you find them, don't complain. Rather, be happy. You know how to complicate your analysis without falling into chaos.

CODA

Now you know all, or most, or anyway a lot, of the tricks I know. Just reading about these tricks will not do you much good. You may be amused. You may even be instructed. But you will not really know how to do them. They will not really be yours.

The way you learn to do these tricks and take possession of them is to make them a daily routine. In other words, practice. The way a pianist plays scales. The way a golfer practices a swing. Don't let a day go by that you don't do one of them (better yet, several of them) seriously. When I was in my early teens, learning to play jazz, I spent a good chunk of my waking hours thinking music. And I don't mean thinking about music in general or about particular players, the way a fan might have done. I mean that I rehearsed songs I knew, or wanted to know, and solos I had memorized by players I admired on records I owned. I went over these melodies in my head, listening to the intervals between the notes they were composed of, identifying the notes specifically enough that I could write them down on a sheet of score paper or reproduce them at the piano. I did it with songs I heard on the radio, in the background in stores, in movies. And then I'd go after the harmony, making sure I had the chords that made the melody sound right, the chords I could use as the basis for improvisation.

The immediate result of such persistent mental practice was that I looked a little strange walking down the street, humming distractedly and not responding quickly to things said to me. The eventual result was that I could hear a song playing in the background as I talked to someone, and later sit down and play it without having to engage in any conscious musical analysis. To this day, I sometimes surprise my companions by referring to the background music in the restaurant or elevator, which I have "heard" and they haven't. It's the kind of skill David Sudnow (1978) described as what his hands learned when he learned to play the piano, and what some others have called, speaking of skills that similarly have a physical component, "embodied knowledge." Whatever the name, the idea is clear. It's what you know so well that you don't have to think about it to do it.

It's easy to see how you can do that with music, but what does it mean to practice tricks of thinking? It means routinely applying them to the situations that come up in your everyday life. For someone who thinks sociologically, for instance, it can mean seeing everything that happens as an instance of collective activity, as the result of many people and institutions acting together. Sometimes, when I'm teaching a class, I'll point to the ever-present overhead projector and ask "What is that doing here? How did it get here?" (You will recognize this, of course, as an instance of the trick of seeing objects as the residue of people acting together, discussed in chapter 2.) That leads us, naturally, to a discussion about university purchasing departments and all their bureaucratic requirements for getting multiple bids. Then we have to ask why they bought it. Who wanted it enough to go through the bureaucratic hassle of dealing with the purchasing department? That sets off another discussion, about teachers who like to write things down where students can see them and students who like to have things written down for easy copying into their notebooks, and what notion of the educational process that implies. I might also talk about teachers who don't like getting chalk on their clothes, although that could provoke a digression about the sloppier dressing habits of teachers in the last couple of decades, so what do they care whether they get chalk on themselves or not? From there, we can get back on the main analytic line and ask who invented the overhead machine and what prior inventions it relies on, not excluding the discovery and taming of electricity (with an appropriate reference to the section on electricity in Kuhn 1970, 13–14) and the development of the science and technology of optics. I've done the same thing noting that a majority of the students in the room are wearing blue jeans, and similarly tracing back the components of that story as far as anyone will allow, or until the bell rings.

I learned to do this in part from watching Everett Hughes teach, but also from a wonderful experience of watching Charles Seeger, the great ethnomusicologist, respond to a student's tentative remark, in a seminar, that he was interested in doing research on American "country music." Seeger proceeded to tell a two-hour story of the first recording of country music ever made. He described the storekeeper in whose store the recording was made. He said something about the financing and distribution of the records that were made. He named the musicians and described their careers, enough so that it was clear how they came to be there, in that store, on that day, making those recordings. He traced the evolution of the songs they recorded from earlier folk models in the United States and Britain. He worked in a short and masterful dissertation on shape note notation (in which the actual tone was indicated not by position on a staff, but by the shape of the printed note), because hymns written in that form were part of the tradition the recording artists relied on to do what they were doing.

I follow the example set for me by Hughes and Seeger, and raise questions like these about the work the students are doing, their research that seems to have come to a stubborn halt, the material they can't make any kind of sociological sense of. When I ask my questions and speculate my off-the-wall speculations, students often act like I've done some sort of magic trick, pulled a theoretical rabbit out of a hat, found a meaning in their data they could never have found. They don't see how it was done, let alone how they could ever do it themselves.

I explain how it was done. I took the fragments of data they proffered, and applied the tricks I've described here to them. That's all.

Anyone can do it, the same way I do, but it takes practice. A lot of practice. And that means raising those questions about everything you see and hear and handle, all day long or as long as you and your companions can stand it. The jeans you're wearing, the pictures on the wall, the lousy food in the school cafeteria, the doctor's office you've just left, the new garden at the house on the corner. Do it seriously, following as many of the suggestions I've made as you can remember, and above all, inventing your own tricks and remembering them.

You won't, of course, follow up all these speculations with research. But you will be in good shape for the serious work you have to do when you confront your own research materials and those of your friends and colleagues. If you get into these habits of thought, and practice them as systematically as I've suggested, you will eventually become a pro, for whom thinking social science is as natural as breathing. This is the frame of mind of the swimming champions Chambliss (1989) described, who were champions not because they were stronger or even because they practiced all the time, but because doing things the way they must be done in competition was second nature to them. That second nature did come from practice, but also from always being serious about what they were doing, never taking short cuts. When they reached the end of the pool, even if they were just swimming laps for exercise, they always touched the wall with both hands, as competition requires, even though they weren't competing. That way, when they were competing, they didn't have to make an effort to remember to do it right; they always did it right, no matter what, and this time was no different. In this they differed from pretty good swimmers, who relaxed a little when they were off duty and so did have to make an effort to remember to do it right in competition, and Chambliss thinks that seriousness is what makes them champions.

Being serious about social science in your ordinary life will probably irritate other people, who will not always appreciate your insistence on understanding what they want and do and say in its full societal context. As I've said elsewhere:

> Interpreting the events of daily life in a university department or research institute as sociological phenomena is not palatable to people who run such institutions or to those who live by them and profit from them; for, like all institutions, universities and institutes have sacred myths and beliefs that their members do not want subjected to the skeptical sociological view. (Becker 1994, 180–81)

I once heard a Zen scholar tell the following story. He was from Japan and did not speak English well, although well enough. He impressed me, at first, with his high good humor. Despite problems of language, he smiled and laughed a lot, and his pleasure in talking to us was infectious. Then he told the following story, which he meant, I think, as an explanation of the Zen idea of *satori* or enlightenment. It is as good a parable as I know for what it means to have gotten a social science way of thinking into your bones. Since I have never been able to find anyone who could tell me where this story has been written down, I have to reproduce it from memory.

> In the middle of the ocean, there is a special place, which is a Dragon Gate. It has this wonderful property: any fish that swims through it immediately turns into a dragon. However, the Dragon Gate does not look any different from any other part of the ocean. So you can never find it by looking for it. The only way to know where it is is to notice that the fish who swim through it become dragons. However, when a fish swims through the Dragon Gate, and becomes a dragon, it doesn't look any differ-

ent. It just looks like the same fish it was before. So you can't tell where the Dragon Gate is by looking closely to find just where the change takes place. Furthermore, when fish swim through the Dragon Gate and become dragons, they don't feel any different, so they don't know that they have changed into dragons. They just *are* dragons from then on.

You could be a dragon.

REFERENCES

Abbott, Andrew. 1992. What do cases do? Some notes on activity in social analysis. In *What is a case? Exploring the foundations of social inquiry*, ed. Charles C. Ragin and Howard S. Becker, 53–82. Cambridge: Cambridge University Press.

Agee, James, and Walker Evans. 1941. *Let us now praise famous men*. Boston:
Houghton Mifflin.

Alicea, Marisa. 1989. The dual home base phenomenon: A reconceptualization of
Puerto Rican migration. Ph.D. diss., Department of Sociology, Northwestern
University.

Angell, Robert Cooley. 1936. *The family encounters the Depression*. New York:
Charles Scribner's Sons.

Barker, Roger G., and Herbert F. Wright, in collaboration with Louise S. Barker
and others. 1966. *One boy's day; a specimen record of behavior*. Hamden, Conn.: Ar-
chon Books.

Barton, Allen H. 1955. The concept of property-space in social research. In *The
language of social research*, ed. Paul F. Lazarsfeld and Morris Rosenberg, 40–53.
Glencoe, Ill.: Free Press.

Bateson, Gregory, and Margaret Mead. 1942. *Balinese character: A photographic
analysis*. New York: New York Academy of Sciences.

Becker, Howard S. 1963. *Outsiders: Studies in the sociology of deviance*. New York:
Free Press.

———. 1970. *Sociological work: Method and substance*. Chicago: Aldine.

———. 1982. *Art worlds*. Berkeley and Los Angeles: University of California
Press.

———. 1986a. *Doing things together*. Evanston, Ill.: Northwestern University
Press.

———. 1986b. *Writing for social scientists*. Chicago: University of Chicago Press.

———. 1994. Sociology: The case of C. Wright Mills. In *The democratic imagination: Dialogues on the work of Irving Louis Horowitz*, ed. Ray C. Rist. New
Brunswick, N.J.: Transaction Publishers.

Becker, Howard S., Blanche Geer, and Everett C. Hughes. [1968] 1994. *Making the
grade: The academic side of college life*. New Brunswick, N.J.: Transaction Publishers.

Becker, Howard S., Blanche Geer, Everett C. Hughes, and Anselm L. Strauss.

[1961] 1977. *Boys in white: Student culture in medical school.* New Brunswick, N.J.: Transaction Publishers.

Becker, Howard S., Andrew C. Gordon, and Robert K. LeBailly. 1984. Fieldwork with the computer: Criteria for assessing systems. *Qualitative Sociology* 7:16–33.

Becker, Howard S., and Michal McCall. 1990. Performance science. *Social Problems* 37:117–32.

Becker, Howard S., Michal McCall, and Lori Morris. 1989. Theatres and communities: Three scenes. *Social Problems* 36:93–112.

Bellos, David. 1993. *Georges Perec: A life in words.* Boston: David R. Godine, Publisher.

Bittner, Egon, and Harold Garfinkel. 1967. "Good" organizational reasons for "bad" organizational records. In *Studies in ethnomethodology,* ed. Harold Garfinkel, 186–207. Englewood Cliffs, N.J.: Prentice-Hall.

Blacking, John. 1967. *Venda children's songs: A study in ethnomusicological analysis.* Johannesburg: Witwatersrand University Press.

Blumer, Herbert. 1969. *Symbolic interactionism.* Englewood Cliffs, N.J.: Prentice-Hall.

Boudon, Raymond, ed. 1993. *Paul F. Lazarsfeld on social research and its language.* Chicago: University of Chicago Press.

Burawoy, Michael. 1979. *Manufacturing consent: Changes in the labor process under monopoly capitalism.* Chicago: University of Chicago Press.

Burroughs, William. 1966. *Naked lunch.* New York: Grove Press.

Cahnman, Werner. 1948. A note on marriage announcements in the New York *Times. American Sociological Review* 13:96–97.

Candido, Antonio. [1964] 1987. *Os parceiros do Rio Bonito: Estudo sobre o caipira paulista e a transformação dos seus meios de vida.* São Paulo: Livraria Duas Cidades Ltda.

Chambliss, Dan. 1989. The mundanity of excellence: An ethnographic report on stratification and Olympic athletes. *Sociological Theory* 7:70–86.

Chapoulie, Jean-Michel. 1996. Everett Hughes and the Chicago tradition. *Sociological Theory* 14:3–29.

Clifford, James, and George E. Marcus. 1986. *Writing culture.* Berkeley and Los Angeles: University of California Press.

Cohen, Patricia Cline. 1982. *A calculating people: The spread of numeracy in early America.* Chicago: University of Chicago Press.

Cole, Stephen. 1975. The growth of scientific knowledge: Theories of deviance as a case study. In *The idea of social structure: Papers in honor of Robert K. Merton,* ed. Lewis Coser, 175–220. New York: Harcourt Brace Jovanovich.

Conwell, Chic, and Edwin H. Sutherland. 1937. *The professional thief, by a professional thief; annotated and interpreted by Edwin H. Sutherland.* Chicago: University of Chicago Press.

Cressey, Donald R. 1951. Criminological research and the definition of crimes. *American Journal of Sociology* 56:546–51.

————. 1953. *Other people's money.* New York: Free Press.

Danto, Arthur. 1964. The artworld. *Journal of Philosophy* 61:571–84.

David, Paul A. 1985. Clio and the economics of QWERTY. *AEA Papers and Proceedings* 75:332–37.

Davis, Allison, Burleigh B. Gardner, and Mary R. Gardner. 1941. *Deep South: A social anthropological study of caste and class.* Chicago: University of Chicago Press.

Davis, Kinglsey. 1937. The sociology of prostitution. *American Sociological Review* 2:744–55.

De Quincey, Thomas. 1971. *Confessions of an English opium eater.* Harmondsworth: Penguin.

Dexter, Lewis Anthony. 1964. On the politics and sociology of stupidity in our society. In *The other side: Perspectives on deviance,* ed. Howard S. Becker, 37–49. Glencoe, Ill.: Free Press.

Driscoll, James P. 1971. Transsexuals. *Trans-Action* 8 (March-April):28–37, 66–68.

Edwards, Lyford P. 1927. *The natural history of revolution.* Chicago: University of Chicago Press.

Elias, Norbert. 1970. *What is sociology?* London: Hutchinson and Co.

Foucault, Michel. 1965. *Madness and civilization.* New York: Random House.

Freidson, Eliot. 1994. *Professionalism reborn: Theory, prophecy and policy.* Chicago: University of Chicago Press.

Frisch, Max. 1969. *Biography: A game.* New York: Hill and Wang.

Gagnon, John H., and William Simon. 1973. *Sexual conduct.* Chicago: Aldine Publishing Co.

Garfinkel, Harold. 1967. *Studies in ethnomethodology.* Englewood Cliffs, N.J.: Prentice-Hall.

Geertz, Clifford. 1995. *After the fact: Two countries, four decades, one anthropologist.* Cambridge: Harvard University Press.

Giallombardo, Rose. 1966. *Society of women.* New York: John Wiley and Sons.

Glaser, Barney G., and Anselm L. Strauss. 1967. *The discovery of grounded theory.* Chicago: Aldine.

Goffman, Erving. 1961. *Asylums.* Garden City, N.Y.: Doubleday.

————. 1963. *Stigma: Notes on the management of spoiled identity.* Englewood Cliffs, N.J.: Prentice-Hall.

Goody, Jack. 1977. *The domestication of the savage mind.* Cambridge: Cambridge University Press.

Gordon, Andrew C., John P. Heinz, Margaret T. Gordon, and Stanley W. Divorski. 1979. Public information and public access: A sociological interpretation. In *Public access to information,* ed. Andrew C. Gordon and John P. Heinz, 280–308. New Brunswick, N.J.: Transaction Publishers.

Gould, Stephen Jay. 1989. *Wonderful world: The Burgess Shale and the nature of history.* New York: W. W. Norton.

Hatch, David A., and Mary Hatch. 1947. Criteria of social status as derived from marriage announcements in the *New York Times. American Sociological Review* 12:396–403.

REFERENCES

Hennessy, Thomas. 1973. From jazz to swing: Black jazz musicians and their music, 1917–1935. Ph.D. diss., Department of History, Northwestern University.

Hennion, Antoine. 1988. *Comment la musique vient aux enfants: Une anthropologie de l'enseignement musical.* Paris: Anthropos.

Herndon, James. 1968. *The way it spozed to be.* New York: Bantam.

Hobsbawm, E. J. 1964. *Labouring men; Studies in the history of labour.* London: Weidenfeld and Nicolson.

Holt, John. 1967. *How children learn.* New York: Pitman.

Horowitz, Helen Lefkowitz. 1987. *Campus life: Undergraduate cultures from the end of the eighteenth century to the present.* New York: Alfred A. Knopf.

Hughes, Everett C. 1943. *French Canada in transition.* Chicago: University of Chicago Press.

———. [1971] 1984. *The sociological eye.* New Brunswick, N.J.: Transaction Books.

Hunter, Albert. 1990. Setting the scene, sampling, and synecdoche. In *The rhetoric of social research: Understood and believed,* ed. Albert Hunter, 111–28. New Brunswick, N.J.: Rutgers University Press.

Jackson, Philip W. 1990. *Life in classrooms.* New York: Teachers College, Columbia University.

Katz, Jack. 1979. Legality and equality: Plea bargaining in the prosecution of white-collar and common crimes. *Law and Society Review* 13:431–59.

———. 1982. *Poor people's lawyers in transition.* New Brunswick, N.J.: Rutgers University Press.

Kornhauser, Ruth Rosner. 1978. *Social sources of delinquency: An appraisal of analytic models.* Chicago: University of Chicago Press.

Korzenik, Diana. 1985. *Drawn to art: A nineteenth-century American dream.* Hanover, N.H.: University Press of New England.

Kuhn, Thomas. 1970. *The structure of scientific revolutions.* Chicago: University of Chicago Press.

Latour, Bruno. 1987. *Science in action.* Cambridge: Harvard University Press.

———. 1995. The "pédofil" of Boa Vista: A photo-philosophical montage. *Common Knowledge* 4:144–87.

Latour, Bruno, and Steve Woolgar. 1979. *Laboratory life: The social construction of scientific fact.* Beverly Hills, Calif.: Sage Publications.

Lazarsfeld, Paul. 1972. Some remarks on typological procedures in social research. In *Continuities in the language of social research,* ed. Paul F. Lazarsfeld, Anne K. Pasarella, and Morris Rosenberg, 99–106. Glencoe, Ill.: Free Press.

Lazarsfeld, Paul, and Allen H. Barton. 1951. Qualitative measurement in the social sciences: Classification, typologies, and indices. In *The policy sciences: recent developments in scope and method,* ed. Daniel Lerner and Harold D. Lasswell, 155–92. Stanford, Calif.: Stanford University Press.

Lazarsfeld, Paul, Bernard Berelson, and Hazel Gaudet. 1948. *The people's choice: How the voter makes up his mind in a presidential campaign.* New York: Columbia University Press.

Lewontin, R. C. 1994. A rejoinder to William Wimsatt. In *Questions of evidence: Proof, practice, and persuasion across the disciplines,* ed. James Chandler, Arnold L. Davidson, and Harry Harootunian, 504–9. Chicago: University of Chicago Press.

Lieberson, Stanley. 1980. *A piece of the pie: Blacks and white immigrants since 1880.* Berkeley and Los Angeles: University of California Press.

———. 1985. *Making it count.* Berkeley and Los Angeles: University of California Press.

———. 1992. Small n's and big conclusions: An examination of the reasoning in comparative studies based on a small number of cases. In *What is a case? Exploring the foundations of social inquiry,* ed. Charles Ragin and Howard S. Becker, 105–18. Cambridge: Cambridge University Press.

Lindesmith, Alfred. 1947. *Opiate addiction.* Bloomington: Principia Press.

———. 1952. Comment. *American Sociological Review* 17:492.

———. 1965. *The addict and the law.* Bloomington: Indiana University Press.

Lohman, Joseph D., and Deitrich C. Reitzes. 1954. Deliberately organized groups and racial behavior. *American Sociological Review* 19:342–44.

Ludlow, Fitz Hugh. 1975. *The hashish eater.* San Francisco: Level Press.

Lynch, Michael. 1985. *Art and artifact in laboratory science.* London: Routledge.

Marcus, George E. 1986. Ethnographic writing and anthropological careers. In *Writing culture,* ed. James Clifford and George E. Marcus. Berkeley and Los Angeles: University of Calfiornia Press.

McCall, Michal M., and Judith Wittner. 1990. The good news about life history. In *Symbolic interaction and cultural studies,* ed. Howard S. Becker and Michal M. McCall. Chicago: University of Chicago Press.

McEvoy, Arthur F. 1986. *The fisherman's problem: Ecology and law in the California fisheries.* Cambridge: Cambridge University Press.

Mead, George Herbert. 1917. Scientific method and individual thinker. In *Creative intelligence: Essays in the pragmatic attitude,* ed. John Dewey et al. New York: Henry Holt and Co.

Merton, Robert K. 1946. *Mass persuasion: The social psychology of a war bond drive.* New York: Harper and Brothers.

———. 1957. *Social theory and social structure.* New York: Free Press.

Molotch, Harvey. 1994. Going out. *Sociological Forum* 9:229–39.

Morgenstern, Oskar. 1950. *On the accuracy of economic observations.* Princeton, N.J.: Princeton University Press.

Morris, Lori Virginia. 1989. The casting process within Chicago's local theatre community. Ph.D. diss., Department of Sociology, Northwestern University.

Moulin, Raymonde. 1967. *Le marché de la peinture en France.* Paris: Editions de Minuit.

———. 1992. *L'artiste, l'institution, et le marché.* Paris: Flammarion.

Nunes, Marcia B. M. L. 1984. Professional culture and professional practice: A case study of psychoanalysis in the United States. Ph.D. diss., Department of Sociology, Northwestern University.

Parsons, Carole W. 1972. *America's uncounted people: A report of the National Research Council Advisory Committee on Problems of Census Enumeration*. Washington: National Academy of Sciences.

Peirano, Mariza G. S. 1995. *A favor da etnografia*. Rio de Janeiro: Relume Dumará.

———. 1991. *Uma antropologia no plural: Três experiências contemporâneas*. Brasilia: Editora Universidada de Brasília.

Peneff, Jean. 1988. The observers observed: French survey researchers at work. *Social Problems* 35:520–35.

———. 1995. Mesure et contrôle des observations dans le travail de terrain: L'exemple des professions de service. *Sociétés Contemporaines* 21:119–38.

Perec, Georges. 1980. Stations Mabillon (tentatives de description de quelques lieux parisiens, 5). *Action Poétique* 81:30–39.

Petersen, Osler, et al. 1956. An analytical study of North Carolina general practice, 1953–1954. *Journal of Medical Education* 31, part ii.

Rabinow, Paul. 1986. Representations are social facts: Modernity and postmodernity in anthropology. In *Writing culture,* ed. James Clifford and George E. Marcus. Berkeley and Los Angeles: University of California Press.

Ragin, Charles C. 1987. *The comparative method: Moving beyond qualitative and quantitative strategies*. Berkeley and Los Angeles: University of California Press.

———. 1994. *Constructing social research*. Thousand Oaks, Calif.: Sage Publications.

Ragin, Charles C., and Howard S. Becker. 1988. How microcomputers will affect our analytical habits. In *New technology in sociology: Practical applications in research and work,* ed. Grant Blank, James L. McCartney, and Edward Brent. New Brunswick, N.J.: Transaction, Inc.

Ragin, Charles C., and Jeremy Hein. 1993. The comparative study of ethnicity: Methodological and conceptual issues. In *Race and ethnicity in research methods,* ed. John H. Stanfield II and Rutledge M. Dennis, 254–72. Newbury Park, Calif.: Sage Publications.

Ragin, Charles C., Susan Meyer, and Kriss Drass. 1984. Assessing discrimination: A Boolean approach. *American Sociological Review* 49:221–34.

Robinson, W. S. 1951. The logical structure of analytic induction. *American Sociological Review* 16:812–18.

Roth, Julius. 1965. Hired hand research. *American Sociologist* 1:190–96.

Roy, Donald. 1952. Quota restriction and goldbricking in a machine shop. *American Journal of Sociology* 57:425–42.

———. 1953. Work satisfaction and social reward in quota achievement. *American Sociological Review* 18:507–14.

———. 1954. Efficiency and the "fix": Informal intergroup relations in a piecework machine shop. *American Journal of Sociology* 60:255–66.

Sacks, Harvey. 1972. On the analyzability of stories by children. In *Directions of sociolinguistics,* ed. J. J. Gumperz and Dell Hymes, 325–45. New York: Holt, Rinehart and Winston.

Sacks, Oliver W. 1987. *The man who mistook his wife for a hat and other clinical tales*. New York: Simon and Schuster.

Said, Edward. 1978. *Orientalism*. New York: Pantheon.

Schaps, E., and C. R. Sanders. 1970. Purposes, patterns and protection in a campus drug-using community. *Journal of Health and Social Behavior* 11:135–45.

Simmel, Georg. 1950. *The sociology of Georg Simmel*. Glencoe, Ill.: Free Press.

Spector, Malcolm, and John I. Kitsuse. 1977. *Constructing social problems*. Menlo Park, Calif.: Cummings Publishing Co.

Stouffer, Samuel A. et al. 1949. *The American soldier*. Princeton, N.J.: Princeton University Press.

Strong, Samuel. 1946. Negro-white relations as reflected in social types. *American Journal of Sociology* 52:23–30.

Sudnow, David. 1978. *Ways of the hand: The organization of improvised conduct*. Cambridge: Harvard University Press.

Sutherland, Edwin H. 1940. White collar criminality. *American Sociological Review* 5:1–12.

Suttles, Gerald D. 1972. *The social construction of communities*. Chicago: University of Chicago Press.

Sykes, Gresham. 1958. *The society of captives*. Princeton, N.J.: Princeton University Press.

Szasz, Thomas. 1961. *The myth of mental illness*. New York: Paul B. Hoebler, Inc.

Thorne, Barrie. 1993. *Gender play*. New Brunswick, N.J.: Rutgers University Press.

Turner, Ralph H. 1953. The quest for universals in sociological research. *American Sociological Review* 18:604–11.

Vaughan, Diane. 1986. *Uncoupling: Turning points in intimate relationships*. New York: Oxford University Press.

Velho, Gilberto. 1973. *A utopia urbana*. Rio de Janeiro: Zahar Editores.

———. 1974. *Desvio e divergência*. Rio de Janeiro: Zahar Editores.

Vianna, Hermano. 1988. *O mundo funk carioca*. Rio de Janeiro: Jorge Zahar Editor.

———. 1995. *O misterio da samba*. Rio de Janeiro: Jorge Zahar Editor.

von Wright, Georg Henrik. 1971. *Explanation and understanding*. Ithaca, N.Y.: Cornell University Press.

Walton, John, and Charles Ragin. 1990. Global and national sources of political protest: Third World responses to the debt crisis. *American Sociological Review* 55:876–90.

Ward, David, and Gene Kassebaum. 1965. *Women's prison: Sex and social structure*. Chicago: Aldine Publishing Co.

Waterman, Christopher Alan. 1990. *Jùjú: A social history and ethnography of an African popular music*. Chicago: University of Chicago Press.

Weschler, Lawrence. 1982. *Seeing is forgetting the name of the thing one sees: A life of contemporary artist Robert Morris*. Berkeley and Los Angeles: University of California Press.

Wildavsky, Aaron B. 1993. *Craftways: On the organization of scholarly work*. New Brunswick, N.J.: Transaction Publishers.

REFERENCES

Wittgenstein, Ludwig. 1973. *Philosophical investigations: The English text of the third edition*. Englewood Cliffs, N.J.: Prentice-Hall.

Zinberg, Norman E. 1984. *Drug, set, and setting: The basis for controlled intoxicant use*. New Haven, Conn.: Yale University Press.

INDEX

ability: drawing, 135–36, 137–38; effect of power on definition of, 136–38; historical variation in demand for, 113–15, 135–36; musical, 113; numerical, 135
algebra, Boolean, 186–89
Alicea, Marisa, 131–32
analytic induction (AI), 194–212: advantages, 196; compared with PSA and QCA, 196, 200; disadvantages, 201, 206–7; in ethnography, uses of, 208–12; method of, 195; multiple processes, analysis of, 205–6; not-so-rigorous, 207–14; redefinition of object of study, 201, 204–5; rigorous, 197–207; truth tables in, 194–95, 200–1, 206
archeology, 69–70
art, modern, collecting, 139–41
attitude, defined, 110

Bakhtin, Mikhail, 108
Barton, Allen H., 164–65
Beck, Anatole, 21
Beck, Bernard, 125–28
Becker, Howard S., 4, 6, 16, 22–23, 204–6
Bellos, David, 77, 78
Biography: A Game (Frisch), 33–35
Bittner, Egon, 101–2
Blacking, John, 73
Blumer, Herbert, on imagery, 10–13
Bourdieu, Pierre, 140
Burawoy, Michael, 89
bureaucracy, defined, 128–29, 130
Burroughs, William, *The Naked Lunch,* 15

Cahnman, Werner, 69
California fisheries, 42–44

campus leaders, 210–11
Candido, Antonio, 29–30
Cardoso de Oliveira, Roberto, 30
cases, archetypal, 84
casting, theatrical, 22–23
categories: problem of, 83–85; racial, 163; residual, 162–63
causality, 63–66, 189–92
Census (U.S.): categories used, 18; undercounted black population in, 130–31; using data of, 101–2
Chambliss, Dan, 217–18
Chapoulie, Jean-Michel, 3
Chicago Community Fact Book, 12
Churchill, Caryl, *Cloud 9,* 22
class, social, defined, 111, 133
Cloud 9 (Churchill), 22
Cohen, Patricia Cline, 135
coincidence, 28–35; in careers of Brazilian social scientists, 30–31; in my own life, 29, 31
colleges, culture of, 54–55, 99–100
combinations, logic of, 212–14
combinatoric analysis, 171–72
comparable worth, defined, 115–16
concepts: definition of, 110–32; as empirical generalizations, 128–32; as relational terms, 132–38
Confessions of an English Opium Eater (De Quincey), 15
conventional ideas, interference of with sociological thinking, 7, 37–38; "everybody knows that," 88–89; other people's ideas, 88–97; hierarchy of credibility, 90–91; "it's trivial," 92–93; "nothing's happening," 95–98; "why them?" 93–95